THE ART
OF BECOMING AN

ARtist

Don't Just Read This Book - Do It.

DARYLYNN STARR RANK

◆ FriesenPress

Suite 300 - 990 Fort St
Victoria, BC, V8V 3K2
Canada

www.friesenpress.com

Copyright © 2014 by Darylynn Starr Rank
First Edition — 2017

Photograph by Dennis Rank,
www.beautyhiddenphotography.ca

ISBN
978-1-4602-9373-7 (Hardcover)
978-1-4602-9374-4 (Paperback)
978-1-4602-9375-1 (eBook)

1. SELF-HELP, CREATIVITY

Distributed to the trade by The Ingram Book Company

Acknowledgements

I would like to thank all of the lovely, lovely people who took my courses. I've learned the world from you. I've learned my courses from you. I've learned this book from you. I've learned my art from you. Thank you.

And I would like to thank my husband, Dennis Rank. This book is dedicated to him.

Table of Contents

PART ONE

The beginning...

Chapter one

So Here's My Problem

So here's my problem.

(There are actually two problems, but I'll start with this one.)

I've taught my course, say, a hundred times. I've taught it in colleges, universities, community centers, social service organizations, non-profits, businesses (including one of the largest computer game designers in the world...), women's programs, adult summer camps, even a tropical retreat. Students have been kids, teenagers, and adults of all ages. (My oldest student was eighty-five, a retired ship designer.) There has been an extraordinary variety of occupations, professions, careers, vocations, and "non-careers." Participants have been enormously diverse culturally and geographically. There may be a few regions of the world from which students *haven't* come. Iceland comes to mind. The Arctic and Antarctica. But not a whole lot in between.

The participants have been interested or active or already professionally functioning in pretty much every creative endeavor imaginable; writing, painting, dancing, sculpting, weaving, photography, acting, comedy, music, animation, graphic arts, computer game design, architecture, landscape design, quilting, all aspects of the television and film industry (I've been living in Vancouver, "the Hollywood of the North..."), cooking, interior design, and so on, and so on, and so on.

The reasons for taking my course, and the challenges facing every group, as well as every individual, have sometimes seemed infinite.

You'd think that with this array of people, issues, topics, backgrounds, and yearnings, the difficulties and challenges for me as the "teacher" would be extraordinarily complex. Which they are. Complexity of the highest order.

But…

Even with all that complexity, there is one thing… There is one thing that I have to do to make this course work, every single time. First and foremost, there is one fundamental and critical aspect of helping you creative types figure out what you need to do to *get* to that creative universe.

Do you want to guess? Okay, go ahead. Take a minute. Think about it. Really think about it.

Then when you're ready, turn the page.

*   *   *   *

Did you come up with the idea of safety?

Highly unlikely. Though that's exactly what I have to do – work as hard as I can to make everyone feel safe! Safety. You have to feel safe.

Quite simple, really. No, not really. It's NOT simple at all… But… It's absolutely essential!

You have to feel safe.

Okay, let the arguments begin.

For example: "I don't want to feel safe. Creativity is about daring and courage and the thrill of danger."

"Safe is *boring.*"

"I want the *adventure.*"

"It's *about* taking risks."

And it is. Partly. But it's not just *about* taking risks. Doing art *is* taking risks. Doing art takes tremendous courage. Plus the thrill of danger is so often there. When you do your art, you're going into a new, unknown world. What's not scary about that?

More arguments?

"If I wanted to be safe, I'd sit at home and play solitaire."

"I don't want to be safe."

Maybe, just maybe, not so much.

I suggest that you won't have the courage to face the danger, if somewhere, somehow, some way, you don't feel safe enough to face it. ***SAFE ENOUGH!***

I believe with my whole heart, that you have to feel *safe enough* to do your art. Safety, safe enough, matters.

* * * *

THERE SIMPLY AIN'T NO SUCH SPORT AS JUST JUMPING OFF A CLIFF

* * * *

Really, there isn't.

* * * *

There is jumping, diving, cannonballing, leaping, back-flipping off a cliff into the warm, cold, clear, murky, blue, green, glacier-fed, volcanically heated, ocean, river, lake, pond, water below. There is sky diving off a cliff; leaping into the air with a parasail, or a parachute, or a *glider*. You can attach a bungee cord to the harness on your body and fly into space. There's climbing down a cliff with camming devices, anchors, and slings. Or climbing down the rocks free-style, with bare hands and sticky, rubber-soled shoes.

There are so many activities, sports, recreations, and practices you can do off a cliff, which involve some kind of safety net. Think the gentleness of landing in water, the gliding support of a parasail or parachute, the strong, braided shock cord of a bungee. Imagine the steel anchors gripping the rocks, or the friction of specialized climbing shoes against the stone.

All sorts of wonderful adventures. With safety net built in.

But… Simply jumping off a cliff is absolutely not one of those sports!

It just isn't something any of us want to do. Unless the actual intent is not to survive the activity. That option is not going to lead to much creativity. And to my way of thinking, suicide will never be a sport …

Again, there ain't no such sport as just jumping off a cliff.

* * * *

So, therefore, ergo, hence, and "*ta da!*" SAFETY is always my first concern. Some feeling of safety, at some level that suits you, is critical.

Now I'm a therapist. One of my main activities is providing a safe environment for my clients. I actually consider this one of my greatest skills, gifts – and obligations – my ability to make people feel safe. Especially in a therapy session. I mean NOTHING worthwhile is going to happen in a therapy session if your client doesn't feel safe. No delving, no struggling, no grappling, no exploring the past, no dealing with the present, no examining their lives – no nothing. Digging in, digging deep, is terrifying. One of the hardest, scariest things one can do. It takes more courage than practically any other part of our lives.

Consequently, my ability to make people feel safe is critical for my clients. People open up with me. They talk. They share. They expose themselves. They explore their deepest-most thoughts and feelings, secrets, and fears.

IF they feel safe.

As I said, I work extremely hard at it, particularly with my clients. Or I used to think, "particularly with my clients." Then I started teaching.

Well, it instantaneously became clear that my *students* needed to feel safe just as much as my clients did. When they didn't feel safe, they didn't open their mouths. Not a word. When they didn't feel safe, their writing or drawing, or this, or that, or whatever art you can think of, stayed at the most superficial, boring, meaningless level imaginable. *If* they could do any art at all.

You may have been there yourself. You're in a class where you're supposed to *express* yourself. Yet expressing yourself hardly ever means free-flowing openness. One often ends up controlling the situation to whatever extent feels necessary. You contain it. You make sure you stay at a comfortable level. You protect yourself from exposure, from other people's opinions, from criticism, and especially from that most awful thing, "constructive feedback," to exactly the appropriate degree. You don't want the teacher to think you're stupid, or untalented, or not sufficiently educated, or, or, or… You certainly don't want to embarrass yourself in front of the other students in the class. After all, you're thinking they are probably, depending on the particular moment in your life (or your day), either profoundly smarter, more well-educated, and more creative than you are; or so stupid and so untalented – cretins, really – that the last thing you can bear to do is to look bad in front of them. If you do express yourself to an uncomfortable level – too fast, too far, too personal, or intense (for that moment) – or if you get a response that is harsh and inappropriate, you either never go back, or you shut down even further for the remainder of the course.

You do exactly what you need to do, to feel – what? – Yes, safe.

A perfectly rational, sane, and healthy response.... Keeping yourself safe is a fundamental survival mechanism, hardwired in from the beginning of the universe.

So there you go. The most critical task facing me, every time a new class begins, is to figure out how to make everyone there feel as safe as possible. "Safe as possible" translates into incredibly, fundamentally, and profoundly safe. The safer they feel, the better the course. Simple as that. Every single time.

And, far more importantly for the purposes of the course, the reason people are there in the first place – the safer they feel, the better the art! Safety means there is less containment. Less shutting down. Less controlling, or disappearing.

Instead, there is digging and delving and soaring through the air.

With their "parachute" providing whatever safety students want and need.

* * * *

Therefore, as I said, every time I start a course, I have to figure out how to make people feel safe. It's my first and primary job. So I do. Almost every single time. That makes me happy.

You see, this course is special. Period. That's why I want to write a book about it. I want to pass on to everybody who has this book what students have repeatedly gotten in my classroom. What I teach means a lot to me. It was a hard fought for process that taught me what I teach in my classes. (More about that later.) I want to show you what that is, as well. I want to spread it around.

* * * *

Back to my original point. Or the first four words of this treatise.
So here's my problem ...
You've got to feel safe.
That's problem #1. More about this later.

*　　*　　*　　*

On to problem #2

This one is more technical. Though still critically important.

Okay. I know exactly how the course is supposed to proceed. (As previously mentioned, there have been many, many courses.) Notice the words, "supposed to." Because, naturally, it never does proceed that way. It's a course on getting to your creativity... It is, therefore, different every time. It's creative.

But I do know the steps that we need to take. Again, notice that I said *steps*, as in, one step at a time, or step by step, or baby steps, or any other way you want to say it. It's a process. That's one of my most important words. Process. We'll be talking process a lot.

Back to problem #2.

I, Darylynn Starr Rank, commonly known as Dari, your teacher, facilitator, guide, and instructor, the creator and author of this course, program, book, workshop, *process, need* you to take these steps in order for you to get what you are supposed to get out of this experience. One step at a time, step by step, even baby steps.

I need you, reader, purchaser of this book, creative human being, person waiting and/or hoping to be helped along in your process, to get to your art, to get further into your art, to unfreeze your art, or get it flowing better, or cascading, flooding, flowing, flourishing. (Flourishing's good. I like flourishing. Think I'll stop there.) I need you to enter into this process. With me. Step by step. Did I mention that?

Now the problem (#2) is that you bought this *book*. People read books. They start at the top of the page or the Kindle or the screen, and go to the bottom of it, then they turn the page, or touch the screen, or hit the button. And they read the next page. And so on and so on. Until they fall asleep, or have to eat lunch, or go to work (the money paying kind. Not art...), or get bored. Then they come back the next time they have the urge, and read some more. Until they finish *reading* the book.

But that's not what I want you to do. I don't want you to read this book. I really, really, really, do not want you to read this book. I need you not to do that.

I want you to *do the process*.

Don't read it. Do it. Just do it. (Hey, haven't I heard that phrase somewhere?)

Please. Trust me. Just for a little while.

If you don't like it after a little while, you can stop. There's nothing that can make you keep going. I certainly can't. I'm not even there. You can stop anytime you want. (Just please do give it a second. There's a whole pile of specific places where people are tempted, at that instant, to cut and run. I'm hoping you'll give it a chance if you hit one of those places. Even a little chance.) Or you can stop. Or you can completely ignore what I'm asking you to *do*, and just keep reading.

But I'm hoping you won't.

I'm hoping you'll trust me just a tiny bit about this request.

So again, my problem. How do I make a complete stranger, you, strictly reading my written words – not even face to face, not getting the opportunity to look me in the eye and have your lovely alligator brain get a feeling for who the heck I am – how do I get you to trust me?

That's my problem #2

Plus, **coincidentally** (not really), how do I make a complete stranger, you, strictly reading my written words – not even face to face, not getting the opportunity to look me in the eye and have your lovely alligator brain get a feeling for who the heck I am – how do I get you to feel safe with me?

Ah, yes. My problem #1.

There is no such sport as just jumping off a cliff.

*   *   *   *

How do I do that? Get you to trust me, at least enough to "do" this book, rather than read it. For a little while, at least. Until you can make a proper judgment about what it's doing for you. Until you can decide if you want to continue doing it. If you feel SAFE…

How? How do I do that? Well – I *could* just ask you. Okay, I will. Here you go. Could you trust me, please? Could you? Just for a while. (While still trusting yourself more, of course.)

Hey, maybe you will. That would be great.

*　　*　　*　　*

Though, just in case that *doesn't* work, I'll try some other things, as well.

Here's what I've come up with. My own set of steps.

*　　*　　*　　*

My Step #1 – Part 1

First I'm going to tell you how I came to develop this course. It's very personal. It's kind of like spewing my insides out on this page. At least it will give you an idea of where I'm coming from. You'll get a bit of an image of who's asking you to trust them…

Some basics. I was born in New York, then grew up in New York and Miami Beach, literally half and half. Nine years in New York, nine years on the Beach (though not sequential), until I went away to school at eighteen.

I was born, I learned to talk and, finally, I learned to write. From that moment on it was pretty much decided what I wanted to do with my life.

I wanted to write.

Which I did. For a very long time.

I wrote poetry and stories, little plays that I put on with my friends. I lived in my diary. Or I read a lot – when I wasn't writing. In junior high and high school I did what a budding writer is supposed to do. I worked on the school papers, the anthologies, and was editor-in-chief of the yearbooks. My early poetry was published in a national high school anthology. I was very proud. My dearest friend in the world and I spent our summers sitting on the beach writing stories about magic people who lived under the ocean.

Plus, I still lived in what, by that time, I referred to as my journal. (I'm not exactly sure at what age I matured enough to give up the *childish* word diary and change it to journal.) But I did keep writing in it.

I wrote.

When it came time to choose a university, it all seemed perfectly clear. I was going to become a journalist, either a foreign correspondent or a critic (wasn't positive which would be more fun), and write novels on the side. I applied to a school in Washington, DC. It seemed obvious to me that if you were going to become a reporter, DC was the place to start. Duh. And off I went.

I took journalism courses, though I didn't major in journalism. The wisdom of the time was that I needed a broader background to become a superior journalist. English and/or history were recommended. It was still all about the writing.

Which I continued to do, for the college paper. Writing papers for class was my joy. Still kept writing poetry (especially when I felt the torment part of life). Of course I continued writing in my journal.

Then suddenly, abruptly, at the ripe old age of nineteen, I stood up and announced to the world – my three dormitory roommates – that I wasn't going to write anymore. That I needed to do something… useful.

Don't ask me…

Or, actually, you can ask me now. I get it now. Though certainly not then. I just knew I needed to do something "useful." Writing was not *useful*.

Please, every writer who has ever lived, accept my apology. Please. Also, every person who has ever read anything, really. Please. I was nineteen and, as it turns out, seriously screwed up.

Revealingly (at least all these years later. Not then!), I went into psychology.

Two and a half years into my studies, my aunt, probably the most important safety net (wow, I actually put that phrase in *unintentionally* just now) in my life, died. Out of the blue – an aneurism at fifty-five years old.

My oldest sister was living in Brazil at the time, and in my grief and panic, and in her grief and panic, we decided I should go visit her for a bit. I took a six-month leave of absence from university and off I went to Sao Paulo – then I decided to live there. Off I went, back to Miami Beach, in order to put in my visa application and wait for the appropriate paperwork to come through.

(As an aside, that was an interesting summer waiting for that visa to arrive. I sat glued to the television in my living room as Neil Armstrong landed on the moon, then I went off to New York to visit my boyfriend, who announced we were going to a little town called Woodstock for the weekend… A truly interesting summer.)

Eventually the visa came through and I went to study, work, and live in Brazil. Until it became apparent, two years later, that living in Brazil was not going to work for me. Sigh. I proceeded to get a job at Pan American Airlines, intending to work there for a year, then get the ten percent plane tickets I'd be entitled to, so I could fly off to Europe.

However, the universe speeded things up. The first major airlines layoff, ever, occurred six months after I started working there. Since I was recently hired, and a gringa (Brazilians, of course, had priority), I was first to go. Lovely Pan Am felt so bad about firing me that they gave me two months' worth of plane tickets for ten percent of the normal costs. Yay!

So backpack, a minimal amount of money, a thick wad of very cheap airplane tickets, and off I went. Two months passed very quickly, as I flew from one fabulous city to the next, then I settled in for the real thing, backpacking and hitching my way around Europe.

But two weeks later I met a guy.

He was from Vancouver, traveling in an empty Bedford van. It took us about three days to start living together. (Living together was not something I had ever even considered doing before, bad hippie that I was.) Obviously I knew something, because about a hundred years later we're still *we*. We drove around Europe for another six months then decided we were ready to go home. Or at least return to North America. Together. We weren't ready to end each other.

Dennis wasn't interested in Miami Beach, so I said I'd come visit Vancouver for a while. After a very long and somewhat traumatic (at the time) trip, (long story – but they would *not* let me into the country), we got married. I went back to school to get my degree. In psychology. Which I did. Then grad school. Then a job as a therapist and research coordinator at a street-kid, drug treatment program (mostly heroin).

However, I truly had *stopped* writing. From the very first instant of my "usefulness" decision. I mean I'd *stopped* writing. No poetry, or stories, no plays. No articles. Not even a journal entry. I'd stopped.

Worse, somehow, I even hated the thought of writing. I hated writing papers for school. English courses or psychology papers. Didn't matter what. I hated it.

I was training as a social scientist, which means research was the be all and end all of my existence. Do the research, write up the research, get the research published. My version, however, was that I tried hard to make a bargain with my advisor. I'd review the literature, I told him, I'd come up with the idea, do the research, I'd even analyze the data, and **all** he had to do was the writing. The deal was, I explained to him over and over, that he'd get co-authorship on the publication and all *he* had to do was write the darn thing. (Mean person that he was, he would not take me up on the deal, even though I kept trying!)

I just didn't want to write.

At the drug treatment program I was promoted to Clinical Director, which meant supervising a staff of therapists. One of the most important administrative aspects of that supervision was making sure the therapists were taking suitable client notes. Keeping proper records. Of course, *my* client notes were the worst. Positively pathetic.

I stopped writing when and wherever I could. I hated it when I did have to write. In hindsight that was shocking. Bizarre even.

But there was something I find even more shocking. To this day actually.

I never even noticed it.

Not a thing. It never occurred to me that I wasn't writing. Never occurred to me that I hated it. I did not notice that I wanted absolutely nothing to do with the one thing I'd loved most in my life (at least until I met Dennis...). I was completely oblivious to the fact that I never wrote a thing. Completely oblivious to the fact that the thought of having to write filled me with horror.

I simply never noticed.

*   *   *   *

My Step #1 – Part 2

Here's where I get really personal.

The moment came when – well, there's simply no better way to say it. The moment came when the shit hit the fan.

My back, which had been an utter mess from the time I was eighteen when I ruptured my disc for the first time, finally exploded. It turned out to be quite complicated. I'd had a degenerative disc condition, so the disc was herniating more and more frequently, my sciatic nerve was in complete trauma, and I had a rather severe scoliosis. Doctors started talking about removing and/or fusing the disc and inserting a steel rod up my spine. I didn't wanna do any of those, so I was trying to work non-surgically. When my physiotherapist (they're called physical therapists in the States) announced that if he laid a hand on me, I was going to end up in a wheelchair for life, and that I had to go home and go to bed – and stay there – I did.

Sort of.

Although not quite the way he instructed me. No way I could just stop functioning. Turned out that was the single most important way I coped. Functioning. (Though again, I had no idea at the time.) I'd either been in school full-time, and working summers, or school full-time and working part-time, or working full-time, since I'd turned fourteen. (Except for my European traveling time…) In other words… *stopping functioning* full out was not an option.

I compromised. I stayed in bed for two weeks over the Christmas holidays, then got up and went back to work. I stole the unused massage table from a back room in the agency, left the legs folded under, put it on the floor of my office, and went on with my job. Me, lying on the massage table on the floor, my clients on a chair. (Fascinating aside: it was a really effective therapy technique. The whole power differential of therapist and client almost disappeared, which was something I'd always been struggling to achieve. But when your therapist is the one lying on the couch, it dramatically changes the dynamic…)

Anyway, I worked fanatically at healing my back. Stretching, strengthening, exercises, etc., etc., etc., and, as it turned out, most importantly, visualizations, meditation, and imagery. The really fun part of that was that as that process proceeded, my entire, very crummy childhood, came up on me in vivid High Definition Technicolor. You can think about that however you want. I think our bodies do store memories. Mine were not fun.

Bottom line. I come from a terribly abusive childhood. Violent, cruel, and painful. And, as it turned out, healing my back meant healing my childhood, as well. Which was even less fun.

But I did it. I cried and screamed and got ragingly angry and terrified. Mortal terror, terrified. I remembered my childhood. I felt my childhood. Remembered. Felt. Remembered. Felt. Of course I continued working on my back.

It was an awful year. (Only the first year of five as it turned out, though it got better and better towards the latter part.) By the end of the first year I was done. Exhausted. Used up. Couldn't even get out of bed anymore to get dressed, go to work, and lie down again.

I then made a huge decision to go on medical leave, and went home to bed. The time to stop functioning in the outside world had finally arrived.

Next really astonishing fact.

That very first night – the very first day I left work – the very first time I'd stopped working and/or going to school in my entire life (except for the travelling time in Europe), that very first night I pulled out a journal and started to write. For the first time in over fifteen years.

I wrote and I wrote and I wrote. When I finished that first journal, I started another one. Then another one.

I didn't stop.

At first the writing was all about pain. And more pain. Memories. Feelings. A lot of hurt. A lot of rage. A massive amount of fear. It went on and on. As I said, my whole childhood came up on me.

Slowly, however, very slowly, my writing turned to other things as well. A thought. An idea. An observation about life, about me, about returning to writing. Suddenly a poem. A cartoon. A funny little story. I wrote about everything. I wrote about anything.

One day I started writing a novel.

I was overjoyed. Beyond overjoyed. I was home…

Of course I still kept writing in my journal.

There I was, going through this extraordinary process, the whole time watching what was going on. I was, after all, a therapist, by definition an observer of human behavior. Plus I was, after all (whether I knew it or not at that time), an artist. Artists are, by nature, observers of human behavior and anything or everything else around them. Consequently, I fulfilled both roles, and I observed.

I observed what I had been going through. What was happening to me. Then I wondered about it. I wondered why I had stopped writing. Then I wondered, more joyfully, why I had started writing again. I began coming up with explanations. With ideas. With theories. Theories about what had happened to me. Theory, after theory, after theory. I kept thinking, and talking, and reading about artists. Combined with wondering some more.

Finally, I started to understand. Bit by bit. More and more. I kept thinking about it. I kept feeling about it. Gradually I started to realize it wasn't only me this had happened to.

Okay, hopefully, my version of it was a fairly extreme version. While there are many other people out there having that particular version (and far, *far* worse), there are also lots of you who aren't.

Yet the fundamentals are the same. It happens to so many of us. The shutting down of our art. The painful, sorrowful, and often oblivious, turning away from our creative selves. It's sad, tragic, spirit-crushing. Whether we're aware of it or not.

I didn't want to keep watching it happen. To any of us. I hated the idea of it. I wanted to do something about it.

So I decided. Or maybe I just knew. I knew that what I wanted to do for the rest of my life was write.

And I knew that what I wanted to do for the rest of my life was work with other people so they, too, could get to their art.

Ah, there it is – the point of this story.

As I said when I started, I was going to tell you how I developed this course. That's how I developed this course.

*　　　*　　　*　　　*

There you are. That's what I've done.

I've been writing. Teaching this course. I've even gone back to doing therapy. My specialty is working with artists.

*　　　*　　　*　　　*

Step #2 – Your turn

What I'd like you to do is introduce yourself to me. The sad part about this is that I don't get to hear what you have to say. I don't get to know you.

But the glad part about this, and by far the more important part, is that YOU do. Get to hear what you have to say. Get to know – and understand – how you answer these questions. Get to know you…

I'd like you to say a bit, or write about (whichever you feel more comfortable doing), who you are. Anything you want to say about who you are.

Next I'd like you to talk about *your* experience with creativity. Your connection. Your history with it.

By the way, in this moment, I am purposefully *not* giving you more details about what I'd like you to talk about. Either about who you are, or about your experience with creativity. I don't want to lead you anywhere in particular. I don't want to point you in a direction.

I want you to point yourself. I want you to go wherever your thoughts take you.

YOU…

Next I'd like you to think and talk (or write) a little bit about what you hope to get out of this book. Please take *__however__* much time you want; a sentence or twenty minutes, an hour if that's what's right…

Now take a pause (really!): think or say or write.

Then, when you're finished, turn the page.

*   *   *   *

Thank you for doing that. I've got a couple of comments. (Cute trick, eh? Since I'm not there and haven't heard a word you've said.) I have them anyway.

Comment #1: Please pay close, careful attention to how you *felt* talking or writing about your history with creativity. Pause now, for a few moments, and remember. . .

Don't be surprised if it made you feel sad, or angry, even scared. It may have made you cry. A lot of people do. It may have made you smile or laugh as you remembered things you haven't thought about in a while, perhaps a very long while. In other words, it could have made you feel anything. It's actually a hell of a complicated, complex, digging, delving question. You could even have felt nothing. (That was one of my specialties – more later…)

Just please pay attention to whatever reaction you had. It matters.

Comment #2: If your description of your history with creativity started with, "I'm not creative," DO NOT trash yourself. Please notice that I am mentioning this without having heard you say it. That's because many, many, *many* of my most creative, artistic, talented students start off that way.

It means nothing about how creative you are.

It *can* have to do with any number of things: how you (or others) see you, what's happened in your past, what values you've been taught. ANY number of things. We will be exploring them. At length.

But it means *absolutely* nothing about how creative you are.

Comment #3: Thank you for going there. It's often quite difficult, or at least odd, to go exploring your artistic past. I'm glad you made the effort.

*　　　*　　　*　　　*

What I would like to do now is discuss what I refer to as a few housekeeping topics:

First: Please use, find, or buy a pad, a journal, a binder, a sketchpad, a notebook, whatever you're comfortable using, and have it as a dedicated writing or drawing instrument for the course. Use it for your thoughts or ideas about the course, for taking notes and, most importantly! use it (if it works for you) for making art, of any and all kinds. Also you can use it for any exercises or assignments I ask you to do.

To be totally and thoroughly annoying, I would prefer that it not be electronic. It's a gut instinct (and I do keep struggling with it). I strongly request no electronics in my classrooms – they seem to get in the way somehow. Ergo, I am going to request the same thing of you when it's any "In Class Exercises." More about "In Class Exercises" below.

(An interesting note is that just the other day, I was sitting in an appointment with a client who happens to be the ultimate techie, discussing the difference between physically doing art – writing on paper, for example, or drawing on canvas – vs. doing art electronically. I suddenly looked down at the spiral notebook I was taking notes in, looked up and said, "Right? Imagine if I had my laptop here between us during therapy." We laughed, the point being instantly apparent. It would be awful for both of us.)

Therefore, do *try* to do your In Class work non-electronically. When it's not an In Class, do it however you want! You still might want to consider doing things electronically some of the time, and non-electronically some of the time. (Hell, you may as well experiment for the In Class as well, if it's really a sticking point…) Though, in general, it might be interesting for you to see what impacts it has. What differences there are between the two worlds when you're working on your art, or working on your way into your art…

Second: Okay. I am about to describe two kinds of activities I'll be asking you to do throughout the book. The first is an **"In Class Exercise,"** and the second is a **"Homework Assignment."**

But one quick slightly strange formatting note before I do. For many of these activities, I want you to do them before you look at any of the discussions that follow. I want only YOUR response, completely uninfluenced by anything I have to say. So a common phrase I use is, "Then when you're finished, turn the page." This way you won't be able to see the discussions until you *actually turn the page*. That means, however, there are some blank pages in the book. Weird, I know. But important.

To continue.

If I ask you to do an **In Class Exercise** (writing or drawing, composing, or whatever works for you)**,** I would like you to do the exercise *immediately*, as soon as you read what it is. Don't put it off until later. In this case, what we're looking for is your immediate reaction. Your first thoughts and feelings.

Also, my hope and expectation is that you take no more than twenty minutes to do it. I would definitely like you to stick to that. These are the assignments that would take place during the actual face-to-face classroom time, so there is an explicit time limit. (The time limit helps in all sorts of ways. No time limit helps in all sorts of other ways. We will, thus, be doing both.)

Lastly, I would request that you do this exercise in a situation in which you will not be distracted. Therefore this is especially when I ask you to turn off everything! Your phone, iPad, laptop, smartphone, even music! Everything. Just 'til you finish the exercise. Afterwards you can go back to all of it!

If, on the other hand, I give you a **Homework Assignment**, that is a truly different animal. I give the Homework Assignment at the end of the class and participants do it sometime, hopefully, before they come to the next class. My *expectation* of homework, is still that it takes about twenty minutes. In this case, though, if you would like to do more, please feel free! You're on your own for homework, whether you're taking the course or doing the book. The only reason for my concern about time here is that I don't want you feeling that you have to work on it for three hours, or four or five days, and if you don't you're a failure… I want no failure feelings for something so irrelevant! Twenty minutes is what I'm looking for. Or less, of course. But if an hour, or a day… is more fun, go for it.

Also, with a Homework Assignment, if you'd like to do it immediately, do it immediately. If you want to wait a day, or three or four, a week, even longer, that's fine. A lot of people need down time, or away time, before they do their homework. We'll talk more about that later.

Finally, do the Homework Assignment in whatever environment you prefer. Whatever suits you. More on that later, as well…

Third: During the course of doing this book, I will often ask you questions. Questions about what you're thinking, or feeling. Or about your reaction to something I've said. Or often, more importantly, I'll ask you a question about something *you've* said, or written, or drawn.

Of course I'm not there to hear your answer. I'd still like you to consider the question and answer it. Because, again, even though I'm not there to hear you, YOU are. That is way more important.

Do please consider each question, and respond. Then pay attention to your response. Think about it. Or take notes. Whatever works. Just pay attention to it.

Fourth: In an in-person class I ask participants to treat the course and their classmates with confidentiality so that everyone feels comfortable revealing and exploring themselves. (Remember how concerned I am about you feeling safe!) So I request that if they do talk to anyone about anything that happens in class to please keep it anonymous – which is exactly what I will proceed to do in this book. (I even occasionally change some of the details of students' experiences to protect their anonymity even further.)

For you, however, in this situation, while you're *doing* this book, there is nobody else's confidentiality you need to worry about.

But do consider confidentiality for yourself, in any event. You may want to carefully pick and choose what you want to share about this process, and with whom. Of course, you might want to talk about it incessantly. To everyone. Either way, whatever is right for you. Just give yourself some time to consider it.

Finally: This last piece of housekeeping is perhaps the most critical! The two most important things I can say to you.

The first one is that during the process of this book, emotional reactions can happen. They probably will happen! A little, a lot, the potential is infinite. This program and this topic have the capacity to be profound. Surprising, powerful, significant. Please pay attention to that part of it.

If "stuff" does come up for you, take care of yourself. Be as gentle and mindful as you can.

If you need to get support, get support: friends, family, teachers, sponsors, counselors, therapists. Whatever kind of non-professional or professional help you think is worth a try.

If you need to get help, get help.

Do anything and everything you need to do to take care of yourself.

Now on a totally related topic, the second most important thing, has to do specifically with the In Class Exercises and the Homework Assignments I've just finished describing. What I want to say about those is, DO NOT GO PAST WHAT FEELS SAFE!

Yes, I do want you to do this book, not just read it, but please only DO the parts that feel okay for you. Your Way, remember? If a particular exercise feels a bit too scary, skip it! If it feels like it's going a bit too far, don't bother going near it.

Sometimes skipping the assignment and just going straight to the discussion after it might be helpful. Or skipping the discussion entirely, as well. You can always go back to any or all of it later. If you want to.

The critical thing is that you're taking care of yourself now!

Stuff does come up. You need to give yourself permission to pay attention to that stuff. In whatever way you need to.

Remember the cliff you would not just be jumping off? If you were going to do it by climbing down the rocks, for example, you'd be teaching yourself how to do it properly. Managing your skills. Attending to your fear. Hell, you'd probably start off practicing how to do it in an indoor gym.

You'd be busily taking care.

So one more time. Do anything and everything you need to do to take care of yourself.

That taking care of yourself may be exactly what you need to do for you, and for the creation of the art that is the purpose here.

We will be talking much more about this as we go!

So, please, do take care.

*   *   *   *

That's it. That's the housekeeping.
That is also the end of the beginning.
I wish you the best in continuing on.

Take care, all.

Chapter two
Dari's Three Principles of Art

When I started putting together the outline for my very first course, I decided to be as pretentious as possible.

No, not really. At the beginning I actually decided very little. It just sort of came. Baby step by baby step. I *did* the course. Just let it come. Pretty much like I'm asking you to do...

What I intentionally did do immediately was to come up with *the* Three Principles of Art. That is a bit pretentious, no? Ah, well.

Here is just a brief introduction to those principles. We'll be working on all of them, continuously, as we "step" our way through this creative universe.

*   *   *   *

DARI'S THREE PRINCIPLES OF ART

Principle #1 - YOU HAVE TO WANT TO DO IT

Write, paint, act, sculpt, dance, compose... Whatever art form you're interested in.

You have to want to do the art.

When I started teaching, the principle actually read, "You have to want to do your art badly, really badly!" Some of you do. You're wanting to create art with your whole heart. You're yearning for it. Often desperate. Even despairing. It's all you can think about. You've been trying to force yourself into doing the art for ages. Or taking a course for it. Or reading a book. Totally committed. Some of you.

Yet, gradually, I came to realize that that is **not** true for all of you. Not by any means. A lot of the "would be" artists who come to my courses think that's exactly what they are. "Would be's." (Please note: I placed quotation marks around the phrase precisely because I don't believe it for a second!) Or wannabes. These students think they're NOT creative. Remember? They take the course on a whim. Or so they think. They would never suggest that they want to do their art badly. They hardly believe they want to do it at all. Most importantly, they don't believe, even for an instant, that they will ever actually do their art.

BUT all of those students, somehow, somewhy, are in the course. They paid the tuition. They came to the class. They took it at night or on the weekends because they're working full time. Or they pushed themselves out of some particular lethargy of doing nothing. Often they made excruciatingly complicated arrangements necessary to have someone be at home to take care of the kids, so they could actually leave the house for three hours.

The point is they are *there*. They are in the course. No matter how little they believed they were interested in it.

Gradually I realized a lot of participants didn't even really know they wanted to do art – certainly didn't think of themselves as artists.

Didn't think about it much. Didn't care about it much. Didn't have a clue in their conscious universe. I didn't. Oblivious, remember?

But there was something. Something made those individuals come to the course, no matter how they thought they felt about their art. Notice the word, "thought."

Something made me return to my journal. Fifteen years after I'd stopped writing in it, without even noticing. And there is something that made you buy this book, or download it, or go to the library for it, or borrow it from a friend. Something.

Often the urge to be creative is barely a whisper. A faint echo in the most distant part of our being.

But it's there. It's there.

Subsequently, **Principle Number One** changed from "you have to want to do it really badly," to a much simpler and less emphatic:

"You have to want to do it."

Maybe it should actually add, "even a little."

Now, all of you who are reading this sentence, *are* reading this sentence. Consequently, you have already achieved the first of Dari's Principles of Art! Somehow, somewhere, somewhen, you want to do your art. You really do.

Isn't that wonderful?!

Principal #2 - PRACTICE, PRACTICE, PRACTICE.

Just wait. Don't turn away. I don't mean it the way I'm pretty sure you think I mean it. The way we were all trained from the age of five or six. Maybe even earlier.

Sung to the tune of, A B C D E F G: "A B C D E F G..." Or sung to the tune of, Do Re Mi Fa So La Ti Do: "Do Re Mi Fa So La Ti Do..." Maybe not even a tune: Just the classic piano scale. "C D E F G A B..."

"I want to dance!": "First position, Second position, Third position...." Over and over and over, and OVER, again.

I don't mean it that way. I don't mean "practice" it. Or the act of learning how to do it. Or learning how to do it better. I don't mean "practicing it" until you get it perfect.

I mean THE practice of it. The act of it. Think Zen. Think "Om." The simple act of doing your art holds great potential.

Practice, Practice, Practice.

Lots more on this later.

Finally, Principle #3 - PROCESS, PROCESS, PROCESS.

Process, process, process is divided into two major categories:
1. Work at finding the things that help you do your art.
2. Work at finding the things that get in your way.
Pretty straightforward, no?
I wish.

The idea may be. The "process" is not. However, it is what we're about. The great thing is, it really, really helps.

There are, in addition, two corollaries to the principle of Process, Process, Process. Also, if you were to ask me, they are two of the foundations of my belief system about the entire universe of creativity.

So here they are.

Corollary 1: Finding the things that help you do your art and finding the things that interfere, are both everlasting processes.

Let me repeat. Everlasting Processes.

You don't "get there." You don't arrive. You don't finish. The process doesn't go away. You don't solve the puzzles, conquer the issues, figure it out, and you're done. I don't think it's ever done. Any more than figuring out your life gets done. You don't solve your life. You live it. And you work on it. It changes as you go along. With each new stage or phase or moment. Each step of your life brings new (you can insert any word you want here: challenges is one of the current buzzwords) issues and worries, joys, topics, people, learning, experiences, desires, adventures, fears, excitements, concerns, ambitions, and so on and so on and so on.

Well, each step of your creativity does the same. Ongoing and everlasting.

Process, Process, Process.

Corollary 2: There is NO correct answer. There can be nothing prescriptive about the RIGHT way to do your art. By its very nature, creativity is about originality. Originality is an individual thing. It's about your thing. YOUR WAY. It has to be.

There are no "shoulds," no rules, no regulations. No laws, or statutes, or edicts, or proclamations.

It's art. It's your art.

And you're the only one in this whole universe who can figure out how you need to create it. How you need to get to it. What you need to do to be able to do it.

There is no RIGHT way to do your art. There is only YOUR way.

It's about you.

Period.

*   *   *   *

There.

Those are my three principles of doing art.

*   *   *   *

Okay, where do I come in? Since it's all about you and your way.

How do I go about teaching this course? Or working with you in this book?

Well, for starters, I don't – hardly ever, with a very few exceptions – tell you how to do it. Your art, that is. I'm simply not that kind of teacher. EVER. (hardly…) If you do hear me giving you a giant *should* on how you should be being creative, or what kind of art you should be doing, even on what or how you need to do your process in order to get *to* your art, you can send ME, your teacher, to go stand in the corner. (I actually dislike referring to myself as a teacher in this context. It's just not what this is about – me teaching you.) Telling you how to do your art, or your process, is not my point, my job, or my task. It's definitely NOT what I want to be doing.

What I want to be doing is helping you figure out the things that help *you* do your art. In addition to that, I want to be helping you figure out the things that get in *your* way. Then you can do your art the way your art is supposed to get done.

Your art

Your way

Those are the principles and the corollaries and the point.

My point.

*　　*　　*　　*

IN CLASS EXERCISE

I would now like to give you your first In Class Exercise. Since this is your very first one, I'm going to repeat the guidelines… instructions… rules…. I know, I know, there aren't supposed to be any of those. I'm still going to repeat them.

*　　*　　*　　*

If I ask you to do an **In Class Exercise**, (writing or drawing, composing, or whatever works for you)**,** I would like you to do the exercise **_immediately_**, as soon as you read what it is. Don't put it off until later. In this case, what we're looking for is your immediate reaction. Your first thoughts and feelings.

Also, my hope and expectation is that you take no more than twenty minutes to do it. I would definitely like you to stick to that. These are the assignments that would take place during the actual face-to-face classroom time, so there is an explicit time limit. (The time limit helps in all sorts of ways. No time limit helps in all sorts of other ways. We will, thus, be doing both.)

Lastly, I would request that you do this exercise in a situation in which you will not be distracted. Therefore, this is especially when I ask you to turn off everything! Your phone, iPad, laptop, smartphone, even music! Everything. Just 'til you finish the exercise. Then you can go back to all of it!

*　　　*　　　*　　　*

IN CLASS EXERCISE

I would like you to write the following:
"I want to do my art because..."
(Substitute in the kind of art you want to do, as in "I want to paint..." "I want to dance..." "I want to write..." because...)

I wish I could answer your questions, but I can't. (And I don't actually want to...) Please, just write about why you want to do your art. "Why?"

Then, when you're finished, turn the page.

*　　　*　　　*　　　*

How was that? Fun? Hard? Boring? Exciting? (Remember about answering my questions…)

This was an unusual assignment because of what I'm about to say next. If you have finished writing (which, of course, I'm sure you have, or you wouldn't be reading this yet…), I would like you to put the piece away somewhere safe. Seal it up in an envelope. Don't look at it again until you've finished doing this book. Most of the time, when you do any writing exercise, In Class or Homework, we'd now be discussing what you wrote. Though not this time. This time I'd like you to just put it away.

In my classes, this is the only piece of work I ask people to turn in. They don't even have to put their name on it. Just a code that they'll recognize. Everyone's work goes into an envelope, which I seal, and then I sign the seal. I explain that I will not be reading the assignment, but rather, will be handing it back to them on the last day of class.

With you, I'll ask you to take the piece out of your sealed envelope and read it when you've finished the book. Put it somewhere safe!

Take care, all.

Chapter three

Snow

All right. Imagine that you've cut your finger. It's just a little cut, but it's bleeding and it hurts. What do you do?

Please feel free to call out the answers. Or write them down. Then turn the page.

*   *   *   *

Below are some pretty typical responses:
You wash it.
You scrub it.
You wipe the blood on a tissue, or toilet paper, or a napkin, a towel.
You put pressure on it to stop the bleeding.
You suck on it... (Everybody goes ewwwww when they hear this, but many of us do it.) It's our own blood after all...
You can put antiseptic cream or ointment on it.
You put a Band-Aid on it.
Anything else?

*　　*　　*　　*

All right. You leave the wound alone for a few days, you take off the Band-Aid (if indeed you've put one on), and you look at the cut on your finger. What's happened?
Do shout out your answer.

*　　*　　*　　*

Generally, everything being equal, it's healed. Or healed a lot. It's on its way.
Please note, *you* have not healed it.
You stopped the bleeding, you cleaned it. You've eliminated dirt from getting in the way of the healing. You put antiseptic on it to ensure that you didn't miss cleaning out any of the dirt or bacteria. You put a Band-Aid on it to protect it from getting re-scraped, or re-hurt.
Yet none of these things that you did, healed it. Your body healed it. Your body healed your finger.
Given the opportunity, your body naturally moves towards healing. It wants to heal. Its natural process is to heal. Sickness is, by one definition, when something gets in the way of that healing.
But the natural process for our bodies is to move towards healing.

*　　*　　*　　*

I believe, with my whole being, the exact same process is true of creativity. Creativity wants to come. It *wants* to be. To exist. It is a natural state.

*   *   *   *

Okay, now we're going to enter the world of your imagination.

(**A NOTE**: I'd like you to think of me as standing in front of you at a whiteboard, marker in hand, writing down whatever you say. Please just pour out your thoughts. Flow. Spew. Whatever comes. Onto the whiteboard on the next page in this book. Or write them down on your own version of a whiteboard. Paper, phone, whatever works.

Keep pouring them out. Until you stop. Then you can wait a minute. Until something else comes to mind. Then spew some more. Take your time. Keep exploring. As long as you want.)

Okay, back to your imagination.

Sit back and get comfortable, close your eyes (if that's comfortable), and imagine that you're a seven-year-old child who is living two hundred years ago.

In the tropics. It's warm/hot, sunny, lush, beautiful. The sky is blue. Sun, yellow. A lovely tropical home.

Remember, it's two hundred years ago. Which means several things.

It means there is no electricity. There are no telephones. No cellphones, even. There is no television, or radio, or movies. There's none of that. There is no mass communication of any kind. There are not, imagine this, not even any computers. No iPads, or smartphones, or Blackberries. There is no Internet, or e-mail. No Facebook. No Google. Nothin'. Not a tech virtual anything.

That is the world two hundred years ago.

Suddenly the day comes when your parents inform you that you're all going to move to the north. Whatever that is. Your whole family packs up all your belongings and you're on your way. You travel. You keep traveling. To the far, far north. Let's imagine it's northern Canada. Siberia. Iceland. Wherever you want. Just really north.

You arrive at night but you can't see anything because it's dark, and there's no electricity. Remember? You go to sleep in your new bedroom and you wake up early in the morning and you run to your window and you look outside.

The world is covered in semi-frozen, white water.

There's snow out there. And you're seven years old. You've never seen snow before, never even heard of it.

So what do you do?

*   *   *   *

WHITEBOARD
SNOW

Write down anything, *anything* that comes to you.

(**NOTE:** Remember, just pour out your thoughts. Whatever comes. Onto the whiteboard below. Or write them down on your own version of a whiteboard. Just keep spewing. Until you stop. Then you can wait a minute. Until something else comes to mind. Then pour some more. Take your time. Keep exploring. Imagine going through the whole day you first see snow. Go through every aspect of the experience.)

Then when you're finished, turn the page.

*　　*　　*　　*

WHITEBOARD
SNOW

This is a typical whiteboard from my classes.
What's actually written on it can go on and on, depending mostly on
the time available…

---

touch it   feel it   taste it   run inside

make snow angels   roll in it   walk in it

slide down it   Look at animal tracks

build a fort   build a castle

Ask your parents what it is   Where it came from

how long it will be there

play in it   get scared   get excited

eat it   take it inside and melt it   draw pictures

pee in it   write your name in it   Listen to it

watch it fall from a tree   Run in it

Make sounds with it   Crunching   squeaking

listen to the silence of it

smell it   throw it   shape it

make snowballs   make snowman

There you are, out in the snow. You'll play all day. You'll keep
coming up with new things to do. Which is exactly what kids do in the

snow. They keep coming up with new things to do: to try, and play, and explore.

Now look at the whiteboards. Yours or mine. (It's not really fair. Your board comes all from one person. My class board typically comes from ten to twenty people. Consequently, if your whiteboard doesn't have as many activities, it's not surprising…)

Here's what your seven-year-old child has done.

You've explored and examined the snow with every one of your senses. You've experimented with what it feels like, looks like, sounds like, tastes like, and so on, and on, and on. Total investigation of the material, of the environment. You've walked on it, run and slid in it. You've felt all kinds of different emotions.

In addition to this, or really as part of this, you have explored almost all of the many various art forms available to you with this particular medium!

Huh?

Yes.

You have looked at pictures from the snow – flakes falling from trees, animal tracks – you've drawn in the snow or made pictures with your body – snow angels. If you're a boy you've written your name with your pee. (The thing I love most about that one is that the guys in the class are *never* the ones who mention it. Only the women.) You've done sculpture. You've created shapes of snowballs and snowmen. Who knows what other shapes. You've explored the music of the snow. The deep, muted silence of the white blanket, or the crunching and squeaking of snow under your feet and in your hands. You've even done architecture – building forts and castles.

You've searched for and found, probably from your parents, stories of origin. Where did the snow come from? Why is it there? What will happen to it? Just like all the other stories of origin. Why does the sun come up every morning? What happens to the moon? Where do the crops come from? Stories of Origin. The official beginning of storytelling.

The beginning of fiction.

Given the material you are dealing with, that seven-year-old child, who has *never seen snow before*, knows nothing about it, has received no instructions on what to do with it, has thoroughly explored this particular new and unknown medium and produced ART.

ART!

I pretty much guarantee that I'm missing some of those art forms. I also pretty much guarantee that that seven-year-old will eventually practice them.

The art of snow.

*　　　*　　　*　　　*

Creativity.

Art.

It's a natural part of who we are.

It wants to come. Given the opportunity, it will come.

We are all creative beings. Just like healing. Our beings naturally move towards creativity.

Water it, give it sunshine, feed it, give it air and space and opportunity, and creativity will come.

*　　　*　　　*　　　*

Onto the next exploration.

We are going to return to the world of your imagination. (I've provided another whiteboard for you on the next page, if you want it.) Sit back, get comfortable, close your eyes, and imagine the following:

Imagine your parents, or parents in general. What would they say? What would they say to that seven-year-old who is going out into that snow?

*　　　*　　　*　　　*

Whiteboard
What parents would say.
Write down anything, *anything* that comes to you.

Then when you're finished, turn the page.

*   *   *   *

Whiteboard
What Parents Would Say

Put on your coat.   Dress warmly.
Don't forget your hat.   Mittens.   Boots.
Don't stay out too long. You'll get cold. Don't get wet.
Be careful.   Don't fall down.   Have fun.
Be careful, it's slippery.
Don't track the snow into the house.
Take your brother with you.
Let's build a snowman together. Don't go too far away.
Don't get lost. Stop making so much noise. Stop yelling.
Shhhhh.   Shut up already.
Bring in the firewood. Go shovel. Come inside for lunch.
Bundle up. Don't fight with your sister. Don't hurt her.
Get in here.   Stop throwing snowballs.   Stay out of
the street.   Stop wasting time.   Do your chores
Don't talk to people you don't know. Stay off the ice.
What do you think you're doing?
Make sure you come inside before it gets dark.

Phew.

As a special gift to me, the first time I did this exercise, there was a Brit (a person from Great Britain) in the class. A lovely woman from England. Right at the end of the brainstorming session she yelled out *her* suggestion for the board, which was about telling the kids to stop making so much noise and be quiet. Or more pointedly to Shut Up!

Until that point, nobody had mentioned the shushing factor. When she did, she used an expression common in British slang.

She yelled out very loudly, **"STIFLE IT!!!!!!!"** (dragging out the word stifle almost musically). It was perfect.

Consequently, from that moment on, this became the "**Stifle It**" exercise.

Look at the list and notice how many, many, many!!! "Don'ts" there are on the board. Don't, don't, don't, don't, don't. There are also lots of instructions, like be careful, it's slippery, slow down, all of which can be translated into another form of don't, as in – "Don't do anything risky."

If you look at the list, however, you can see there are also some perfectly lovely instructions, too. "Have fun," or "Let's do something together." Wonderful. Loving. Encouraging creativity. Encouraging exploration together.

But sadly, in every brainstorming session I've ever done, on every board students have filled in, the "don'ts" dramatically outnumber the nice suggestions. More than dramatically. The ratio of don'ts to lovelys is huge. Every single time.

That lovely, excited, exploring, experimenting, expanding, creative seven-year-old, gets stifled. A lot! There was a television series called *Curb Your Enthusiasm*. These days it always makes me think of that...

Here's an interesting lesson I learned when I started doing this course. I would introduce this brainstorming session by saying the following:

"I'd like you to imagine that the seven-year-old you, from two hundred years ago, who has just traveled north, and seen snow for the very first time, had mean, terrible parents."

(I realize now, that was *my* fundamental reference point, so that was how I imagined it.)

Yet I quickly realized from listening to students' responses – students who came from every conceivable type of family background – that it didn't matter if we were talking about terrible parents or wonderful parents. Nasty, aggressive families, or warm loving ones. It just didn't matter much at all.

We were simply talking about parents.

These don'ts are not necessarily examples of parents being mean. A great many of the comments and instructions (depending on the parents, of course), were simply parents being parents. Good parents, in fact. Parents doing the job they are supposed to do. Parents who are taking care of their children. Keeping them dressed properly, keeping them safe, secure, keeping them out of harm's way.

Being parents.

Yet those instructions, that care, those don'ts, still close down behaviors, slow the child down, impede the child's free spirit. That happy, creative kid is now paying attention to a whole bunch of other things. Dressing properly, being cautious, behaving appropriately. Paying attention to time and distance, taking care of younger sibs.

They are no longer just diving creatively into their new exciting world.

If the parents *are*, in fact, mean, if they are the other kind of parents, if the comments are actively aggressive, or excessive, like some of the comments on this whiteboard (comments which are all too familiar from my courses), the process is often crushing. Instead of the patient (or impatient…) groan of the child who's accustomed to being pestered to take care, who's simply being parented and now has to stop and think about what they are doing in the excited exploration, the child of mean or abusive parents experiences the bubble-bursting, spirit-flattening, soul-stomping defeat and despair of their joyful creative self.

These kind of experiences, both the taking-care of the child ones, and the soul-stomping ones, go on throughout childhood. Schools, for example, have to have rules. They have to keep the children safe. They have to keep some order. Ergo, there are a lot of don'ts in school. *Lots*. There are a lot of don'ts and rules in extra-curricular activities, too; in clubs and sports, choir and band, all of them. After school's out, it's the same thing. There are rules in practically everything, whether it be math tutoring or dance classes.

Now, all of these rules are merely ways of keeping order. Of course, that's only if every teacher and sponsor and coach is a human being.

When they're not, when they're mean or abusive, it's a whole other world that crushes one's creativity. (We'll explore that more deeply, further on.)

And then, then, we grow up. The same thing happens in the work-place. Rules and regulations. "Appropriate" behavior, attire, work habits. When driving. There has to be some order on the road. (Thank goodness, right?) Lots of rules.

There are rules about pretty much everything. Or guidelines, at least. Recommendations for the proper way to function in any given situation. The world becomes absolutely filled to the brimming point with DON'Ts. Some reasonable. Some, completely nuts. Some better. Some worse. Sometimes often, sometimes rarely. Though never without consequences – and never without memories.

Our happy, exploring, creative universes, really do get curbed. Cut off. Discouraged. Shut down.

STIFLED.

Now let me repeat.

Water it, give it sunshine, feed it, give it air and space and opportunity, and creativity will come.

But we have to figure out how to do exactly that.

Therefore, part of our job is to explore all the different kinds of things that interfere with that watering and that sunshine, that air, that space and that opportunity, so that creativity does come.

Because it really *does* want to.

Take care, all.

PART TWO

Principle #3
Process, Process, Process

1. Work at finding the things that help you do your art.
Sounds like a good idea…

This section will be devoted to this topic. Work at finding the
things that help you do your art. Figure out the things that help you
be creative.
While the whole book is essentially devoted to this very same issue, it
will just go about things from many different angles.

*   *   *   *

(Note: No, I have not accidentally skipped Principle #2 – Practice,
practice, practice. It will come. Again and again and again…)

Chapter four

This'll Help

A NOTE: The following instructions will sound familiar. It's what we did for snow and stifling. This is just a reminder.

There I am. Standing in front of you at a whiteboard, marker in hand, writing down whatever you say, whatever your thoughts are, whatever comes. You write them onto the whiteboard in this book. Onto your own piece of paper. Whatever works.

Keep spewing until you stop. Then you can wait a minute, until something else comes to mind, and then do some more. Take your time, and keep exploring. As long as you want.

*　　　*　　　*　　　*

This time, I'd like you to think of anything that can, or does, could or would, or even *just might*, help you to be creative. Anything that would encourage you to be creative, improve your creative environment, stimulate you, or inspire you. *Whatever* it is. *Whatever* it might be. If the thought surfaces, any thought, write it down. If the image appears, put it on the whiteboard. If the whisper whispers, repeat it in writing. ANYTHING. EVERYTHING.

If you think it might help you do your art – WRITE IT DOWN!!!!!!

*　　　*　　　*　　　*

Whiteboard
Enhancing Your Creativity
Write down anything, *anything and everything,* that comes to you.

Then when you`re finished – for now, at least – turn the page.

*   *   *   *

Whiteboard
Enhancing Your Creativity

Reading

Memories

A perfect chair   Feeling comfortable

Friendly people   clutter

café/coffee shop   COFFEE

Quiet   Solitude

No distractions   No disturbances   Privacy

Graphic Novels   Riding a bus   My favorite pen

Other Animals   Daydreaming   Movies

Other people's writing

Nature   groups   a view   love   romance   emotions

music   Libraries   Vacations   Traveling   evening

Silence!

tidy   tragedy   travel   meditation   middle of the night

beer   babies   heartbreak   experiences   photo album

a beautiful view

light

other people   exercise   watching children

quotations

Airports   A sharp pencil

Early morning   Beautiful Light   good food

happiness   art classes   others' art

privacy   chocolate   Special occasions   anger

a walk   a glass of wine   a drink

afternoon   joy   Tea   Sleep

the ocean

Being alone the forest   meeting someone   emotions

smoking a cigarette

photographs   new friends   Yoga

writing in my journal   reading my journal

the mountains   Art books   Dancing

my garden   cleaning my room   Magazines

Art Galleries

staring at the fireplace

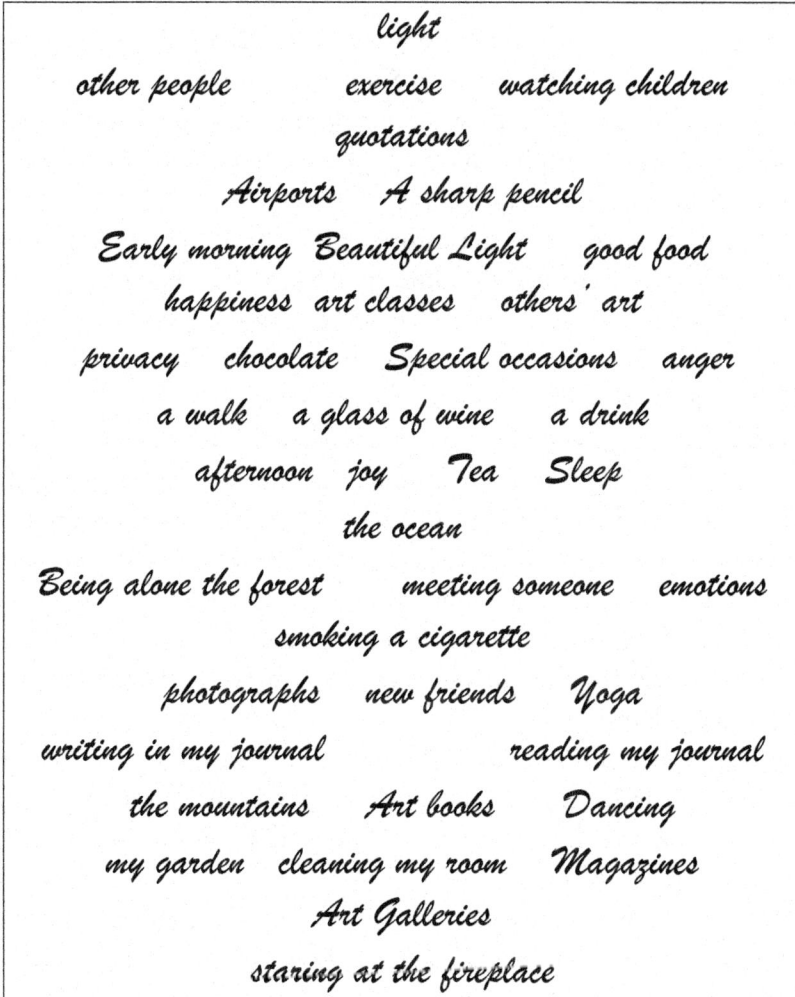

Above is a typical whiteboard from this brainstorming topic.

Let me make a few comments about this board, and then I'll go through my own personal list.

As you can see, the things that help you be creative can be just about anything. Probably, they can actually be *actually* anything… An infinite world of possibilities.

How much the same or different is your board?

My guess is, some the same, some different. That, of course, is one of the major points of this process. Some the same. Some different.

First, and absolutely most importantly, there ain't no right answer. None. *Anything* can inspire you. Experiences, emotions, environment. Sounds, feelings. People, not people. Anything.

If you do this particular brainstorming session a second time, you'd almost definitely come up with other anythings. When you actually do your art, you'll probably notice that something entirely new and different is helping you at any particular moment. Something that is not on your list, or the course list, or my list. Pretty much anything and everything can help you do your art at any particular moment.

The second point is that I'd like you to imagine you are sitting in the class that brainstorms this particular whiteboard. Someone calls out, "I need everything organized. Neat and tidy. Otherwise I can't relax."

Three minutes later, someone else calls out, "I need the environment to be a bit cozy. Cluttered. Filled with stuff."

The need for absolute quiet comes up in almost every class. As does music. Even clatter.

In one corner of the room is an early riser. She loves to paint before everyone else wakes up. In the other corner is the late-night artist. Midnight is best for him. Or three o'clock in the morning. Remember, there is no right answer.

What works for you may absolutely not work for anybody else. Your friends, classmates, family. They may all do it completely differently.

Their way.

It's also important to remember that we're all human. We ALL doubt ourselves. At least some of the time. Sometimes, all of the time. Consequently, it is more than easy to think that "they" are doing it the right way. That *their* environment is the correct one. That yours is not. That you're sabotaging your process by using the wrong techniques.

But that ain't it.

If it works for you, it's the right way. Period. Their way may actually be bad for you. Vice versa, as well. Try not to doubt too much, or assume their way is right and yours is wrong. Try not to second-guess yourself. Please do feel free to experiment. Try their ways if you feel like it. It might be a whole new discovery.

The bottom line is quite simple. **Your way** is the right way for you. The only thing that matters for your creativity, is what helps *your* creativity.

One more general comment, then I'll get on with *my* list.

What works for you today, or this year, or on this particular piece of art – writing sculpture, tapestry – may absolutely *not* work tomorrow. Or on that other piece you're working on.

What does work can depend on a myriad of things. What's happening in your life, the specific moment, the mood you're in, the time of day, the time of year, and oh, so frequently, the specific piece you're working on.

Personal example. I often listen to music when I write. It's usually, almost always, a particular piece of music for a particular piece of writing. If I try to listen to a different piece of music, it doesn't work. If I hear that particular piece of music, in *any* context (it's happened in restaurants, airplanes, in a movie), a piece of music that I listened to when I wrote a particular story, I get utterly confused. I am instantly back in that story, that setting, that world – and it always takes me a minute to figure out where I am, what I'm doing, what the hell is going on.

It's part of *that* story. Plus it is definitely part of *writing* that story. The worst possibility of all is that if I listen to that piece of music when I'm writing something *else*, I freak. I can't write. Nothing happens. I can't settle in. However long it takes me to figure out what the problem is, not a single word gets written. When I do figure it out, the relief is enormous. Oh, no, I think, I'm not crazy after all. It's just the wrong piece of music...

Therefore, pay attention to whatever works for you. Pay attention to the particular moment. Remember that it can, and probably will, change throughout your life. Just like so much else in your life. Finally, after all of this effort and analysis figuring out what helps you do your art, try not to get stuck thinking, "Oh, this is the way I'm supposed to do this, so I *have* to do it this way."

If it's not working, try it another way. Just change the bloody music. And breathe.

*   *   *   *

Remember, there ain't no right way… Only your way.

Take care, all.

Chapter five
This Helps Dari

Ways to Create A Creative Environment
Dari's Version

This chapter is filled with my list of the topics, places, activities, issues, concepts, objects, and so on and so on and so on, that have come up for me as significant facets of enhancing my creative process and environment.

I need to add here that many of these topics, places, activities, issues, concepts, objects, and so on and so on and so on, have only occurred to me because of ideas that have come up in brainstorming sessions in various classes.

I mean who knew I liked my studio a bit cluttered-looking? It's just my studio, filled with what it's filled with. I'd never considered clutter, one way or the other. It was only in a brainstorming session in which one student said they needed a messy, comfortable, somewhat cluttered environment to work in, and someone else practically groaned, that the topic even occurred to me. The groaner then said that their working environment had to be incredibly neat and tidy, almost sterile (their word), or they'd sit and focus on the mess, instead of their art.

I instantly knew that focusing on the mess just wasn't me. On further observation of my studio later that night, I realized that some amount of clutter was definitely what makes me happy and productive. Thus the topic of neatness versus clutter got added to my list.

Consequently, I've worked at exploring the alternatives to my actual preferences, since the topics so often come up in the whiteboard sessions. I say music, someone else says silence. I say focus, another artist wants distraction. The alternative possibilities that my explorations allude to are often someone else's "way."

Therefore, my list is organized along the lines of the general categories that resonate with me, and also along the lines of many that happen to be the opposite of mine or, even just somewhere in the middle.

"My list" simply means that it's the list I've written down to explore all the possibilities.

Herein I begin my (and everybody else's) list:
(I won't bother writing more on the topic of clutter… Consider it covered.)

PHYSICAL SPACE – LOCATION, LOCATION, LOCATION

For me, that definitely means Virginia Wolfe's "A Room of One's Own."

My physical space is my studio. Over the years, as I've lived in different places, I've had four different studios. Each one has been magical.

When I returned to my writing after that seventeen-year gap (hole, void, abyss, silence…), my first writing location was the dining room table in the middle of our semi-open-planned house. The typewriter (for those of you who don't know what one of those is, please proceed to Wikipedia… ☺), happened to be sitting out on the table the day – that glorious spring day – when I sat down and started writing fiction. There I was, typing my first words, while gazing through the sliding glass doors into my garden. The very first sentence described the lush purple hyacinths blooming in front of the textured cedar fence.

Over time, that location taught me a number of useful concepts for future studios.

Useful concept number one: I did not like being in the middle of a large open space. I wanted privacy. Aloneness. Isolation. Complete withdrawal from the other parts of my world. I wanted and needed a "A Room of One's Own."

Useful concept number two: I wanted and loved a view. At that point the view was a lush, colorful garden. The lusher and more colorful the better.

Useful concept number three: The view worked best when I was looking at it through sliding glass doors. It took me a while to figure that one out. It turned out that I didn't like the view getting cut off at a window's edge. A window frame meant I looked at my garden only partly, and then partly at the wall beneath it. I loved the expanse of the wideness and the tallness of the glass doors. Total visual focus straight to the outside.

Useful concept number four: I loved the feeling of working at our round oak dining room table with a center base (rather than four table legs – who'd have thought that would make a difference, but it did!).

Profound or ridiculous. All four concepts gave me a great deal of useful wisdom when we moved to a house with a two-car, free-standing garage. My husband and I proceeded to convert it – half into a workshop for him, half into a studio for me. To be honest, my half was a little bigger than his. He was very sweet when designing it.

Thus my first real studio was a converted garage. (A dear friend terrorized me by suggesting, in the middle of our massive efforts to convert it, that I would never get rid of the smell of the gasoline. Fortunately, he was wrong. This resulted in – *Useful concept number five:* A reminder to me to listen to others, but trust myself.)

We put glass doors in, on two adjoining walls, forming a corner with an enormous expanse of glass through which I got to gaze at the garden and forest beyond. That was my first actual studio. As I said, magical.

For my next studio (no free-standing garage), I went so far as to build an addition on the back of our little house. Glass doors. Enchanted garden.

My third studio is an old converted storage room, but I get to stare through more sliding glass doors at the open ocean.

I'm writing this chapter in a "half-bedroom" as in "a three and a half bedroom" of living space. The room is pretty small, but I'm gazing out onto a marsh inhabited, at the moment, by thousands of migrating snow geese. Again, magical.

All of my studios have held the magic. My studio. My space. A room of one's own is totally what works for me.

For many of us, the perfect physical space truly is "a room of one's own," if you're lucky enough to be able to manage that. Sometimes it's more of a *space* of one's own, a *corner* that's ours. A place where we won't be disturbed. (Note: That was definitely a bit difficult in the dining room…)

On the other side of the coin, a lot of people *want* and *need,* their space to be in the middle of the living room, where they will be disturbed. A place where everyone hangs out. Where the activity of their lives is taking place. Family, kids, friends, other animals. That's where the magic happens for them. If they were alone, shut away from the world, they'd go crazy. They want to know and be part of what's going on. It feeds their creative process.

As for those creative types who dread the idea of working on their art at *HOME,* of entering an isolated, quiet space at *HOME,* who need to get the hell out of the house to do something creative – and there are lots of you – pretty much anywhere else you choose can work perfectly.

It's not a particularly odd idea, or a new one. Think back to Parisian artists' cafés. The ones where people like Van Gogh hung out. He even did a painting of one of those cafes; *Café Terrace at Night,* also known as *The Cafe Terrace on the Place du Forum.* It's a beautiful piece. Other artists, like Sartre and Guy de Maupassant, also hung out in cafes. They connected with other artists. They did their work there. At this point, many of those cafés are tourist attractions for heaven's sake. Way back in 1927, writer and habitué of Vienna's Café Central, Alfred Polgar, wrote an actual essay, *Theories des Café Central* on the topic and described the café as a place where "Its inhabitants are, for the most part, people… who want to be alone but need companionship for it."[1] Dali, Kafka, Munch, even Freud, loved their cafés. These days think coffee shops.

I've lived in Vancouver for a lot of my life, and there are certain areas of the city, Kitsilano is one of them, the "Drive" is another, where artists have their special hangouts. In both neighborhoods there are coffee shops, cafés, restaurants, where, if you walk into any one of them, they'll be filled with writers and visual artists, musicians, performers, all working away at their computers, or on their scripts, or in their sketch pads. It's the activity and the "life," the bustle, the camaraderie, that make these spots an attractive physical space to do one's art.

Pubs in London. Marketplaces in the Middle East. There's always somebody doing art in those locations.

There are endless kinds of artists' "watering holes."

One, infinite, last example of a physical space that can be quite inspirational for doing art, for lots of us, is practically any place outside. You know, nature. The beach, the forest, Walden Pond, the top of a mountain, a Caribbean island, Key West (think Hemingway), the Mississippi River (I can't help it. Mark Twain's one of my beloveds.). The list is as infinite as the settings on the earth.

Sometimes when I'm absolutely stuck, and not a word will come in spite of my magical studio, I will bundle up (it often seems to happen in the middle of winter), and go to a particular beach I love. I sit there staring at the waves, the sand, the birds. Waiting. Usually freezing.

Sure enough, after a while, the words will come. Finally! (I did mention I was freezing?)

The point of all this?

The particular physical space you are in when doing your art, may be a very, *very* important thing to consider.

It can be ANYWHERE.

TOOLS

This is a funny category.

If you're a painter, a sculptor, a woodworker, I can almost hear you thinking, "duh!" Tools are fundamentals of your work.

Most artists instantly understand that their tools are of the utmost importance!

Of course, you're right. You need the proper brushes, the proper canvas, the right clay or marble, the right knives, and files, and hammers, the perfect piece of wood. (There's a wonderful woodworker in Key Largo whose property, nestled in a grove of trees, is filled with dozens of piles of the most beautiful, fascinating, lush, pieces of wood you can imagine. Gathered from different forests, different countries, different continents. Each stack is lovingly labeled and covered to protect it from the weather.)

Artists need their tools. They often seek endlessly to find the perfect ones. Photographers need the right camera to do their work. They need precisely the correct lenses, filters, film and slide film (at least in the old days, though you'd be surprised at how many photographers still cling to their hoarded supply of rolls of films as they fight the fight against digital photography), memory cards, computers, tripods, even the proper packs and bags for all this gear. (I could go on and on about this one. My husband's a nature photographer, and OMG!)

Dancers' shoes are critical. As is as the surface they dance on. The exact fabric and style of what they wear is essential to their ability to move the way they need to.

Think musicians and their instruments. A Stradivarius violin sold for $3,600,000 in 2010. It was made with three kinds of wood, but the mystery of the magic varnish remains.

So, duh. Tools are important. Artists need the perfect ones.

It's important to take them seriously. Honor your needs and preferences. Even trust your impulses when it comes to suddenly needing a specific thing for a specific piece of art. Your intuition often knows things before you do. (More about that further on...)

One more time, tools are important. Most artists are fully aware of this.

Unless you're a writer. Those of us who are writers hardly ever think in terms of the importance of tools. Or that we use them or need them or need to think about them. Yet many of us actually do. We do need them and we do need to think about them.

The rest of this section, therefore, is particularly devoted to writers. Although I hope it will offer support and justification to all of you other artistic types, who often have to struggle with the should-I-or-shouldn't-I? "indulgence" of purchasing a new tool. A really common and frequent "issue." Giving yourself permission to spend money on your art… (Please note, I am using the word "issue" in quotations because I am mocking the diagnostic tone of it!)

Or, it may also offer support for finding the different kinds of tools that aren't obviously associated with your art. The ones that you just don't think about.

My husband, the nature photographer, likes doing extra, extra (as in tiny, tiny, tiny) macro-photography. This requires a perfect tripod (okay, that was a fairly obvious requirement), that he sets up with his camera and spectacular (read expensive) macro lens. Then he stares into it for an inordinate amount of time (it can take him half an hour to set up), in order to get the perfect shot. Often he's down close to the ground in some convoluted, contorted position. It took him quite a while, and a *lot* of back pain, to realize he needed to carry a super-lightweight, folding stool to sit on during this process. A simple, even seemingly silly tool, that lets him focus (pun intended) much better on his process, just because he's not rushing to avoid being in pain for so long.

But this particular list is for *my* tools. I'm a writer, so they do focus on writing…

For any writing I do by hand, I use a very particular type of spiral notebook. They're all over my house in reds and blues, greens, aquas, purples. I use them for therapy notes, one per client, household notes, and for writing fiction and columns and this book (part of the time). They have to be the right color for the right purpose. Color-coded as it were. Even the right thickness. I hate it when I can't find my particular favorite kind of spiral in stores because they're temporarily off the shelves.

Pretty old-fashioned, I know. Yet I'm not the only writer who has a thing about notebooks. I even had a friend who had to order his most special journals from England. (Though he wasn't well off at all.) There was only the one special journal that worked for him. My husband has to have his little Moleskin notebooks. Not just the regular ones, oh no. The Van Gogh edition with the colored silk covers, naturally four times the price of the boring old black ones, is what he needs to be happy. Once, when we were spending several months down in the

Florida Keys, he ran out of them and we actually had them shipped down from Vancouver. (He *tried* to use the cheap black ones, he really did. Or so he says.)

I also have a pen. A special kind of pen. *The* pen. They too, are all over my house. I have them in black and red, purple, green, blue. They're a felt tip pen, a bit expensive to buy in the numbers I need, so I searched and found refills in bulk online for them.

(Total aside. I recently had a horrendous experience with a shipping company. I had shipped a white banker's box from Key Largo to Vancouver, filled with many of the class notes I have used as source material throughout this book. *Thousands* of pages. Ten days later I received a large brown carton instead, inside which my white banker's box had been placed, wrapped in multiple layers of plastic. When I removed the plastic and opened the original box, I found most of my spirals soaking wet... The box had gotten wet somehow, and then it had been wrapped in the plastic, ensuring that every piece of paper remained as wet as possible for the entire journey.

Needless to say I was horrified, devastated, panicked. You name it.

Yet the glorious happy ending was that not one word of the notes that I had written with my perfect special pen had smeared even a little. There was dye from file folders all over everything, but I could still read every word of the handwritten notes! I'm betting I will never write with any other pen for the rest of my life...)

Now here is my official, most embarrassing, revelation about my own important tools. I am a perfectly capable person on a computer. Not spectacular, not a computer freak expert (like so many of my friends), but competent. Please keep that in mind as I embarrass myself.

For many, many, many years, when I wrote fiction, long past the time (really, truly, long past the time when it had gone completely out of use), I persisted in using WordPerfect 5.1. It was a DOS program for those of you who even get what that means. For those of you who don't, it's OLD! I absolutely had to keep using it for writing fiction.

After struggling to give it up – I was sure I was just being silly and fussy – I finally figured out why it actually was so important to me. There were two reasons. The first reason goes way back in time.

I learned to type at the age of thirteen. I supported myself through university as a secretary. (Remember my time at Pan Am.) I'm a very good typist. Very fast. Touch typing all the way. (That means using all ten fingers, for you smartphone typists.)

When I was writing fiction I never, ever, even *glanced* at the keyboard. Or at the screen. Just fingertips to the keys. I was utterly absorbed gazing out the window, or the glass doors, at the magical garden in front of me, or the magical ocean, the marsh (depending on which studio I was in).

Of course, what I was really gazing at, was the fictional world I was writing. It's what I see. I'm lost in that world, framed by the beauty of what I'm staring at.

What does that have to do with WP5.1 you may wonder…

WP5.1 did *not* require the use of a mouse, a touch pad, or a pointer; for all of those, one *has* to look at the screen. (Try using any of them without visually tracking the movement. It simply doesn't work.) But in WP5.1 you only used the keyboard. Which I NEVER had to look at. I could simply keep peering out my sliding glass doors into the world I'm writing. Which is exactly what I needed to be doing.

My second reason for wanting WP5.1 is the writer's precious "blank sheet of paper." In WP5.1 there were no icons, no toolbars, no nothing. The only thing on the screen, other than blankness, was the name of the file, very tiny, in the bottom left of the screen, and the page number and position on the page, in the bottom right. Nothing else. Just a blank screen – and a lovely shade of blue, at that.

Apparently, I *needed* that blank sheet of paper.

There you are. My embarrassing revelation about the importance of my particular computer tool. When I couldn't keep focusing on the world outside my window, it would interfere enormously with my writing process. These years I have finally adjusted to the reality of Word. I've given up Word Perfect 5.1. But to this day, I truly do miss it.

If you're a writer, think about it. The perfect tools may matter to you just like they matter to almost every other kind of artist.

Plus if you're every other kind of artist, think about it anyway. I'm guessing there is inevitably some guilt and struggle about taking your specific needs quite as seriously as they may need to be taken.

SOUND

As I mentioned before, some of us need quiet or we can't concentrate. Absolute quiet. No sounds at all. I've seen a ticking clock drive students crazy when they're trying to write in my classroom.

Others people need music. Different kinds of music for different moods, different pieces of art. It can even be critically important whether there are lyrics, or it's strictly instrumental. (The words of the lyrics often get in my way.) Also, as I said previously, the choice of a specific piece of music can be crucial.

To do their work, many artists need the sounds of their families, their kids, friends, and roommates, or the clank and clatter and buzz of a coffee shop. (There's even some research suggesting that many coffee shops have the perfect decibel level to foster concentration and creativity.)

Sometimes the best sounds are simply the sounds of nature. I'll often turn off the music and open the doors and windows so I can hear the birds, the wind in the bamboo, the waves on the shore. Only when I can listen to the outside, will my written words pour forth.

Sound is one of our basic senses so it can be a critical part of doing art. Nothing much more to say about it. It's critical for me. I need the right sound at the right time.

SCHEDULING

For many people, the only way they can work is to have a schedule. It's often difficult to fit their art into their lives (or vice versa). They need a plan. Okay, "I'll paint two hours every day, from 7:00 to 9:00 in the evening." "I will make time for my writing every Saturday morning." We'll talk, further along in the book, about a bunch of issues that come up around this topic. Taking the time for yourself, taking your work seriously, and so on... Still, for now, having a schedule really helps some of us get to our art.

Or not...

The other side of this particular coin is that scheduling art is anathema to many others of us. Three a.m., when inspiration strikes, may be the only appropriate time to even consider doing art.

Just think about what works for you.

PRACTICE, PRACTICE, PRACTICE

It really can help!

Remember, I don't mean like practicing scales.

I mean the practice of your art.

Francis Bacon, the Irish/British painter, said, "As you work the mood grows on you."[2] I hate to admit this, but – in an effort to be as open with you as I want you to be with me – during all the years I've been teaching my courses, I always assumed the quote was from the wonderful philosopher, Francis Bacon. When I was writing this sentence for the book, however, I went searching the Internet for the official reference to it. It turned out not to be the philosopher Bacon, at all. It's a completely different fellow, the Irish/British painter. Sigh... At least somebody really said it. Thank you, Mr. Bacon.

One of my favorite quotes, one of the most meaningful concepts in my life actually, and the very first handout I give in all of my courses, is from Henri Poincaré, the Nineteenth Century French mathematician.

Please note: I love the fact that the very first handout I use in my courses on *creativity* is from a mathematician!

*   *   *   *

".... These sudden inspirations... never happen except after some days of voluntary effort which has appeared absolutely fruitless and whence nothing good seems to have come, where the way taken seems totally astray. These efforts then have not been as sterile as one thinks; they have set agoing the **Unconscious Machine** [my emphasis] and without them it would not have moved and would have produced nothing."[3]

*   *   *   *

I believe, with my whole heart, in the process of the unconscious machine. It has been by my side for all of my written work.

It's still fascinating to me how and when I became truly convinced of it, and committed to working with it. Here's what happened.

I wrote newspaper columns for many years. The columns had to be submitted to my editor by late Thursday afternoon. My normal pattern was to think about the column and start writing it on Tuesday mornings. I would work on it during the day, often throughout the day if I were having trouble. Wednesday I would edit it, which took at least a couple of hours, then I'd send it off to my husband, my personal editor, for his comments. He'd send it back to me and I'd make the changes I deemed necessary... Thursday I would do a final edit and send it off. It almost always took many, many hours of work over the course of the three days.

The interesting thing happened, by chance, on a Friday afternoon, when my husband and I were out sculling (think rowing with two oars each, and sliding seats) in English Bay, a protected ocean area between Vancouver and West Vancouver. Some salmon were jumping above the surface of the water, and the seals were getting appropriately excited. The gulls were singing overhead. An eagle flew by and I saw a great blue heron standing by the shore waiting for some fish to swim by.

It all started me thinking about the incredible joy of seeing all these wild, beautiful beings in the sea, on the sand, in the sky. How astonishing it was. More magic.

Abruptly I had to focus back on the paddling because the waves were getting a bit challenging, sloshing over the sides of our small boat. All thinking about anything but keeping the boat afloat stopped.

I went through my weekend without a wisp of a salmon thought, then spent all of Monday working with my clients and courses.

When Tuesday morning arrived and I sat down to write my column, I ended up writing about the glories of the sea. It took about two hours. The whole thing. Started, finished, edited. By *far*, the fastest column I'd ever written.

Dennis, husband, had little to comment on in his editing, and by Wednesday morning the piece was done.

I was so surprised by the ease of writing that column that I started thinking about where it had come from. I paid attention to the fact that I had first thought about it, for approximately five minutes, four days prior to writing it. I wondered if that were significant.

Consequently, being a good empiricist (I was first trained as a social psychologist – translation: a researcher), I tried it a second time. The following Friday afternoon, I chose the topic for my column, thought about it for about five minutes, then let it be. Didn't think about it at all over the weekend.

Again, when Tuesday morning arrived, the column slid out of my keyboard.

It became my pattern. Friday afternoon – make a decision on the topic, think about it for a few minutes, then, fergit-about-it…

My fastest column ever took eleven minutes.

I *know* it was because I allowed my unconscious machine to do its work.

Whether by working at your art – practice, practice, practice – or working at the practice of "mindfully" giving your unconscious machine room to do its practice, it can help your art.

Here's another story, apocryphal but useful, on the practice of your art.

Once upon a time, the story goes, there was a famous Chinese artist. Her paintings were renowned throughout the land. One day a gentleman came to her door and asked her to paint a rooster for him. She said she would, that it would cost $2,000, and he should come back the following Saturday to pick it up. He agreed, went away, and returned the following Saturday.

"Can I have my painting?" he asked. "Yes," she said, "but give me the $2,000." He scooped the money out of his pocket and handed it to her. (She was quite well-reputed, after all.) She turned away, picked up a blank canvas, put it on her easel, grabbed her brush, and in a few brief strokes, painted the most beautiful rooster ever seen. The gentleman gazed at it lovingly, but then looked back at her with a bit of doubt on his face. "Excuse me," he said. "The painting is quite beautiful, but don't you think it is a bit excessive to charge me $2,000 for something that took less than a minute to create." She smiled at him, a bit smugly to be sure (but she *was* a very famous artist), gestured with her index finger for him to follow her, walked to a door in her home and opened it, then stepped aside to let him look inside. What he saw, on the floor, on the walls, on easels, all over the room, were hundreds of paintings of roosters.

Practice, practice, practice.....

OTHER ART

My studio is filled with prints and paintings, favorite quotations, books, calendars, (my endless source of new inexpensive art every year), photographs, woven rugs, and tapestries. The walls and shelves are covered in small art cards. Whenever I travel, almost every town, village, city, and my particular favorite, inhabited tropical island, have cards for sale created by local artists. The cards reflect the culture, the colors, and the memories I take home from holidays. For me, it's a terrifically inexpensive and easy-to-carry source of new art. Art cards now pervade my studio.

Reading is unavoidable for me. Books are a major ongoing form of art in my life that helps, encourages, inspires, teaches me, fills me with joy. They're all over my studio (and the rest of my house).

Of course there's nature's art. All over my studio, as well. Little piles of sand from various tropical holidays (I'm a snorkeling/diving fanatic). Stones, shells, dead coral washed up on the shore. Feathers of endless species of birds. Plants that have dried, naturally and beautifully.

There are contributions from friends and family. All my loved ones give me something of themselves for my studio. Often it's art. A clay sculpture from my twelve-year-old niece. Photographs and paintings they've done.

I gaze at all this art constantly. I'll lose myself staring at a particular picture, and the losing leads to writing.

I'll read a quotation from an artist I adore, and suddenly the words come. My words.

Whatever art inspires you, can inspire you.

FOOD OR DRINK

Some people like their perfect snack when they go to their space to do art. Their perfect piece of chocolate. Some like/need coffee or tea, cappuccino at the coffee shop, a bottle of wine, a beer, a drink even. (It's funny how shy everyone gets, when the brainstorming is happening, about any mention of alcohol. I always have to reassure them that it's not as if not a single artist in the entire world would, or has ever, used any and all substances to do their art...)

Drinking and eating is a natural accompaniment for many artists. They love it, they need it. It comforts them, inspires them, and helps them get to their art!

But it's a total distraction for others.

In therapy, for example, I won't even allow my clients to bring water to a session (unless it's a health matter), because taking a bit of food or a sip of something can interfere with their process. When I was younger and practically everyone I knew smoked, I noticed how frequently a drag on a cigarette was a perfect way to deal with (think "avoid") a sudden emotion that would come up in a conversation. I've seen that happen repeatedly in therapy. Then I saw the same thing happening with *my* writing.

Hence, I never take any consumable article into my studio.

PRIVACY AND SAFETY

You already know how important I think safety is. Remember my version of jumping off a cliff? But it is an infinite topic.

I've seen the results of not feeling safe to do your art again and again and again. It never, ever appears to be a good thing.

A close friend of mine, a writer, was married for thirty years. After many years of working strictly at being a wife, a mother, and a homemaker, she struggled to get back to her writing. Finally, she did. She was soooo happy. Until one day, about three or four months after she started, her *beloved* husband said to her, "I'd be interested in writing, too, if *I* were comfortable with the idea of being mediocre..."

The good news is, she's now a published author, and still writing. As well as a loving mother and grandmother. Though she's not married anymore. (Perhaps more good news, in her case.)

Safety from, and with, people around you is a real issue. To put it simply, some of the people close to you, much less those not close to you at all, can be bad for your art. Whether they are looking over your shoulder or making comments. Or not making comments, in that pointed sort of way some people have. Reading your writing. Staring disapprovingly at your paintings. Not bothering to look. Closing the door on your music.

All of these have surprisingly powerful potential to shut down your work.

A student of mine in a journal-writing class announced that after having written in her journal for her entire life, she had not written a word in it for eleven years. I asked her if anything in particular had happened eleven years ago. She informed the class that she'd gone traveling for a couple of weeks and, while she was away, her boyfriend had read her journal. Of course we all groaned in sympathy. It got worse as she continued.

"Then he edited it," she said. "He edited my journal."

Eleven years.

He wasn't safe. So she wasn't safe. Neither was her art.

Alice Walker talks about the fact that she wrote her novels in her head. By the time she wrote them down on paper they were pretty much done. Revised, edited. The whole works.[4]

Amazing.

And awful.

Turns out that when she was a child her brothers would destroy her writing in numerous ways. She subsequently adapted to this particular form of not feeling safe by not putting her work down on paper/computer until it was completed. Amazing. Wonderful that she found a way to keep her beautiful novels safe, her writing world safe. Astonishing that she was able to write and edit a novel in her head!

A horror, nonetheless. The time and effort and energy it must have taken. Who knows what else she might have used that for?

The painful stories of having one's art damaged and attacked really are infinite. The effects can be devastating.

I now offer you the following.

You don't *owe* showing your art to anyone. You're not being a coward or a wimp. It doesn't mean you're not taking your work seriously if you won't expose it to the world. The moment will likely come when it's time to expose it to the world. But it has to be your moment. Not pressure from someone else.

Trust yourself. Trust your instincts.

My own personal version of "the moment" came after I'd been writing for a year and a half. I hadn't shown a word of my writing to anyone. Not a syllable. I mostly didn't even tell anyone I was doing it. Including my husband, for heaven's sake. Then one day, when I was reading over my work from the day before, a smile flowed over my face, and over the rest of me for that matter. A thought suddenly fluttered by. "I like this. I like what I'm writing."

The moment was precious. For me that meant it was time. I was now safe enough to expose my writing to others. Because my writing now belonged to me. *I* liked it. And, no matter what – and there have been a lot of "what's" – in some fundamental way, I was safe. Please, therefore, think about what you need to do to keep yourself safe. Privacy needs to be cherished. Just as much as sharing.

LIFE

Sounds kind of silly, but not.

Anything. Any life experience, any memory, any emotion. All of it is the primal fount of our art.

During the brainstorming sessions on "What helps you do your art?" you can always hear the realizations happen. "Love," someone inevitably calls out. Everyone smiles and laughs, thinking of all of the art in the universe about love. Immediately thereafter, or sometimes only several minutes later, "Heartbreak," is called out. Probably an equal amount of art on that topic, no? Special moments, birth, death, marriage, of course. Ordinary moments, a walk, a conversation. Joy. Sorrow. Adventures. Terrors. This particular list is truly infinite.

Huge topic. Not much to add.

Any moment in our lives, any emotion, any experience, any memory, can inspire our art.

ACTIVITIES

Pretty much any activity can enhance our creativity. But there may be certain ones that work best for you. Going for a walk may be the single best thing for you to do to clear out the cobwebs, loosen up your body, and get you in the mood to create.

Really, it can be anything.

I was at a writer's retreat in Vancouver, in a workshop with Dionne Brandt, a wonderful Canadian poet and novelist. She had grown up in the Caribbean and spent a lot of her childhood with her grandmother. Her grandmother loved to make soup. She'd spend hours putting all the fresh vegetables and tropical fruits into a huge iron pot, then stand at the stove stirring it. And stirring it. And stirring it. Dionne talked about watching her do it.

She also talked about her writing. Dionne would sit and write and write and write, and then she'd stop. It didn't matter what she did or what she said to herself, she was stopped. Stuck. Not a word would come. No matter what she did.

She'd actually give up on her writing for the day (or so she thought). She'd close down her computer and decide to make soup. She'd put all the ingredients together, lovingly chopping and slicing and straining, just like she'd watched her grandmother do, then she would stand at the stove stirring the soup, staring at the fluid swirling in the pot, the bits of vegetables circling; stirring, staring, stirring, staring. Abruptly she would turn off the burner, go back to her computer, and watch as the words poured out of her...

Any activity that works.

I had a chaise lounge in my garden studio. When I got stuck with my writing I'd go stretch out on it, staring up through the skylight at the apple tree growing overhead. I'd think about Van Gogh's apple blossom painting and fall asleep. Usually for about three and half minutes. Then, lo and behold, back to my computer, unstuck. Three and half minutes!

Exercise can be astonishingly useful. It often helps you flow. Go to the gym, go walk, cycle, kayak, swim, ski, run, rollerblade, sail, scull... Play a sport. Whatever you like. You've heard people talk about exercise getting the juices flowing. Those very juices can actually be your artistic ones.

Go anywhere. Do anything.

Go someplace wonderful. Museums. Art galleries. Bookstores. A concert. Anything that helps you be creative.

NATURE

Again, go someplace wonderful. It doesn't have to be big, or far away.

Over and over and over and over. Nature's the one thing that inspires so many of us.

Breathe the salt air by the ocean. Or the moist greenery in the forest. The crisp smell of snow. The dry, baked scent of the desert.

Stare at the birds in the trees, or the marsh, on the sea. The ants crawling along a sidewalk. Look at the worms in your garden soil.

Touch the leaves, or the sand, or the rocks at the base of the mountains; dip your foot in a nearby pond, or river, or lake. Feel the crops growing in the field.

Walk in it, run in it, ride your bicycle. Sit in it, lie down.

Nature can so often take us where we're trying to go.

OBSERVING OUR WORLD

Whatever is going on around us.

Parents can spend hours staring at their kids, then the moment hits (the kids are often asleep when it does...), and the art comes. So much can flow from watching them, seeing them explore the universe, exploring their universe.

Watching people anywhere. At home, on the street, on a bus. People-watching is often a surprisingly rich source of inspiration.

Watching all the other animals. Our cats, our dogs, our birds, and fish. Laughing. A lot.

Just paying attention to what's going on around us.

*   *   *   *

Just a few more things on the list. But important.

FOCUS

This is a bit of an odd category. Let me explain.

I believe that focusing on anything that takes you inside yourself can be a truly wonderful source of getting to your art. Just going inwards.

The very first suggestion I include in this category is breathing. Breathing. The simple, extraordinarily magical act of taking a breath.

Breathing deeply. Slowly.

Relaxation techniques. Yoga breathing techniques. Meditation. Visualizations. Uttering mantras. All of these "focus" activities can take you inwards to your art. In service of this possibility, I will be including examples of some of these techniques throughout the course of the book.

I have another category I call "focus toys." None of these objects were purchased with the purpose of being a focus toy. In the beginning they were just things I had that I liked to look at. Only gradually did I realize what they were doing for me.

I usually bring examples of these to class. At first everybody laughs at the idea of an artistic "focus toy," and laughs at me (or with me I prefer to think) for believing in them, until I pass them around the class. Then *I* get to laugh as I watch person after person become so engrossed in what they're gazing at, or listening to, that they ignore me as I continue with the "lecture."

One of my personal focus toys consists of "moving flowing sand pictures." (I searched the Internet trying to come up with a proper name for it. "Sand toys" was my primary effort, but resulted in a terrific array of pails and shovels and beach balls. "Sand pictures" or "sand paintings" take you to some wonderful sites of artists' works who use sand to paint, while other sites have you creating pictures in sand...)

It was Googling "moving flowing sand pictures" that finally did it. I'm talking about the objects that are framed in metal or wood or plastic, have two pieces of glass sealed inside the frame, and sand and fluid sealed inside the glass. You make the sand flow by tilting the whole thing, or turning it on its side, or upside down. Each time you do, it creates a new picture. The focus part is that you sit there watching it flowing and forming that picture.

Even the advertisers of the product get it. An excerpt from an online ad…

"Gently falling sand forms unique individual landscapes. The visual effects soothe, relieve stress, develop imagination, create aesthetic impressions…"[5]

Another toy of mine, the first one I got, though I didn't realize what I was getting when I bought it, is a clear plastic rectangular box divided in half with blue oil on the top and yellow oil on the bottom. You turn the rectangle upside down and the oils gently drip into each other. It even makes a rhythmic bubbling noise as it flows. (Sorry, I couldn't find a name for this one anywhere…) I watch and listen to the bubbles flow. Entranced. Soon enough, I start writing.

I almost always burn a candle when I write. I stare at the flame. Think fireplaces or campfires. You know the state you go into? It can be great for doing art.

Any objects, "toys," like these can help you focus in. There are tons of them out there. Metal balls that click against each other, time after time after time. Birds who peck repeatedly at the water. Wind chimes, spirals, mobiles. All sorts of "toys."

The last example I'll give you of a focus activity is a personal story of my creative process. I had a writing pattern from early on. When I went out to my studio to write, I'd go out there, sit down, turn on my computer, and… waste time.

I'd play computer games. This was early on in the computer game process. My favorites were the Sierra Quest games. King's Quest, Queen's Quest, Space Quest. I loved them. You didn't even have icons back then, so you typed in words for all your questions and answers and attempts to solve the various riddles and problems. I'd sit there at the computer, feeling guilty as hell every minute, and play for at least a half an hour. Sometimes an hour. Sometimes even more. Feeling even more guilty.

Here I was, with this precious amount of time to write, and I was frittering it away. Throwing this opportunity into the virtual garbage.

So I'd try to stop playing. I'd go out to my studio and try to get right to my writing. But I couldn't. I'd just sit there. Trying to write. Failing. Inevitably, I'd give up and either go inside to do something else, or start playing a computer game. Finally I came to realize that, if I stayed out there in my studio and played those bloody computer games, eventually I would settle in and write. The real thing. Almost every time.

Also, eventually, I figured it out.

One way to approach my realization is to look at the right brain/left brain dynamic, where the right brain is said to be more skewed toward creativity. (It is necessary to note here that the research has found that the topic is much more complicated than everyone thought, so this analysis has to be taken with a significant grain of salt.) It is, however, a useful image for me. When I wasn't in my studio, I was doing other things that were more part of the regular, logical, linear world. At that point I was working part-time as a consultant, evaluating science and technology research with my husband. Or analyzing the benefits of community programs. Or doing the normal things one does, taking care of house and home, doing bills and paperwork, and so on.

Then I'd go out to my studio and try to write. I would endeavor to make this significantly abrupt transition from the practical world into my creative, fictional, fantasy universe.

But it was hard... Really, really hard.

Turns out that the games were my way of traveling partway to that universe. I'd leave the regular, more systematic world, and start playing computer games. I'd go off on a virtual quest, in medieval times, or outer space. Solving magical riddles, exploring distant landscapes. Definitely more on the side of fantasy...

Gradually I would leave my "normal" world, my daily reality, and make the transition into the world of fiction and creativity that I needed to make in order to start my writing.

The guilt finally went away.

Therefore, for all of you who live for computer games and get in trouble with everyone you love, try thinking of it more as a transition activity. Do it for a while, then stop for a while, and see if anything interesting happens… (And yes, you *do* have to stop at some point for this to work!)

All of these bits and pieces, these "focus activities," the breathing, the relaxation techniques, the toys, the computer games, have helped me focus inward and move inside myself.

And it's there that I need to go to write.

*   *   *   *

Counting down – three more topics on my list.

OTHER PEOPLE

"Other people" got somewhat of a bad rap in the section on privacy and safety. I really do believe it's a critical consideration to at least pay attention to the individuals and environments that are bad for your art.

The other side of the coin, however, is that other people can be one of the greatest sources of support and enhancement and encouragement of our creative work. In fact, it's often hard to be creative without that help.

Friends and family, colleagues, and fellow artists – if they're the ones who are SAFE – can be gloriously supportive, helpful, encouraging, pragmatically useful (think my husband/editor), and necessary. We all need praise, reassurance, care, encouragement. Did I mention encouragement? Let me mention it again. We all need encouragement.

Family, friends, classmates, fellow artists – take a course, join a group – can be a wonderful and integral help with our art.

Absolutely integral!

I'LL NAME THIS CATEGORY *AFTER* I TELL YOU ABOUT IT

Personal story: When I grew up in the early sixties, I had a fundamental gender problem. I saw this image all around me about exactly how it was that I was supposed to be a "girl." For example, I was supposed to play with dolls, care about clothes (hell, we had to wear skirts or dresses to school – no pants, ever), dream of my future wedding, and grow up to be a loving wife and mother. That's who girls were supposed to be.

For me, there were major problems with that image.

The problems were, I hated dolls, loved jeans, didn't ever want to get married, and knew for sure I didn't want children. I didn't ever want to stay home and play house. All I wanted to do as a kid was play outside. (Except, of course, when I was curled up in my room reading, or writing, or listening to music.) Otherwise I wanted to be doing something physical. They couldn't get me off my bicycle. Or, especially, out of any body of water.

When I thought about growing up, what I did want was a career. I wanted to go to university, go to grad school, be a professional. Journalist and writer, remember.

But back then, girls just weren't supposed to be like that.

Only boys were. Boys got to play outside and go search for their lives. Boys had choices and options and adventures ahead of them. Boys were active.

I wanted to be active.

Girls were the opposite. Or so they told us. And the opposite of active is????

"Passive," obviously.

Of course I absolutely, positively, didn't wanna be passive.

Since this was in the days before the "Second Wave" of feminism had hit, I didn't understand enough to call myself a feminist. The expression we used back then was a "male-identified female."

If I were a male-identified female, I didn't have to be passive. I wouldn't be. I was active as hell. Extra active.

Even in high school I got in trouble because I was involved in "too many" extra-curricular activities. Can you imagine that now? It's the name of the game, now. Back then I was considered weird.

It morphed into a total lifestyle. I studied too much, worked too hard, played too hard. Went on too many adventures. I became a classic workaholic. Functioning, functioning, functioning.

Then the day came when, as I described earlier, my back blew up. I had to stay in bed for a very long time.

One of the weirdest things I remember about the earliest part of that process was that when I finally returned to work, lying down on the folded-up massage table placed on the floor to take care of my back, I suddenly started noticing the clouds outside my office window. I'd lie there on the floor staring up at them. I started seeing pictures in the clouds. I'd completely forgotten about that. I'd spent so many hours of my childhood lying on the grass looking at pictures in the clouds. Alone. Or with friends. We'd even try to see the pictures the other person was seeing. We'd make up stories about them. Adventures. It was so much fun.

I thought about how long it had been since I'd done it. Or even remembered doing it.

Over those next few "bad years", lying in bed at home, or on the massage table at my office, or on the grass outside in my garden, I spent a lot more time staring at the pictures in the clouds, the images in the stucco on my bedroom ceiling, the sketches in the wood grain of the doors.

A lot of time not "functioning." Just lying there, staring at those pictures.

It always made me happy.

It always took me away from my pain into another world.

Another change had to do with reading. As I said, I loved reading. A lot. I didn't drive until I was twenty-eight, and I never sat on a bus on in a subway without a book in hand. Never. Basically never left the house without one. Waiting rooms, lunch on my own, standing on line alone, I was always reading.

During the bad years, I slowly realized I wasn't doing that so much anymore. On my periodic doctor's visits, I'd sit staring into space while I waited for my appointment. I still read like crazy but my purse was often weirdly light, and I realized it was because I wasn't carrying a book with me every single time I left the house.

I'd find myself just sitting, wherever I was, staring out the window, or into nothing at all.

The concept crystalized for me a little while later. I was finished with the bad years and into the good years, writing. Exploring this whole other universe. Then I went traveling.

My sister and her family were living in Chile, and Dennis and I went to visit them in Santiago. My sixteen-year-old niece had spent the previous summer in the desert, and loved it. Beyond love. She wanted to take us there to see it, so off we went about a week after we arrived in Santiago; my niece, my husband, and I flew north to the town of Antofagasta on the Atacama Desert, rented a pick-up truck, and drove out into the desert.

There are two things you have to understand for the rest of this story.

One. Dennis, my husband, is an outdoors FREAK. He grew up in Vancouver, across the street from the forest. He loves the mountains, the ocean, the woods. His first job, when he was in university, was prospecting in the bush, in British Columbia, for two full summers. He worked way out in the bush, living in tents for months at a time. He loved it.

His normal Saturday morning now is a four-hour bike ride, fifty to sixty miles. He skis, cycles, swims, hikes, snorkels, and scuba dives down to 180 feet. He used to run. He grew up camping out in the great outdoors and as an adult would go up and camp, alone, in the mountains, in *very* cold weather. Did I mention, alone? A complete outside freak. He thinks bears are beautiful, and describes sharks as puppy dogs. (Though he did steal that phrase from me...)

I have never seen him be anything but happier being outdoors.

And I've never, never, never, heard him be afraid of it. (Talk too much about emotions and he'll run, but never from nature.)

The second thing you have to understand is that the Atacama Desert is the driest desert in the world.

I am officially a water freak. I love the ocean. Can't get enough of it. Yet there we were, driving through this desert, not a drop of water in sight, and I was transported. Completely gone. In another universe. This desert was breathtaking. I was filled to the brim with the beauty of it; the colors, the shapes, the textures. The flow of the sand, not moving, but flowing anyway. Think of the deserts in the movie *The English Patient* if you've seen it. Bland, in comparison.

There I was, moving through this place, oblivious to everything but the exquisite beauty surrounding me. Full up with it.

Gradually, after I have no idea how long, I realized Dennis and my niece were talking away. I heard Dennis' voice, with a strange edge to it, talking about it being "spooky." A bit "creepy." That it was "Barren. Empty. Even a bit frightening." Even more gradually, I understood that he was talking about the desert we were driving through!

I actually winced, not grasping, not being even faintly capable of understanding, what the hell he was talking about.

He tried to explain. Though all he kept saying were things like, "There's nothing here. Not a blade of grass, not a leaf, not a tree. Nothing."

There I sat, however, so all consumed with the fullness of what I was experiencing. I couldn't understand.

Until finally, I did. Dennis had grown up in British Columbia. An amazing, astonishing rainforest.

The Atacama was the driest desert in the world. There wasn't a tree, a leaf, a blade of grass growing there. It was sand and the occasional rock. It was empty of all things Dennis identified as living. Barren.

For me that desert was filled with everything.

Amazing shapes and textures. Movement. The colors were luminescent. Later that day we were sitting on a hill, and my niece and I were digging little holes in the sand with our hands. Under the surface there were literally clumps of green sand and pink sand, orange, blue, yellow clumps. Separate colored chunks of sand in one small hole. Obviously each one was some different kind of mineral, which together glowed with the most astonishing colors. (Interesting fact. I just went to the Internet to see what I could find out about those minerals; copper is a major one. The Wikipedia site said, "Due to its otherworldly appearance, the Atacama has been used as a location for filming Mars scenes." There you go.)

I even loved listening to that place. Remember the muted silence of snow that we talked about? This was some other kind of silence. Sand silence. It brushed gently over my ears.

The place was lush with its presence. Lush with its emptiness.

For me, that emptiness was filled with voices.

It was in the Atacama that I finally understood the most fundamental part of me that I had lost for so much of my life. Lost until I had entered, and then gradually emerged, from the bad years. I had lost the part of me that was once again able to stare at clouds and see the faces in them and look at the animals wandering through the sky.

The part of me that saw and felt and smelled, even listened to that barren, empty desert. The driest desert on the earth.

I found the part of me that didn't need to be active, ALL THE TIME. That didn't want to be active. That didn't want to be that kind of active.

The part of me that could be quiet.

Hearing the voices. Inside and out.

Finally I had discovered the true opposite of the word "active." It wasn't passive. That wasn't my only choice if I were a girl.

The true word, that state of being, was "receptive."

I discovered receptivity.

Receptivity was the crucial part of me that had been missing all those years when I wasn't writing. I simply couldn't go inside and hear the voices.

I believe receptivity; the choice to go into that place when you need to, the ability to be there, to hear all those voices, is a critical part of being an artist. Of finding one's creativity. Thus the name for this item on my list is:

RECEPTIVITY

Now when I go into my studio to write, Dennis and I always speak of it as me "going into the desert."

*   *   *   *

Last item on my list of things that can help you be creative.

JOURNALS

It's a simple one. Fundamental to many of us. Writing, or drawing, or scribbling, WHATEVER, in a journal, can help you with your art. You can spew your feelings, your joys, your frustrations. Anything. Write your schedule for the day. Write your accomplishments. Write or draw your ideas, your thoughts, your designs, your plots. Bits of conversations you've heard. Descriptions of things you've seen.

Your life plan. Your art plan. Anything. Anything. Anything at all.

Get it down on paper. Or on your screen. On your canvas. It can be the place where you express your deepest, most intimate thoughts and feelings. Fears and joys. Accomplishments. Doubts.

I think a journal is one of the things that can get you to more places than just about anything else. It can be the one thing you can hang on to.

If it works for you…

Well that, for now, is the end of my list…

*   *   *   *

Homework Assignment

Your assignment is now to think about all of this!!!! Think about the things you thought might help you be creative while you were doing *your* brainstorming session on your personal whiteboard. Next, think about all the things on the class whiteboard that people thought might

Darylynn Starr Rank

help *them* be creative. Then think about my list of things that help me be creative.

See if any of those ideas resonate for you when you consider what might help you be creative.

After you've gone through all of that, picture anything *else* that might occur to you that might help you be creative.

Keep picturing. Keep turning these ideas over in your mind.

Once you've done all this thinking and all this resonating, I'd like you to "**make a list**" of ten things that you believe might enhance your creativity. From your whiteboard, or the class whiteboard, or my list, or your new thinking.

A list of ten things.

Do not worry about leaving out an important one. If you come up with eleven you can use eleven. If you change your mind next month, you can change your mind next month. Or tomorrow! This is simply your first draft…

That is Part A of your Homework Assignment.

"Make a List of Ten Things That Might Help You Be Creative"

Part B is, that after you've made your list of ten things (or seven, or eleven), I'd like you to

"Do Three of Them"

I do not mean do them, and then try to do your art. I do not mean do them in order to do your art.

I mean JUST do them.

Do three of the things that you believe might help you be creative.

Also, notice yourself doing them. Okay, yeah. Do them mindfully… I love the word, and even more the concept. Observe yourself. Notice yourself. Give yourself the attention.

90

Come back to this book after you've done them. Later today. Or tomorrow. Or next week. Just come back after you've made your list and done three of them.

Enjoy!

Take care, all.

Chapter six
Did it? This Also Helps

How'd it go?

Did your list have ten things? Or seven? Or seventeen?

Hard to figure out the things you think will help? Or hard to narrow them down?

Did you keep changing the list? Or did you absolutely know, right away, the ones that you wanted to try?

I hope you came up with something. If not, you will eventually.

And now for those of you who didn't even try to do the list, and who may be sitting there reading this, feeling like you're back in second grade and you didn't do your homework and you're a bad little child, I have something very important to say! You are not allowed to sit there feeling like you're a bad little child. That's not what's happening here.

In my classes, there were always some students sitting there with that particular look on their faces. And when it came time for them to read their list, they'd say something like, "I didn't make the list. I started thinking about this other thing and I forgot." Or "I just didn't feel like doing the homework but I..." Or "I got completely distracted and..." The description of what they did do, or did think about, always ended with, "I'm sorry."

Well, that wasn't okay. Not my point at all! When we investigated a little more, we often found that what they thought about or got distracted by was absolutely fascinating. Far more valuable to them at that moment than the actual assignment they were "supposed" to have done. And usually totally, completely, and profoundly on point for the actual assignment, even if it didn't start off sounding that way.

Finally one day it became clear to me what was, in fact, taking place. The following is what I would say to every class from that moment on:

"First, you are not allowed to sit there feeling like a bad little kid because you did not do your homework. Second, when you start discussing your homework, you may discuss the Assignment you were given that you actually did, or you can provide us with a thorough description, explanation, or exploration of something entirely different. This is what we subsequently officially labeled as, "Observations On Your Fallow Time."

Some of you may not remember what the word fallow means. (Many of the in-class students didn't.) Unless you're from the prairies or the mid-west… So, for them and for you I'd explain thusly:

Fallow is the time that occurs *between* harvesting a crop of pretty much anything at all, and planting the next crop of pretty much anything at all.

It is during that time that the soil rests unseeded, gathering nutrients and water and bugs and oxygen and glorious sunlight, in order to recover its *natural* fertile state. It does all of this before it begins its next process of *creating* food, or cotton, or whatever crop will be growing there. Fallow time is critically important in agriculture. It's how the earth regains the richness, the abundance, the fruitfulness it needs to create something new.

Now, notice the word "create." Fallow time is crucially important in our kind of creativity as well! Very, very frequently what is occurring when you don't do your official Homework Assignment, when you cannot bring yourself to write or paint or sing precisely what you were asked to do, it's because you are busily preparing for what needs to happen next. You are gathering your forces, and sunshine, and air to nourish your next creative step.

Consequently, not doing your actual assignment may very well be the most creative activity you can do!

So in class I'd ask students from then on to tell us *either* about their actual Assignment *or* give us observations on their fallow time.

Now I am repeating it to you as well. Just in case...

Back to the rest of your homework. The three things. I'd like you to spend a few minutes thinking about the three things you actually *did*. What were they like for you? Were any of them things that might actually help you get into the mood? Did you start thinking about artistic things? Daydreaming?

While you did them, or after you did them, did you feel like maybe, sort of, perhaps, just a little bit, that you might actually want to sit down and do some art? Did you think about your sketchpad and maybe something you could conceivably, perhaps, if only for an instant, draw in it? Any urge to dab a bit of paint on a canvas? Compose a few notes on your guitar? Knock a few blocks off a piece of marble?

Or, were you mostly thinking, *OMG, this is a complete waste of time*????

If you did have any artistic urges, then – soon, if possible! – do the same thing again. If not, you might want to try it another time anyway. Just in case it works the next time. (This is a learning experience, as they say.)

OR... change your list. Adjust your list. Remove the thing that felt like a complete waste of time, and try something completely different.

There are so many possibilities.

No matter what, I want you to keep thinking about that list of ten – and doing them. A little at a time. Notice how you feel. How your creative parts respond – or don't respond – to them. Please keep adjusting the list and the things you do however you need to. If one of them leans you toward your art, even a little, count it as something you want to do to help you. If it hurts, or puts you off in any way, shape, or form, dump it!

Some things help us be creative. Some things don't. Keep refining your version of what helps. Keep experimenting.

Do work hard at not questioning yourself if this doesn't work right away. Work at not doubting yourself, or deciding you're just not trying hard enough. Some things work. Some don't. There's no good or bad to what works. No good or bad to what doesn't.

Remember: There ain't no right way. Only *your* way.

Most importantly, I'd like you to OBSERVE what happens.

OBSERVE your process. Notice it. Pay attention. You're an artist. Artists are observers. Use that tendency, that skill, that ability, that *drive,* to help you learn about you. Learn about your art. Learn what helps you. Learn what inspires you.

It is actually a learning process. You know some things automatically. You just know instantly that certain things will help your art. But the rest of it? Nope. We seldom think in terms of learning about our *process*. Of studying what helps us do our art. But I want you to do exactly that.

So, one more time:

OBSERVE YOUR PROCESS.

*   *   *   *

Breathing Exercise

(Please note: I've recorded an audio file of this "Breathing Exercise," as well as other visualizations exercises further along. If you would like to listen to me saying them, they are available for listening or downloading to anyone who has purchased any version of this book. Please go to my website, http://www.theartof-becominganartist.com/visualizations and enter the word – Breathe – where it asks for the code word. If you don't want to do that, simply read a paragraph or two below, then do the visualizing, then read one or two more, and so on.)

What I'd like you to do is get as comfortable as possible, and listen to the file, or read the script if you prefer. If it's okay for you, I'd like you to turn off the lights, then sit down, sit back, lie down, whatever works best for you, and relax. At any point during this exercise, please readjust so that you are more comfortable, more relaxed, and nothing's hurting.

Okay, eyes closed.

Now take a breath. Breathe in and breathe out again. Breathe in and breathe out again. Breathing however is most comfortable for you. Breathing, relaxing. Breathing, relaxing. Take the breath into your body and let it out again. Breathing Relaxing. Take the breath into your body, down into your stomach, and out again. Breathing, relaxing. Adjusting your body to be as comfortable as you can.

Now what I'd like you to do is start watching your breath. Follow it, pay attention to it as it goes into your body and comes out again. Down through your chest, into your belly, and out again. Watching it, feeling it, relaxing. Follow the breath moving through you. Feel it relaxing your chest, relaxing your belly. Breathing in and breathing out.

Feel the breath moving through you; filling the spaces, relaxing, breathing, relaxing, breathing, filling the spaces. Relaxing and breathing. Now I'd like you to follow the breath as it moves down into your legs, breathing, relaxing. Moving down through your thighs into your calves, breathing, relaxing. Moving down through your ankles, into your feet, out to the tips of your toes, breathing, relaxing, filling the spaces, breathing, relaxing, breathing relaxing. Feel the breath move up through your feet, through your ankles, your calves, your thighs, and up into your bum, breathing, relaxing. Filling your belly. Moving up into your chest now, and into your back. Feel the breath filling your back, moving through your spine, your shoulder blades, relaxing your back, filling the spaces. Breathing, relaxing. Breathing, relaxing.

Now follow your breath as it moves up into your shoulders. Relaxing your shoulders, breathing into your shoulders, filling the spaces, relaxing, breathing, relaxing. Now follow the breath as it moves down into your arms, down through your wrists, into your hands, and out to your fingertips. Breathing, relaxing. Filling the spaces. Your arms relaxing. Your hands relaxing. Your fingers, out to your fingertips, filling with air, feeling relaxed.

Now follow the breath as it moves back up through your arms, into your shoulders and up into your neck. Relaxing your neck. Filling your neck. Breathing in. Breathing out. Relaxing. Breathing, relaxing. Breathing. Your neck feeling more comfortable. Feeling relaxed.

Now feel the breath as it moves up into your jaw. Moving up into your face. Feel your jaw muscles relaxing. Feel the breath moving into your mouth. Into your tongue. Your lips relaxing. Breathing, relaxing. Feel the breath moving into your ears. Into your cheeks, your sinuses. Relaxing. Breathing up into your brow. Your eyes relaxing, breathing. Filling the spaces. Relaxing.

Feel the breath moving into your skull. Your whole head, feeling the air, filling the spaces, relaxing. Breathing, relaxing. Breathing. The air moving in through your body, and out again. Breathing, relaxing. Breathing, relaxing.

Your whole body now filled with air. Filled with breath. Relaxing. Easing. Breathing. Comfortable. At ease. Relaxed. The breath moving through you. Relaxing you. Calming you. Moving through you.

Moving in. And moving out again. Breathing, relaxing.

Take a minute now to keep breathing, relaxing.

Then when you're ready, come back here.

*   *   *   *

How was that?

I personally think breathing, real breathing, is a bit of a miracle. I'm always surprised by how different I feel afterwards.

If you feel different as well, it's useful to notice that. Very useful. Hardly any of us pay attention to it. Unless you're in the middle of a meditation.

You just did some focused breathing for a very few minutes. Now you feel different. Pay attention to what that difference feels like. It might actually help you get into a creative place.

And it's a pretty simple thing to do to get you there.

*   *   *   *

In Class Exercise

I'm going to ask you to do another In Class Exercise.

This one is weird. Officially weird. Though it can be incredibly useful.

I call it the "Two Pads and a Bump" technique. (In order to be accurate it should actually be called "Bumps and Two Pads", but I'm a writer and the other way *sounds* better.)

I'll tell you what the topic is after I describe the technique.

*   *   *   *

The **technique**: What I want you to do is have two pieces of paper in front of you or, if you're on your computer, two documents open on the screen at the same time. If it's a journal or a notebook that opens sideways like a book, you can just use one page as your writing page, and the other page as your second piece of paper. The point is, you need two things on which to make marks...

I am going to ask you to write or draw a picture. (Remember you'll get the topic *after* the explanation of the technique. Just bear with me.)

(Note: To avoid my having to write "paper or canvas or screen or Word Document or any other surface" *every time* I explain some exercise throughout this book, I hereby declare that I am going to use the word "paper" as the universal shortcut to describe all of the above. Please feel free to do your work in or on whatever medium you prefer! The other shortcut is that I'll use the word "write" to describe writing or drawing or painting, or typing or texting, or whatever other process you use to create your assignment. I will use the word "pen" to describe the tool you're using.)

To continue: As you write – each time you find yourself pausing, really, **each and every time** you find yourself pausing, even a tiny little bit, hesitating, glancing away, stopping, ***anything!*** ***for any reason whatsoever***, for any length of time whatsoever, I want you to switch immediately to your other piece of paper.

Then write down or draw ***whatever*** thought or feeling, idea, physical sensation, or anything else you experience or are aware of in that pause. ***WHATEVER*** it is. The pause can be absolutely fleeting. Nearly invisible. Or, it can last five minutes and send you far, far away. It's simply that the pause is different from just pouring out your assignment on to the paper.

So: any pause and off you go to the other piece of paper. Be aware of the pause and write down what happened during it: an idea, thought, feeling, awareness of something, a physical sensation, anything. Just get it down on the other page.

When you've done that, return to the original page and continue what you were writing or drawing in the first place.

When you find yourself pausing again, same thing. Over to the other page, get it down. It may be the same thought, or a different one. The same feeling, or a totally different emotion. Doesn't matter. Just put it on the Bumps page. The second page is now officially the "Bumps" page. Ah, there it is, "Two Pads and a Bump."

Then back to the original piece.

It doesn't matter how many times this happens. How many pauses you encounter. Or how few. Just go to the Bumps page every time it occurs.

Most importantly, it doesn't matter how many bumps you have, or how few. Nor does it matter at all what they're about. There is

NOTHING evaluative about having or not having bumps. There is nothing good or bad. There is nothing about them that's either successful or failure-ridden. They just are. Or are not. Period.

We'll discuss this in much more detail after the exercise.

For now, please, try not to create any pauses you don't really have, just so you have some pauses to write down. Also, please, avoid trying *not* to pause because you don't want to have any!

Okay, that's it. "Two Pads and a Bump."

On to the actual topic for your In Class Exercise.

What I'd like you to write about, or draw, is:

"Your Weekday Mornings"

Simple as that. Make it as realistic as you want. Or not. As detailed as you want. Or not.

Work on it right now, for about fifteen to twenty minutes. Of course, don't forget the bumps. Then when you're finished, come back here and turn the page.

*   *   *   *

Okay, how was that?

It's a strange process, isn't it? But often quite useful. Sometimes even transformative.

All right, in front of you, you have your description of your weekday mornings and your list of bumps. (Or no bumps?)

It's whiteboard time. Below is a whiteboard for you to write in your bumps.

After you've finished writing them in, look at the whiteboard on the following page. It's filled with the bumps of a typical class doing this first Two Pads and a Bump exercise.

*   *   *   *

Whiteboard
Weekday Mornings
Two Pads and a Bump
Write down all of the bumps that you experienced

*   *   *   *

Whiteboard
Weekday Mornings
Two Pads and a Bump whiteboard from my classes
WRITTEN – For those of you who *WROTE* this exercise

Rereading   how to phrase the next line   itch
looking for a word   spelling
trying to remember what happens in the morning
exasperated   this is bad   I don't know how to end it
It's awkward   what to write next   phrasing
my wrist hurts   grammar   remembering to write bumps
too much detail   too little detail   don't write about
that   I don't know how to write
this doesn't flow   it's too long   I'm lying
I don't feel like writing this negativeness
I'm not writing fast enough   too much emotional family
relations   not good
incorrect orde r I'm worrying about what people will
think   their opinions My fingers are sore   I'm cold
I'm hungry   tired   bored   random thoughts
run-on thoughts   no thoughts

All I'm doing is complaining   whining   always
socially conscious   afterthoughts   rushing   anxious
this is crap   lying   selfish   self-centered
don't know stuff   this is so useless   can't do anything
good   my hand is sore   what's next
I'm thirsty   I'm thinking   it's not good.
this sucks.
my neck is tight   the clock's ticking.
it's distracting   boring   that's not true
my mornings are really boring, or hectic, or stressful,
or rushed   my husband is so lazy   my wife is irritating
I'm frustrated by the other students   writing is pointless
I have no talent   the kids are so slow   I hate my job
it's too short
and on, and on,
and on

*   *   *   *

Darylynn Starr Rank

Whiteboard
Weekday Mornings
Two Pads and a Bump whiteboard from my classes
VISUAL ARTS – for those of you who *DREW* this exercise

---

the line's not straight   that's too small
perspective's all wrong   it's the wrong color
I left out the window
I forgot the clock, the bed, the sink, the mirror,
the coffee pot, the closet, my wife, my husband, the
children!!!!!
That doesn't look right   it's too tall
I just can't draw
I can't even draw a stupid square, circle, box, bed,
dresser, pair of socks   I'm not wearing any shoes
the shading went outside the lines   that's too big
it doesn't look like that!!!!!   My hand hurts
my back is killing me   my neck is so sore
I hate my job

My bedroom is so ugly   My house is so ugly
That just doesn't look like what I'm looking at
This picture is really boring
My life is really boring
I don't know how to do this at all.
There's not enough detail   There's too much detail
There's nothing outside the window
This is so useless
I'm so slow   I'm so useless
and on

*   *   *   *

Okay, let's talk.

You've just written or drawn something that no one but you will ever see. Even in my classes, I tell everyone ahead of time that they will not be reading this piece out loud. Or showing their drawing.

Obviously, those of you doing this book don't have to worry about that. You've written or drawn it for yourself only. No one else ever has to see it.

You wrote about or drew your weekday mornings. When I started teaching the course, I thought that giving a more intriguing or challenging or even interesting topic would be better. Gradually, I realized that was the opposite of the point. So I chose the most ordinary, mundane thing I could think of. Something that everyone has every day of their lives. Their typical weekday morning. That way there would be no challenge to come up with something unusual, or intriguing, or even creative. We all have our mornings.

Finally, I told you it didn't even have to be factual or accurate. You could just make it up.

Yet look at the boards! Either yours (if your bumps surprised you a bit), or the class boards. Trust me. This is truly an example from a typical class experience.

(There, of course, *is* the possibility that you didn't have any pauses at all, and therefore, the bumps just aren't there. There is also the possibility that you had pauses but chose not to write them down. It happens for some people. I'm guessing the point, or points, of this discussion will still be meaningful. I'm hoping you will, please, hang around.)

I've broken down some of the bumps into a few general and quite common areas of concern, in no particular order. These areas almost always end up, in one form or another, on the class whiteboards.

First, there's the fundamental issue of, "Accuracy." Are you writing or drawing or [fill in the blank] correctly? If you're writing, are you spelling the words correctly, is the grammar perfect, is it the right word, how should you phrase your next line? In your drawing, are the lines straight, is the perspective correct, are they the right colors, is the shading accurate? All of these concerns made you pause in your writing or drawing.

Second is the concern with "Quality." This is your evaluation of your writing or drawing ability. It's awkward, there is too little detail, too much detail, it's boring, it's not good, it's crap. I have no talent, I don't know how to draw, this sucks, this doesn't flow, it's too long/big, it's too short/small. That sentence is too run-on. The bed looks crooked. I don't know how to end it. This just doesn't look like what I'm looking at! I don't know what to write next. Draw next.

There's the inevitable "Questioning of purpose." Why am I writing at all? Why am I doing this? What's the point? This is stupid, useless, meaningless. A total waste of time.

There is concern over the actual "Content." Difficulty remembering exactly what happens in the morning (even though one does these things every day of one's life). Is this in the correct order, should I include this or that or something else? Or shouldn't I? Do I describe all the actual objects in the room?

This is about the accuracy of the content, rather than the accuracy of your skill.

There is "Emotional Evaluation" about the content. I shouldn't write about that. Oh, don't draw that in. I'm just complaining, whining, selfish, self-centered. That's not true. My husband would say I'm lying.

There are "Emotional Reactions" to the actual nature of the mornings. Jeez, that's so boring, the kids are sooo noisy, the kids are so slow, my mornings are really stressful, rushed, hectic, my husband's so lazy, my wife complains so much, my parents are horrible nags, I should do this or that or something else differently. My job is so hard, boring, stressful. I hate my mornings. I hate my family. My job sucks. I hate my life!

There is the "Distraction" of what's going on around you. That ticking clock is driving me crazy. That is really annoying.

And finally (finally only for the purposes of this list – there will always be more bumps…), the "Physical." I'm cold, I'm hot, I'm thirsty, hungry, tired, itchy, sweaty. My hand hurts. My wrist is sore. My neck is so tight.

Please note, these comments are just a small sample of what comes up during this exercise.

What the heck does this mean? Remember, no one will ever read this but you. No one will ever see this drawing except you. It's about something everyone experiences every weekday of their lives. Every one of us. It didn't even have to be accurate.

But look at the board!

This messy tangle of things is going on in people's heads, hearts, and bodies, even when they're doing this very simple exercise. The most trivial creative act generates a slew of conflicting, perplexing, upsetting, and sometimes just plain nasty thoughts that are NO HELP AT ALL. Worse, they are for the most part completely hidden from view unless we work really hard to recognize them.

Just imagine what would be going on if you were trying to do something complicated!

THIS IS WHAT MANY, MANY, MANY OF US ARE CARRYING AROUND INSIDE US, EVERY TIME WE TRY TO DO OUR ART!!!!!

OMG

IT'S A BIT OF A MIRACLE THAT ANY ART EVER GETS DONE AT ALL!

*   *   *   *

Let's look at some of these bumps in more detail.

*   *   *   *

Bump – Writing or Drawing Correctly

Let's start with the spelling and grammar issue.

This may be an apocryphal story (I simply cannot find my reference), about Jacqueline Susann. (Still I read this somewhere, sometime, where

I believed it, so I'm guessing there is probably truth to it.) Jacqueline Susann wrote a novel called *Valley of the Dolls*, which broke all sorts of sales records and was the bestselling work of fiction for 1966. It is still recognized as one of the best-selling books of all time![6]

It was basically the first time someone wrote a novel about drug use in Hollywood ("dolls" are pills). Imagine. The first time.

In any event, Susann's writing ability was generally not considered to be the best. Even Don Preston, the editor assigned by her publisher to work on the book, judged it harshly, calling Susann a "painfully dull, inept, clumsy, undisciplined, rambling, and thoroughly amateurish writer whose every sentence, paragraph and scene cries for the hand of a pro."[7]

Here's the part for which I cannot track down the reference. One of her publishers, when asked in an interview, "Why, with all the great writers in the world, did you publish something that was so badly written?" (Think spelling, grammar, phrasing, sentence construction…, all those issues that keep coming up for writers.) The publisher's response was the following: He pointed at the building that housed his huge publishing company. (I know. The world is changing. Back then, however, some of the publishing houses were huge!) "You see this building," he answered. "There are a thousand people in there who can edit this manuscript. Can correct the spelling and the grammar and the sentence structure. Can make the writing ept, adept, and professional. But there is only one Jacqueline Susann who can write this story."

Back to the present. You've got spell check and grammar check on your computer/tablet/phone, whatever. Plus dictionaries and thesauruses online, at the library, in bookstores, and quite likely if you're a writer, in your home. You can use a ruler to draw a straight line. You've got thousands of books out there that can show you how to achieve proper perspective, or how to construct a proper sentence. Or. Or. Or. The point is, forgive me all you dear English teachers, all you lovely art instructors, all you charming editors, compared to getting to your "creative voice," grammar is **TRIVIAL**.

You can study and learn proper drawing techniques as well. Worrying about being able to draw a straight line, ABSURD. Who cares? (Use a ruler next time…)

Worry about the correct spelling of your artistic expression, **LATER**!!!!! For now, it might be a great idea just to worry about getting it expressed!!!!

How's that for an awkward phrase? (I say, who cares? I can fix it later!)

*　　*　　*　　*

I have now described numerous other categories of bumps that appear on the whiteboards. Many of these concerns are profoundly serious issues; e.g. evaluation of your ability, talent, and skill; concerns over the accuracy and truth of your art; what is and is not "appropriate to depict," and so frequently, the meaning and purpose of your art. We will explore these concerns extensively and throughout the flow of this book. The issues that appear in your bumps are often some of the most powerful issues that artists confront daily. **They did not pop into your head by accident…**

We'll be examining them at length.

Before we move on, though, I want to make a couple of other general comments about some of the topics on these whiteboards.

My first comment is that doing art often does bring up life issues. You write a simple piece about your morning activities and find that, quite unexpectedly, you react to, or question your whole existence. You're upset, tired, bored, stressed, happy, or miserable. You love your mate, you hate him/her. You're not sure you should have had kids in the first place. Your parents are the most annoying people in your whole world.

I had one student (true story) who kept pausing while she wrote this exercise. Over and over and over again. She did what she was "supposed" to do, and went to the bumps page and wrote what she was experiencing. Her first bump was "my job is boring." Back to writing about her morning at work. Pause. "My job is so boring." Back to writing page. Pause. "Boring!" Write. Pause. "Really boring." Write. Pause. "Really, really boring!" Write. Pause. "I hate my job. I hate it. I absolutely hate it."

After several more boring/hate pauses, she simply stopped writing about her mornings. Instead, she went over to the bumps page and started drawing a picture. Turned out to be a butterfly. The whole time she was drawing it, she was grinning.

The next day she gave notice, quit her job, and went into a fine arts writing program at the local university.

Art brings up "stuff!"

We'll be talking about this "stuff" at length.

It's a great, joyful, rewarding part of doing art. You get in touch with your feelings, your hopes, your dreams. You often figure out so much of your world. Art is a way inside.

This stuff is also a hard, lousy, difficult part of doing art. You get in touch with your insides, your feelings, your disappointments, your dreams that you haven't been taking care of. You figure out your insides.

My second comment is more physical.

The sore hand, sore wrist, and so on physical bumps were particularly interesting to me when I started out. I guess it was because of my back history. Everyone's comments about these physical reactions were almost always something along the lines of, "I'm not used to writing so that's why my wrist, hand, fingers, arm, etc., is sore." I was always surprised by these bumps because I couldn't believe that anyone would be so unused to the act of writing, even in this computer age, that fifteen minutes would actually cause pain. Soon I started hearing other physical comments about perspiration, soreness in backs and shoulders, breathing difficulties. One student even said his chest got so tight he was a bit nervous that he was having a heart attack.

Then it struck me.

Fear. It was mostly about fear. Tension, tightness, fear. A great word when trying to do one's art. People got so scared and nervous and tense doing their art for the class that they'd be gripping their pens extra tight, or tensing their muscles, tightening up every part of their body, and so, the pain. Hands, wrists, neck, shoulders, chest.

Also, of course, the lack of breathing. Fear does that. Impedes the flow of air into your being. This is a perfect example of how frightening getting to your art can actually be.

We'll talk a lot about fear during the course of this book.

As well as about all the other bumps…

All of this from simply observing your pauses while doing a piece of art, and a pretty dull one at that!

*   *   *   *

It is important to remember that bumps can be an extremely useful tool for observing, and subsequently examining, exploring, becoming aware, and over time, dealing with, the myriad things that get in your way when you are trying to do your art.

Bumps may be repetitive. You may find yourself repeating the same ones over and over. That would suggest to me that that particular bump is a significant topic for you, and something that needs to be worked with.

Bumps can also change over time as new issues come up. Or they can change depending on the piece you're working on.

Bumps can often be extremely deceptive. You could pause and write a bump that simply says, "thinking of what to write next." Sometimes that's exactly what you're doing. But sometimes there's a world going on underneath that pause. A world that's telling you that what you're doing is bad, or wrong, or frightening. Stupid, or utterly without talent.

Bumps can be layered. The first time you write one, you may think the bump is about the word, so you write "word." Yet if you look a little deeper, you discover it's actually about your lousy vocabulary; and deeper still, it's "What the hell makes you think you can actually write?!!!"

Here's a story about the first time I asked someone to do the bumps exercise. (My poor husband, of course. He gets thoroughly exposed in my courses. He's my official guinea pig.)

I had been thinking about bumps and was just on the verge of trying it with my Saturday morning class the next day. It was Friday night, date night, and Dennis and I were at a favorite restaurant. I was talking about how nervous I was about the exercise. My hopes were high that it would be really interesting and effective. Consequently, I was anxious as hell.

Dennis offered to try it.

Yay!

He used the paper placemat and started writing about his mornings while I watched from across the table. He wrote a few words, then he paused, then a few more words, then paused, then a few more, and he paused again.

"Hey," I asked softly, "what are you doing?"

"I'm doing the exercise."

"But you're pausing. And you're not writing down the bumps."

"No, I'm not. I'm not pausing."

"Uh-huh," I said, "you are."

"Oh, okay. Sorry. I'll start again."

I smiled sweetly.

He started writing.

This time when he paused he went over to the bumps page and wrote something. I smiled more. He wrote more. He paused, went over to the bumps page and wrote something. I couldn't see what he was writing because I was across the table looking at it upside down, but I watched it anyway. Write, pause, bump. Write, pause, bump. Gradually I realized that every bump contained the same word. Not ones that I could read, upside down, but the shape and pattern of the words were identical to the bump before it, and the ones before that.

"Um, Dennis," I interrupted.

"Yeah?"

"You keep writing the same words?"

"Yeah, I know. I keep trying to remember what I do in the morning."

"Oh." I paused, thought about it, and then: "But you do it every morning of your life. It can't be that difficult to remember... Can it?"

He just stared at me.

"Is it possible that something else is going on?"

The truth was that I was starting to get nervous. If this was what was going to happen with my students during this exercise, it was going to be a boring mess. Even worse, the whole thing was going to be useless.

My husband's a very sweet man (although with an occasional tendency to emotionally shut down, which is kinda what I thought/hoped was actually going on). He thought for a moment then said he'd start over one more time.

Stupid things kept happening!!!!! Really stupid. Still he kept trying. Still I kept watching.

By the fifth try, *I* was holding back tears of defeat and failure, and *he* was ready to blow.

"I will do this one more time!" he said through gritted teeth.

"Yes, okay," I mumbled, through my own grittedness.

He proceeded to write without pausing, though his knuckles were turning a bit white, then he suddenly whipped his pen over to the bumps sections and wrote something in HUGE letters with underlines and exclamation points, and threw down his pen.

Quick digression. Part of what Dennis does for a living is program evaluation and strategic planning for science and technology research… Just try and imagine what a report on something like that normally looks like, especially to us non-physics type human beings. Pure scientific vocabulary, jargon, gobbledygook! Often completely incomprehensible. My husband, however, prides himself on writing so well that even lowly artistic commoners (e.g., me), can make sense out of every word. He's well known in his field for just that. He writes great reports! End of digression. Back to the exercise.

He wrote his last exclamation point, looked at me, shaking his head, and said, "I don't believe it. I just figured out something that I have *never* realized before! Though I've been doing it my whole life!!! Forever!!!!"

"What?" I asked, with bated breath.

He swirled the placemat around 180 degrees so I could see what he'd written on his bumps page. It read, "Whenever I get frustrated writing, I just give up and start writing **CRAP!!!!**"

"Wow!" I said grinning.

"Wow, indeed!" he said, though not grinning quite as broadly as I was. "Yes, Dari, your bumps exercise was very useful… It sucks realizing what I do, but it will probably be *very* useful in the future. Thank you, dear…" The sarcasm of the thank you was dripping, but behind it was a congratulatory grin.

I immediately stopped wanting to cry, stopped myself from standing up in the middle of the restaurant and cheering, and proceeded to use the Two Pads and a Bump exercise in all of my classes.

Bumps can be extremely surprising, useful, even enlightening. I mean, hell, you're accessing your "unconscious machine."

As I've suggested several times now, a true key to this creative process is observing and becoming aware of what's going on for you when you're doing your art.

Bumps can be an excellent way to do that.

In general, when you are doing writing/drawing In Class Exercises or Homework Assignments for this book, I'd like you to have a bumps page going. It can be a never-ending source of information.

$$* \quad * \quad * \quad *$$

Homework Assignment

As this is your first official Homework Assignment (other than the list of ten things, and doing three of them), I'm going to repeat my expectations of a Homework Assignment:

I give the Homework Assignment at the end of the class and participants do it sometime, hopefully, before they come to the next class. My *expectation* of homework is still that it takes about twenty minutes. In this case, however, if you would like to do more, please feel free! You're on your own for homework, whether you're taking the course, or doing the book. The only reason for my concern about time here, is that I don't want you feeling that you have to work on it for three hours, or four, or five days, and if you don't you're a failure… I want no failure feelings for something so irrelevant! Twenty minutes is what

I'm looking for. Or less, of course. But if an hour, or a day… is more fun, go for it.

Also, with a Homework Assignment, if you'd like to do it immediately, do it immediately. If you want to wait a day, or three or four, a week, or even longer, that's fine. A lot of people need down time, or away time, before they do their homework. We'll talk more about that later.

(Just remember the "Unconscious Machine.")

Finally, do the Homework Assignment in whatever environment you prefer. Whatever suits you. More on that later, as well…

*   *   *   *

Okay, your Homework Assignment is to:

Do a Postcard

It can be *from* anywhere *to* anywhere. From *anyone* to *anyone*. About *anything* you want your postcard to be about. I'm suggesting a sort of standard postcard, which is, of course, very small. Though if you like, it can be an oversized postcard. Whatever size you like. But a postcard.

Also please do bumps. The whole bumps process.

Second part of your homework is to do "three more things." Remember? "Do Three Things" from your list. Same or different. Whatever you prefer.

See you later.

Take care, all.

*   *   *   *

I'm hoping you've done your homework, and that is why you are back here going through the book...

Therefore, please read your postcard out loud. If it's a drawing look at it. Get more light on it so you can really see.

What do you think? Did you go someplace wonderful? Or strange? Even weird. Students have done every type of postcard imaginable. From the simplest, "Hi, having a ball, see you soon," to amazing adventures on top of a mountain, in the middle of a jungle, exploring an ancient fort. Several students have even written postcards to a dead loved one. From anywhere to anywhere, remember?

How was it doing it? Think about what you felt, what it was like for you, writing or drawing, or painting.

Postcards are a true art form for a lot of people.

Do please pay attention to the bumps. Make note of them. Maybe a bumps section in your journal, so you can truly OBSERVE this part of your process.

One final comment on the topic of bumps.

They can obviously be an excellent way to help you do your art. They can also obviously be an excellent way to help you figure out what gets in your way.

Consequently, bumps are both the end of Part Two *AND* the beginning of Part Three.

Take care, all.

PART THREE

Principle #3

Process, Process, Process

1. Work at finding the things that get in your way.
Sounds like a good idea...

This section will be devoted to this topic. We will be working at finding the things that get in in the way of you doing your art. That interfere with your creativity.

Though again, as with "finding the things that help you do your art," the whole book will essentially be devoted to the very same issue.

It will just go about things from many different angles...

(Please note: Obviously, the bumps exercise will almost certainly be part of identifying the things that get in your way. They may also be things that help you figure out what to do next. Or they may be ordinary occurrences, like a *real* pause for thinking. Just pay attention to them.)

Now on to a few of the other topics that can interfere with your creativity.

Chapter seven
I Suck

Bump – Doubting Your Ability

I do not think that there is an artist on this planet or throughout the entire course of human history, who has not, at some point in their creative process, doubted their ability.

I believe that every single artist who has ever lived, has questioned their talent, insulted their art, and been absolutely positive that they were just not very good. Or for that matter, any good at all.

In my courses I always use a variety of quotes to illustrate topics, and I intend to do the same thing throughout this book. I have *many* quotes from many artists on this particular topic. Let's be gentle and call the topic:

"My art just isn't very good."

(Please feel free to substitute whatever wording comes more naturally to you on this particular subject... Mine tends to be rather caustic, harsh, vulgar... Whatever.)

One of the quotes I always use comes from William Saroyan, novelist and playwright. For years, I would read this quote in class along with all the other quotes on the topic of "my art just isn't very good." It was simply a statement about our endless doubts about our ability.

Yet the more I read this particular quote, the more something about it nagged at me, though I could never quite grasp what it was. Until one night (three o'clock in the morning is generally my "oh, of course!" moment), I figured it out. So before I go on with the other quotes about our infinite certainty about our absolute lack of talent, ability, and skill, I am going to explore this particular quote.

The quotation is:

"All writers are discontent. That's because they're aware of a potential and believe they're not reaching it."
William Saroyan[8]

This statement is usually perceived as a statement about writers' doubts. Writers (think all artists), often believe they are failing to achieve their potential. A perfect example of the topic of self-doubt, or belief in our general and pervasive lack of ability and talent. Right?

Maybe not. Maybe it is actually much more than that. Let me explore.

Okay, picture it: You have inside you an image of a piece of music you want to compose, a picture you want to paint, a sculpture you want to mold or carve into this perfect entity, a story you want to write, or, or, or...

Okay, the fact is that human beings are extraordinary beings. Our brain is the most complex computer ever even imagined. And that's just our brain. Our mind. There's also the rest of us. There are our emotions, our physical bodies, our senses, whatever our spiritual beliefs give us – a soul, a spirit, a sense of the universe, consciousness; however you perceive this category. There is all of who we are.

There we are – we imagine this piece of art, with *all* of who we are.

Well, this piece of art is filled with our universe. It has the visual image, the colors, shapes, textures, all our senses – sound, taste, feel, looks, smell – it's multidimensional. It's got the history of our whole lives in it. It has the knowledge of all our learning. It has all of the emotions we feel that are attached to the image. For some of us it's got the unnamable parts to it, of where creativity comes from. Some kind of spiritual communication to or from the universe. All in all, it is the most vivid, astonishing creation imaginable.

It's our imagination toiling in its profound complexity. We know exactly what this piece of art is supposed to be. Exactly. And we want to create it. In our art. Exactly. Then...

Then we take our piano or our guitar and choose a chord or a melody that depicts it, or we dab our perfect brush in the perfect color oil or acrylic and stroke it on to the canvas, or we chisel the perfect piece of marble just so, or we take our pen and dabble *little black marks* (these marks are more commonly called letters...) on a piece of paper, in order to reproduce this extraordinary image that exists inside of us.

But we can't do it! No way. It's not possible. It's simply not possible.

Oh, sometimes we can go a huge distance in capturing its essence. We can even attain greatness in creating something that is powerful and beautiful and real. We actually have a name for it. It's called a masterpiece.

But we cannot, in our art, reproduce the complexity of that image that exists inside us. We just can't. No matter what we do.

We try. We work at it. We grapple with it. Our job is to create art that is as close to the image inside us as we can get it. We keep continuing the struggle to get it as close as we possibly can.

We struggle and we edit, we practice, we rewrite. We recompose and polish and smooth the piece to make it as perfect as we can make it. We see inside us what it is actually supposed to be. We work it and work it and work it. But it never does reach "its potential." And we know it. So finally we stop. Even though we're not there...

I believe this unattainable perfection is the root of one of the more famous quotes in art:

"A poem is never finished, only abandoned."
Paul Valery[9]

(Though many of us believe the quote is actually, "Art is never finished, only abandoned." There are, in fact, numerous versions of it.)

There is a famous story about Picasso (perhaps apocryphal). A small gallery in Europe exhibited his early works. He was told he couldn't go inside that gallery any more, because every time he entered, he would "fix" something on one of his pieces. I guess he kept trying to make it "right."

Back to Saroyan's quotation.

"All writers are discontent. That's because they're aware of a potential and believe they're not reaching it."

Given that I believe there is complete accuracy in realizing the impossibility of achieving our potential in our art, I have chosen Saroyan's comment as my official "GENTLE UP" quote.

You cannot get there. It's true. NONE of us can get there. No matter what we do.

We recognize, deep inside of us, what the real image is. That image that we cannot achieve. We keep trying for the closest version of it we can get. Until we decide it is time to abandon it. That this is absolutely the best art we can create!

Consequently, instead of damning our art as a failure, instead of demanding we do the impossible, it really might be worth it to "gentle up." Recognize the fundamental glory of our image. Recognize the impossibility of achieving it outside of the magnificent internal organism that is us. Appreciate how close we actually came…

What do you think?

Yeah. So?

Gentle Up!

*   *   *   *

Of course none of this gentling will stop us from questioning our talent, doubting our ability, or worrying that we are just lousy artists.

We all do it. It's part of the process.

Consequently, just so we don't feel so alone in that doubt, just so we understand it's completely 'normal', here are some comments from other artists on this topic of doubt:

"I feel like I am all thumbs in my studio – feel foolish and inadequate, starting to lose control." Judy Chicago[10]

"I have written one quite tiny piece, but I do not know what I shall call it. I have a particular aversion to showing you anything that I have composed; I am always ashamed." Clara Schumann[11]

"And although you are physically by yourself, the haunting Demon never leaves you, that Demon being the knowledge of your own terrible limitations, your hopeless inadequacy, the impossibility of ever getting it right." William Goldman[12]

Neil Welliver, the landscape artist, apparently told his students: "Doubt is a central factor all the time. There's always the doubt: What the hell am I doing out here in the middle of the woods, all alone, painting?"[13]

How about some encouragement about those doubts:

"The primary benefit of practicing any art, whether well or badly, is that it enables one's soul to grow." Kurt Vonnegut Jr.[14]

"If you can't write a good poem, for goodness sakes write a bad one. There's something important there." E. A. Nesbit[15]

To sum up, this section was about the following:

Gentle up.

Be kind to yourself when you're hating your art, doubting your skill, your ability, your talent. Understand that you are not alone in those feelings.

Take care, all.

Chapter eight
Back to the Beginning

In Class Exercise

Remember, this is an In Class Exercise, so I'd like you to do it right now, for about fifteen to twenty minutes only. With bumps, please.

Please write about an experience you had in school that was not good for your creative expression.

Try and go back as early as you can. If it has to be later on, in high school or college, then do write about that. Still, if you can, try to think of something earlier.

If you can't come up with something specifically about "creative" expression, just think of any experience that wasn't good for your self-expression in any area.

Don't forget bumps...

And just a reminder of something I've mentioned before.

You always get to choose whether to do an assignment or to skip it.

This will be the last time I'll mention this, but please always keep it in mind.

Then when you're finished, turn the page.

*   *   *   *

What I'd like you to do now is read what you wrote, out loud. Say the words out loud. If you can, slow down a bit while you're reading it. Actually try to read it with feeling.

Please do pay close attention to what **you're saying**.

Then read on…

*   *   *   *

I usually hate giving this assignment.

In general, it's often the single hardest, most painful exercise in the book. Not always, of course, but far too often. When students start reading the assignment out loud, the tissues come out, the room gets hushed. Involuntary grunts are the only sounds heard from the other students. Shock, dismay, sympathy appear on their faces. Adrenalin flows. Crying happens.

Even after the first several times I did this, knowing what was likely to come, I often sit there with gritted teeth, trying not to join the Kleenex brigade. Or to start cursing.

However, before I continue with the tirade about some of the terrible creative experiences kids have in school, I need to interrupt with a (fairly) brief comment from the other side of the universe.

In my courses, in my life, I have also heard (and experienced!) wonderful, brilliant, kind, loving supportive stories about students' school years. Stories about teachers mentoring creative children, helping them, supporting them, encouraging them, standing by them. Even, for many young artists, a particular teacher being the bottom line as to why they actually became adult artists. Very often it's exactly because they had that perfect, loving, and caring teacher who helped them.

In my universe, at least a good part of why I survived, period, much less why my art survived, is because of some very special teachers. School was my wonderful safe place. Filled with wonderful, safe people. Hell, one of the closest people in my life, all these years later, is my professor from university, my advisor, my mentor. He is one of my closest friends, essentially family, and certainly beloved. What he taught me and gave me is immeasurable. In many ways this book exists because of him.

Ergo, the contents of this section are not in any way a condemnation of the field of teaching. I could never even think of doing that. It's simply (Hah! Really simple, no?) that the contents of this section are about the things that get in your way. Not about the many good or even wonderful parts that I hope were in there, too.

Second comment. Not all of you will have a terrible story about something that happened at school that was bad for your creative expression. That makes me very happy. If you had to go searching for something that was not good for your creativity in some other arena, that means that school, at least, was good for you. That part, too, makes me very happy.

But much too frequently, the stories that come out of this exercise are awful. They are mean, or cruel, or at the very least insensitive and thoughtless. Worse, they are frequently crippling, not just at the time, but long-term.

Unfortunately, I'm also guessing that if you have written about one of these kinds of experiences, if this is the thing that occurred to you when I gave the assignment, that it has affected your ability to get to your art! To do your art. To love your art.

"Work at finding the things that get in your way." Remember?

Sadly, very, very sadly, this exercise often points out something important that gets in your way. Or even a thousand of those things that get in your way, coming from that one moment. The effects of what happens to you when you are a child, or a teenager in a classroom, from your teacher, from the other kids, are often multilayered and complex.

And, I'm sorry. I'm terribly sorry.

I'm sorry it happened. I'm sorry that it had to come from school. A place that is supposed to teach you, and nurture you, and encourage you.

Still, even more importantly, I want you to know it. I want you to remember that it happened. To understand how it made you feel. So that you can start realizing what it did to you, that little kid, or young teenager, or college student. That artist, human being, who is you. So that you can now be able to start working through it.

And please remember, as you are working through it, you may very well need support to do that. You may need help or support from your family, help or support from your friends, help or support from a therapist. Things come up, of course. And this could be an important one. So take care of yourself as much as you need to!

After the discussion below, I'll give you a Homework Assignment that will hopefully help you start working this through. No, let me correct that statement. I believe that writing about that experience has already helped you start doing that. So, to rephrase, after the next section I'll give you a Homework Assignment that will hopefully help you *continue* working this through.

*　　*　　*　　*

Dari's Nerd/Geek/Outsider Theory of Being a Young Artist.

Welcome to my world.

There I was, putting my course together, and trying to come up with some way of framing a particular set of ideas I have about being an artist-type kid, and the impact that it has on us growing up. I was working at coming up with some way of putting my ideas into a theory. The theory has evolved enormously over time. Where I start with it here is a small piece, with incredibly creative "variations on the theme" from the very people I'm talking about. I learn something new about it in every class I teach.

It's complicated, and complex, and it isn't an all or nothing theory. It's true some of the time about a lot of us, or a lot of the time about some of us, or, or, or... Also, as I've been very clear about from the beginning (think "children in the snow"), since I believe that creativity is a natural and innate part of every single one of us, it gets really, really complicated.

Consequently, while you're reading/thinking about it, please make an effort to not be too black and white about it. This part of the world is not binary!

Artists, by their nature, often tend to be somewhat marginalized.[16] They have a general tendency not to fit in. Art is, pretty much by definition, creative, therefore original. Therefore, it's not what's already out there. It's not a proper profession. It's not practical. It's not what people have seen/heard/etc. before. It's not a bunch of things. Artists tend to be outside the mainstream. This starts early. Kids who are artistic types often don't fit in, even in school. *Glee*, the TV show, has gone a long way to help performing artists have more of a "popular" place in school, but even there, think of the number of slushies they've had thrown in their faces.

There is a whole slew of noticeable differences between some artistic types and more "normal" people. It starts pretty early. You can choose which of the following you relate to.

In my own course outline – a *very* loose document – I generally have a heading for each topic, and below that, a phrase or a sentence summing up the topic (then I continue on with various details about the topic). In this case, the sum total of the phrase I use, under the heading of Dari's Nerd/Geek/Outsider Theory of being an artist, reads:

"You're tooooooooooooooooooooooooo…"

Now let's complete the various sentences.

You're too sensitive, for sure. Whether it's, "you're too sensitive" so you cry all the time, or too sensitive so you shut down and don't say a word or you disappear, or too sensitive so you get super angry… You're too sensitive, so you get afraid of things. Whatever. According to the rest of the world, you're often just too sensitive.

You're too serious. (Lighten up, they say.) Too dramatic (as in, you take things too seriously…) Too intense. Certainly, too emotional.

You may have spent a lot of time in school (and at home, outside, etc., etc., etc. – it's just that we're talking about school right now) off in fantasyland. Daydreaming. Making up stories in your head. Going on journeys in your head. Just going off into La La Land. Too much time *not* paying proper attention. Especially in class.

You spend your hours of class time doodling. Drawing pictures. Doing graphic design. Hiding the images whenever the teacher walks by.

Or instead you watched everything that was going on around you. You watched the teachers. The other kids. A whole other way of not paying attention in class. You became completely absorbed in watching the leaves on the trees outside the classroom window. The clouds in the sky. Whatever.

Part of the problem is you'd already started being an observer.

(Please note: the following idea came well before Sponge Bob came into existence - ☺.)

You tend to be what I call a sponge person. It's part of being "too sensitive." You walk into a room filled with other people and you instantly start sponging up everyone else's feelings. Sometimes you're practically vibrating from it. It can feel really weird or utterly overwhelming. You're super aware of other people's moods or feelings, whether you respond to them or shove them as far away from you as you can. You react to what's going on inside them. You pick up on other people's "stuff."

Which I think is totally unfair given how much of our own stuff we have to deal with so much of the time...

Personal story: I was in graduate school in psychology. You have to take statistics in grad school in order to get your degree. Relatively advanced statistics (it was grad school, after all). Try and imagine how much all we gentle, taking-care-of-other-people types, loved statistics. I failed the mid-term. Failed it. Bottom of the class. Hadn't done much failing in school. I worked really hard at being a good student. I was totally freaked out by that "F." Consequently I got more and more tense as the days went by and the final exam loomed.

Dennis, husband if you've forgotten, tutored me. He was actually the teaching assistant for the course because he'd come over to psychology from working on a master's degree in particle physics. He was a bit better at math than the rest of us... (By the way, everyone was very jealous that I got to go home with the statistics teaching assistant.) Anyway, I'd gotten so tense about statistics that he would actually have to whisper when he was working with me, otherwise it sounded like his voice was booming inside my head.

Needless to say, I studied and studied and studied for the final. Non-stop. I was totally freaked out by the idea of it preventing me from getting my degree. Maybe even more so, I was horrified by the idea of taking statistics for a second time. Yet as much as I studied, I was still panicked.

Ultimately, I did one of the weirder things I'd ever done at school. I walked into my statistics professor's office and pleaded with him to let me take the final exam alone. I told him he could have me take it before everyone else took it, or after everyone else took it. He could give me the same exam or a different one, so I couldn't cheat no matter what. I'd do whatever he wanted me to do with the exam. If he would only, please, please, please, let me take it alone in a room with no other students around me.

You see, I'd come up with another theory. What I thought I'd figured out was the following: There I was, a true sponge person. I was always picking up on feelings from other people. If people around me were sad, I felt miserable. If they were happy, the world looked sunny. It's just the way it was for me from the time I was little.

And there we were, a class of about twenty or so psychology graduate students, sensitive, caring, helpful types, almost every single one – with the "rat runner" people, the true scientist types, being the only exceptions who weren't quite as scared of math – all of us panicked about passing the required graduate statistics course. All gathered together in this little room, taking an exam that would determine whether or not we were allowed to get our degree. So there was a bit, *A BIT*, of nervousness. A *TINY* little amount of adrenalin, floating around in that space. Let's face it, there would be panicked perspiration pouring out into that environment.

And I would be sponging up every nano-atom of it. And I would become paralyzed with fear.

Which is exactly what I decided had happened with the mid-term. I'd blanked out. I could barely see the problems written on the paper in front of me.

I had to do *something* for the final.

Which is why I basically pleaded with the statistics prof to let me take the exam alone. Which he did, though I'm sure he thought I was a nutcase. But hell, he was a psychologist, and so, in this case, very understanding.

Happy ending. I got the highest mark in the whole class. Even better than Dennis… (For which he'll never forgive me.) Apparently I had found ways to manage my own anxiety about the stupid exam. However – and this is the key point – I could NOT manage everybody else's.

Sponge people…

Another aspect of artistic types can be a strange sensory phenomenon called synesthesia. Merriam-Webster's definition is: "a concomitant sensation; *especially*: a subjective sensation or image of a sense (as of color) other than the one (as of sound) being stimulated."[17] In other words, this is where one sensory system connects with a different one. It can be anything with anything. There are dozens of forms of it that have been heavily researched. One of my own versions is an excruciatingly strong connection of colors with feelings. I think this type of synesthesia is much more common than many of the others. Many of us have emotional reactions to particular colors. Mine is just a bit more irritating to those around me than the norm. Example: I was looking for a backpack that wasn't grey or black or burgundy or navy blue. Those were the normal backpack colors I kept finding in all the stores. (Especially in gray Vancouver…) I'd go into store after store, and ask if they had any backpacks in pink, or green, or red, etc. They would point me to the dullest greens and reds you can imagine. Eventually I gave up asking for my particular set of colors (after a solid year of searching), and simply started walking into stores and asking if they had any happy-colored packs… They mostly grinned and shook their heads. Yet they knew what I was talking about. Until one day, a very nice guy pointed to a corner, where hung a fantastically happy Caribbean aqua pack. To this day, I grin every time I open the closet.

Another example. Husband, Dennis, who got his first degree in engineering physics (translate that, one more time, as good in math!), learned to count and do arithmetic as a child by having a picture associated with every number! (He didn't try to do this, it just happened.) I e-mailed him while I'm writing this to ask him for an example that he remembers. Here's his response:

3x6 = 18, was swaddled in something warm

2x9 = 18, was sort of spiky

3x7 =21, was just safely over the lip of a cliff

3x8 = 24, was a white horse in a green grassy field

(I love that one.)

What's important to understand in the context of this chapter on artistic types, is that, in addition to being from the world of physics, Dennis is also a professional nature photographer... Yup. An artist. (I think there's often a strong relationship between physics and art.)

One of my very favorite examples of synesthesia in literature is in a Swedish novel called *Simon and the Oaks*, written by Marianne Fredriksson.[18] It takes place in the 1940s. An uncle takes his young nephew to attend his very first concert. The boy sits down in the theater, looks around at the intimidating room, listens to the scratching sound of the musicians tuning their instruments, and feels like running from it.

Finally he sees the conductor raise his baton and hears the music start.

The rest of the chapter is very strange. (Please note, this novel is in no way any kind of science fiction.) Instantly the reader is in the middle of another country, another time, a strange and fascinating kingdom, a story profoundly different and at odds from the novel I'd been reading. An ancient story about priests and goddesses, kings and knights, birds that speak, temples that are destroyed, and flooding rivers. The tale is absolutely gripping and the reader is thoroughly immersed in this other story until, abruptly, this chapter ends.

The next chapter begins, and the boy is back in the city with his uncle, completely confused. The music has ended, the concert is done.

While the music played, the boy saw, felt, and heard the story of this other place. It's how he heard the music.

There turns out be a reasonable amount of research evidence that there is a strong connection between artistic types and synesthesia.[19]

I think you're getting the idea. There seem to be a number of characteristics that artist types tend to have, or have somewhat more than the norm. These characteristics show up right from the beginning. Ask your parents, if that's a safe thing to do. They'll talk about your relationship to music. Or your compulsive drawing. Maybe how sophisticated your ability to talk was from the very beginning. How clever you were. How funny.

It starts early. The child artist with the unusual tendencies.

There you are, a young child in school, who feels somewhat different from the other kids, but doesn't understand why. Plus, there they are, all the other young children who feel you're somewhat different from them, but they don't understand why either.

What I think happens is that everyone tends to attribute that difference, that "not fitting in-ness," to more obvious, more easily identifiable characteristics. You're all young kids, for heaven's sake. Perhaps not the most sophisticated analysts ever.

So instead, you're seen by the other kids as too tall or too short. Too thin or too fat. You wear glasses, you're an egghead. Whatever… That's what's wrong with you.

You're weird. Because of, whatever! You buy it, and they buy it. It's one of the ultimate attacks. You can carry it with you forever!!!!!

There it is, my nerd/geek/outsider theory of being a little person (child) who's an artist.

While all along, what is really going on is this wonderful, difficult, lovely, disturbing, creative thing about you.

There's so much to say about this. So many stories. Here's one that was particularly useful for me.

A lot of people in my courses listen to this theory in a state of shock. Their childhood comes up on them, hard. Really hard. They remember so many of their experiences all too well.

In this one particular class, as usual, a couple of people had tears in their eyes as this other way of understanding their school years clicked.

Then one young woman, in her twenties, started sobbing. She said she'd hated herself her whole life for how she was perceived in school. She'd always felt like a complete outsider. A nerd. A geek. Most profoundly a complete and absolute loser.

Yet she was connecting with every syllable of what we were all saying. It was making sense. Describing exactly who she'd been. Still was. But with a completely different explanation. She left class that night smiling softly.

The next week she came back in to class and announced that I'd changed her life. That she'd been reinterpreting so much of who she'd been and who she was. That she was feeling SOOOO much better. She'd also started doing a whole bunch of research on it and had found a book that she thought I might find interesting.

The book is *The Highly Sensitive Person*, by Elaine N. Aron, a psychologist.[20] It turns out that Elaine Aron has been doing an extraordinary amount of research, pretty much all of which supports my Nerd/Geek/Outsider Theory of being a young artist.

Her research shows that about fifteen to twenty percent of the general population score as "Highly Sensitive" people. You are not alone!

It also means that you are somewhat different than about eighty to eighty-five out of every one hundred people you meet. Remember feeling like an outsider?

Professionally, highly sensitive people, tend to be... You want to guess? We often tend to be healers, teachers, scholars, and, YUP, artists.

A particularly interesting set of results is the cross-cultural research done in this area. When asked to rate their reactions to highly sensitive people, different cultures have different reactions. In North America, we are not considered "wonderful." The majority of North Americans will not choose highly sensitive people as the favorite type of person to hang out with. Whereas in some other countries, like Sweden, China, and Japan, highly sensitive characteristics are prized.

It's so often not the set of characteristics that is the problem; it's how they're perceived. By others and by ourselves.

My silly favorite demonstration of the proportion of the sensitive artistic people who take my course – remember the course is on creativity – is to ask how many of the people in my class like going to huge parties, or big parades, or any other kind of large noisy event. The most frequent response is that not one person raises their hand. Sometimes, one or two people, at best, say they like parades and huge parties.

Remember, not all the characteristics will be true for everyone! It doesn't matter. It's the tendency that we're interested in.

Another interesting and related study I heard about, although I cannot find the source for this one (there are many studies on this topic), was about schizophrenics. The study showed that diagnosed schizophrenics had an "attenuated stimulus filter system." Translation: their filter system was not adequate to deal with the amount of stimulus that was coming in. Or, stimulus overload. Sound familiar? Overwhelmed. Overloaded. "Tooooooooooooo sensitive…"

The clever researchers proceeded to do the same study on a group of artists. Do you want to guess? Same results. "Attenuated stimulus filter system." Sensitive artists, taking in lots and lots of what is going on around them, and not quite able to filter it sufficiently…

*   *   *   *

So, that's my theory.

I'm confident about it, to a great extent, because of the extraordinary response I repeatedly get from students, artists, friends. Also myself. I've been thrilled that I get such a positive response. When I found so much validation for it in Elaine Aron's work, as well as other people's research, I felt even better about the theory.

Still, joyful humility is often waiting just around the corner.

I found an amazing and fascinating quote a few years ago. It's by Pearl S. Buck. It is especially wonderful in the context of my thoughts on the topic of who artists tend to be. My wonderful *"new"* theory.

It took me a *lot* of searching to figure out exactly when she wrote the quote. But she won the Nobel Prize for Literature in *1938,* so I figured it couldn't be all that recent. I was guessing it was from the 60s or 70s.

I finally found the original source. It was in a speech she gave in *1937.* She clearly already knew all about the nature of artists.

Here's the quote:

> **"The truly creative mind in any field is no more than this:**
> **A human creature born abnormally, inhumanly sensitive.**
> **To him, a touch is a blow,**
> **A sound is a noise,**
> **A misfortune is a tragedy**
> **A joy is an ecstasy**
> **A friend is a lover,**
> **A lover is a god,**
> **And failure is death..."**
> **Pearl S. Buck**[21]

Pretty cool, no?

*   *   *   *

Okay, now let's go back to the original In Class Exercise. It was:

Please write about an experience you had in school that was not good for your creative expression.

While you are thinking about it, I would like you to keep securely in mind what I've been talking about. Dari's Nerd/Geek/Outsider Theory of Being an Artist. That means that a great part of what was happening in those early years is that you were always who you are now – a creative young'un... (Okay, maybe now, you're not quite such a young'un – you may be older than 18... – but you were *always* creative.)

I'm going to share a few stories with you about various people I know, artists and non-artists, including several students doing this very exercise. I'm also going to include one from my own history, a major motivation for me including this exercise in my courses. Afterwards, I'll give you homework.

Some of the stories are so simple, so elemental, you could blink your eyes and not notice what happened. Until a long time later.

Some of them are so painful that they may shut you down on the spot in hurt and anger, fear and shame.

One of my first students was retired. She'd been a teacher first, then a school principal for over twenty years. She knew all about the educational system. She sat in my classroom many, many years after that (she was in her mid-seventies), at a kid's small school table (that course took place in a community center), and read her Exercise out loud.

She told us about a moment when she was in the second grade, and her class had been told it was time to do art. Yay! That made her very happy. All the seven-year-olds enthusiastically got out their crayons and started to draw. She started coloring joyfully along with the rest of the class, while the teacher wandered up and down the rows of children. My student was busily drawing a picture of the outside of her house and her garden, a perfect early landscape of where she grew up.

Abruptly the teacher stopped, stood over her, looked down at her picture and asked accusingly, disapproval dripping deeply from her voice, "What is *that?*" She pointed at the upper part of the picture.

"It's the sky!" answered my student, staring up at her teacher, both excited by the drawing, and confused by the tone of the question.

"But the sky is blue!" retorted the teacher, her voice dripping even more deeply with disapproval. Abruptly she turned her back and continued walking around the class, shaking her head as she went.

My student, this lovely woman, a retired professional who had devoted her life to educating children, over seventy years of age, finished reading her assignment and looked up at me with tears flowing down her cheeks. Almost seventy years later.

I shook my head, gave her all the sympathy I could, and listened while the next person read their assignment. At the time I remember feeling shocked at the powerful impact that story still had on the woman. A brief moment, almost seventy years earlier, and here she was sitting, in my classroom, in front of a group of still virtual strangers, crying.

These days I'm no longer shocked.

After years of teaching these courses, of hearing story after story of creativity-crushing experiences, of seeing the raw painful reactions of so many students as they remember the event for the first time in years, or say it out loud for the first time ever, I now understand how powerful, far-reaching, and long term the effects can sometimes be.

That woman never felt the same about doing her art. She was hurt and confused. She was "bad." What she had done with her picture, with her art, was simply wrong. She proceeded to shut it down. (It was, of course, more complicated than that. Though that was a very profound and painful beginning of it.) So much so, that she had literally waited until she was in her mid-seventies to take a course on getting *back* to her art.

Her awakening was astonishing. The smile on her face when she started taking back her artistic work was glorious to see.

Another student had painted a picture of an Apollo space walk for a homework assignment in junior high school. He'd spent day after day working on the project, both because he loved painting and because he was fascinated by space travel. A fairly typical thirteen-year-old obsession. He'd studied all of the photographs he could find of the experience and reproduced them with fanatic care. He brought the picture into class one Monday morning and (need I say it?), he was very excited. Very proud of what he'd done.

The teacher looked at the picture, yelled at him for leaving about a third of the painting blank, and ripped off that part of it!

Yes, of course. The "blank" part of the picture was space...

Another story: An Irish student moved to Canada when she was a child. In fifth grade, she stood up in front of the class and read a poem she had written for homework. The teacher told her the piece was garbage and started imitating her Irish accent.

And another. One student who was passionate about music from early on was in the choir in elementary school. Sister Gabriel instructed her to "Not sing." Rather to only "mouth the words" because her voice was not good enough... As an adult this woman now sings in several different choirs. It's a major part of her life. To this day, however, every week at practice, she relives the experience. She still sees all the six and seven and eight-year-olds, gathered around the piano as the nun gave her those instructions. And she is always embarrassed to sing out loud.

Another. This student had a twelfth grade English teacher who my student felt was fundamentally out to get him. He was a straight "A" student except in that particular English class. Finally, in desperation, he traded his paper with another student and handed it in under his name. He got a "C" on her paper, she got an "A" on his... At least that student figured it out. Though he always wondered why that teacher disliked him so.

Many students; smart, competent, adult professionals told stories of being held back, or put in classes for intellectually challenged kids, or labeled with various forms of learning disabilities, all inaccurately. Those were the nicer versions.

Far too many students were called hurtful names, or simply had their work insulted by their teachers! They were called, and these are all quotes; stupid, boring, retards, trite, simplistic, lazy, silly, wrong, wrong, wrong...

One student read a paper she had worked on fiercely for several days. "You must have had help from adults," she was told.

A thirteen-year-old child, who had studied the violin for three years with the same teacher, experienced the humiliation of being told, in front of the entire school orchestra, that he was simply tone deaf.

There are a myriad stories at home as well. But just one for now.

At a family gathering, one student played a guitar piece she had learned and perfected at school. She played it perfectly. "Thank god that's over," said her uncle.

These kinds of stories are endless. Horrible and endless.

Then we get to move on to another topic.

One student was sitting with several other kids in a reading group. They were laughing about something they had read, and the teacher *slammed* my student on the arm with a book. This was the first time I'd heard a story about physical abuse in the classroom from this writing assignment. Over time I heard many more!

I was completely shocked to discover how many experiences of physical abuse students had in school. At first, I thought it was because

I was an American living and teaching in Canada. (Please note, I said, I *thought* that was the reason.) Where I grew up, New York and Miami Beach, I never saw students subjected to corporal punishment. I heard and read stories, numerous novels, of terrible treatment in British boarding schools. Though not in America. Never in America.

Yet there I was teaching in Canada, at least as *civilized* as the USA... and listening as the assignment brought up story after story of students strapped, paddled, and even more severely beaten for expressing themselves in the most harmless ways. As with any kind of physical abuse, the impacts of the abuse were long-lasting and devastating. If the abuse were related in any way to artistic expression, it frequently ended all artistic expression from that moment onward.

It's just insane. Beating a student for the way they did an assignment. Story after story. Being beaten will screw up your art, for sure.

As it turned out, I was completely wrong about American schools. Corporal punishment has been going on all along. At the moment I am writing this, there are still nineteen states that allow it. Apparently I was very lucky in the schools I attended. It is a terrible thing that this was a normal, accepted part of the culture in so many schools. By the way, Canada banned corporal punishment in schools in 2004...[22,] something I was very happy to discover.

My own worst experience of my artistic expression being damaged (fortunately!) did not involve physical abuse of any kind. I didn't even remember that it had happened until many years after the fact. I had no idea, actually. That in itself is a not a good sign. It was pretty devastating to find out about it even after all that time. Imagine what it must have felt like when I was thirteen years old.

As I've mentioned, I came from a very difficult childhood. Ran away from home at thirteen, from my physically violent mother in New York. Fortunately I had a non-violent father I could go live with in Miami Beach.

So, one dramatic escape later, I went to Florida, went to school, and went on with my life. No one considered the possibility of sending me to a therapist. Still, I was just so happy to be out of the "difficult" part, that I squared my shoulders and made good!

In eighth and ninth grade I had an English teacher whom I idolized. We all did, actually. There was this little group of "gifted" writer types, who kind of worshipped him. We formed a creative writing class and proceeded on our way.

Many, many years later, I was visiting my dad when my stepmother told me that she was clearing out all of our (the kids) things. She said there was a box of my papers from school on the closet shelf, so could I please go through them and do what I wanted with them.

It was more than twenty years later, and I'd had no idea that the box even existed, much less what was in it... I sat down on the floor in my bedroom and started going through schoolwork from the eighth grade on.

Then I found it. I had written a poem, a sonnet, actually, shortly after I arrived in Florida. It was about leaving my mother and getting rescued by my new life. Of having a real chance to survive. Literally. I wrote a bit about the cruel woman I had left (a profoundly understated description, and certainly the first time I had written down anything about it in public). I wrote about the gratitude I felt for being rescued, and about my determination to do the best I could with this new chance at life.

I was surprised, even shocked, that I had actually written a poem about it. I hardly ever even talked about it back then.

As I finished reading the poem, I looked down at the bottom of the page and saw the comment my "beloved" teacher had written.

"Melodramatic! Just write your poem about the effort you make as a teenager to live a good life."

Wow. I'd had no (conscious) idea he'd ever said anything like that.

All I could think about was that hurt thirteen-year-old, me, having the courage to break the silence on such an abusive childhood, and write down just a tiny, utterly understated, piece about her childhood feelings, probably for the very first time. Writing it down on paper and getting that response. "Melodramatic." (He had NO idea....)

Talk about shutting me down!

When I read this comment twenty years later, I was, as the Scots say, gobsmacked! My teacher's comment was both insensitive and irresponsible. A thoughtless moment from such a wonderful teacher.

The horror stories from so many people seem infinite.

It appears from many of the class assignments that humiliating children during presentations is considerably more common than I ever imagined, even in my more pessimistic moments. And it's terrible. *Even if* they were only momentary, careless lapses from otherwise perfectly okay teachers.

Sadly, of course, there were also numerous stories about bullying. Bullying from other kids. Bullying that hurt, and damaged, and devastated, and certainly, beyond the shadow of any doubt, shut down people's artistic expression.

If I had to pick a topic in the news these days that makes me the happiest and the most hopeful about where our world is going, it would be on the topic of bullying. I am so joyful and so grateful that this cruelty is being talked about, exposed, and confronted.

In one class there was a young Japanese woman who gave me a lesson in another form of stifling. A stifling that shuts down even the concept of creativity.

This student was about twenty-two, and she was attending college in Vancouver to prepare for the TOEFL, the Test of English as a Foreign Language, the exam that is necessary to attend university in many places in North America. Her English was pretty bad, but her determination was wonderful. So wonderful that she took my course in creativity, just for her own sake, even though she had to write and read out loud in English, in a class filled almost entirely with native English speakers.

In her assignment she described some typical practices that took place in the schools she had attended growing up in Japan. The really terrible example had to do with her Japanese classes. (Think English class in most of North America. You usually take English every single year.) As many students do, she cried painfully while she was stumbling through the reading of the assignment out loud in our class. In her case, it seems that a common activity throughout her school years was that the teacher would read a story out loud, then ask the students to do a homework assignment. The assignment was to describe what the main character was thinking at a particular moment in the novel or story.

A perfectly wonderful opportunity to use one's imagination, I thought. Go inside the mind of a literary character and create the cognitive, emotional, and psychological world they were acting in. Wonderfully creative, I thought!

Not so much. The problem? There was only one right answer to the assignment! Only one!

That **CORRECT** answer was written down in the teacher's **INSTRUCTION MANUAL!**

Every other answer that anyone came up with was *wrong*. Incorrect, inaccurate, false… Absolutely, unarguably *wrong*…

Can you imagine?

I have to admit. The personalized Homework Assignment that I came up with for her as a result of what she read in class, was one of my favorite assignments I have ever come up with.

(Please note: in my courses I often give out individual assignments based on what a particular student has written, or said, or come up with in some way, during class. It's a challenging, but lovely, part of my courses. Of course it is based on my fundamental premise that this whole gigantic package has to be YOUR WAY. Therefore, individual assignments are often the *only* way.

By the way, I do hate that it is so much more difficult to do that for you, since you are doing this book and not attending my course. We'll keep grappling with that…)

My Homework Assignment for this young woman, was to go home and select a novel or a story that she loved, to pick a moment in that story that she wanted to explore and, yes, to write down what she thought the main character was thinking. But, and here was the great part, she had to come up with fifteen different thoughts!

Of that same moment.

Consequently, at least fourteen of her fifteen thoughts would have *had* to be "wrong!" if she were doing this in her old school! Yay! She chose *The Little Prince*, the novella written by Antoine de Saint-Exupéry in 1943.

When she came back to class a week later and read her homework out loud, she had come up with fifteen cute, funny, sad, moving, beautiful thoughts. It was gloriously creative. And she couldn't stop laughing. The whole time. It was the most wonderful laughter of joy and freedom. And she couldn't stop crying. The tears were streaming down her face. I think that the laughter and the tears were also tinged with some truly righteous anger.

The other stories from this assignment go on and on, but I am going to stop here. The point is that the ability of these experiences we have in school to shut down our art can be truly devastating. As I said, it's often the hardest assignment I give. The one I hate listening to the most. And one of the ones for which I am again reminding you the most strongly; get whatever support and help you need to take care of yourself.

Still, it is often one of the most important moments in this process of reconnecting with our creativity, our art, and our joy of expression.

*   *   *   *

One last little moment from my academic life that I've thought of frequently during my writing of this book and during many other pieces of writing I've done. It wasn't devastating. Partly, I think, because I was in my mid-twenties, instead of ten years old. Though it rankles still.

This one was in university; a question on a quiz in my very favorite topic, *statistics*. One small essay question. I wrote a short paragraph in response. I got back the following comment:

"Brief, therefore superficial."

I felt awful. Stupid and simplistic and... superficial! Yuck! But some phrase in Latin kept drifting through my head as I read it and for days afterwards, as I inevitably kept thinking about it, then thinking about it some more... After a while I grabbed the phrase from my brain to examine it.

"Cogito ergo sum."[23]

"I think therefore I am."
(That's the common translation. "I am thinking therefore I am" is the literal translation.)

The phrase is a fundamental principle of western philosophy. Pretty much as brief as it gets. Also, the profound opposite of superficial!

Which brings me to another profoundly profound point about lots of things we are taught and of what we experience or have experienced in school about our art. What was said to you, or taught to you, or done to you...

IS FREQUENTLY ABSOLUTELY WRONG.

So do keep that in mind when you are thinking of your own school experiences.

*   *   *   *

Next, I'd like you to read the following story. Afterwards we'll get to your homework.

*   *   *   *

The Brown Flower

Once upon a time, a small boy had been going to school for a few weeks when his teacher said, "Today we are going to make a picture." The boy thought about how he could draw lions and tigers, trains and boats, houses and suns, and all kinds of pretty things. He took out his crayons and began to draw.

But the teacher said, "We are going to make flowers." The boy stopped drawing, turned his paper over, and thought how he could draw all kinds of different flowers; some with big leaves, some with pink leaves, some with pink and orange petals, some big purple ones and some little yellow ones, and he started to draw happily.

But the teacher said, "I will show you how." She drew a flower on the blackboard. It was brown with a green stem. "Now you may begin," she said.

The little boy liked the flowers he had drawn better than the teacher's flower, but he took out a new piece of paper and made a flower just like hers. It was brown with a green stem.

On another day the teacher said, "We are going to make something with clay." The boy thought about how he could make snakes and snowmen, elephants and mice, donuts and lots of other exciting things. He began to pull and pinch his ball of clay.

But the teacher said, "We are going to make a dish." The boy liked that idea too, so he started to make dishes of all shapes and sizes. But the teacher said, "I will show you how." She showed the class how to make one deep dish. "Now you may began," she said.

The little boy looked at the teacher's dish, then he looked at his own. He liked his dishes better than her dish, but he crushed them back into a big ball. Then he made a deep dish, just like the teacher's. And so it went for many weeks.

Then it happened that the boy's family moved to another city. On the very first day at his new school, the teacher said, "Today we are going to make a picture." The boy thought about how much fun it would be to draw a picture, and he waited.

But the teacher didn't say anything. She just walked around the room. When she came to the little boy, she asked him whether he wanted to draw a picture. He said that he did, and he asked her what he should draw. "Anything you want to," said the teacher. He asked her what color he should use. "Any color you want to," said the teacher.

The little boy looked at his blank paper and thought hard for several moments. Then he picked up his crayons and started to draw. He drew a brown flower with a green stem.

Based on a poem by Helen E. Buckley[24]

* * * *

There's a lovely answer to this in a Peanuts cartoon by Charles Schulz. Charlie Brown paints a superhero in spite of the teacher's instructions to paint a flower. He calls him Sunflower.

*   *   *   *

Homework Assignment

All right. Here is your Homework Assignment. Do it right away or do it later. Whatever works best. (Of course, please do not continue working in the book until you've done the assignment, or tried to do the assignment, or decided you don't want to do the assignment. Or until you've done something entirely different that felt more like it was the right thing for you to do...)

I wish I were there to hear what you wrote for the original assignment and then to scramble through my own being to figure out what would be a truly useful Homework Assignment to give you in response to your experience.

But I'm not. So I can't.

What I can do is make a suggestion. It's a technique I use fairly frequently for this assignment. It's often the point. (Though not always. More about that after.)

I'd like you to think about the person or persons that caused the situation you described in your assignment.

AND I DON'T MEAN YOU!

Many of us spend our whole lives holding ourselves responsible for causing ourselves harm, and letting the actual wrongdoer off the hook. You were a kid. Or a teenager. Even a young adult in university. They were the authority. The person in charge. The person who had the power.

You didn't cause the situation. Even if you'd like to think you did. Really, you didn't. There is a much more than excellent chance that you had nothing to do with what happened!

The assignment is to think about the teacher, or the principal, or the other kids, or whoever did that thing that harmed your creative expression, and write her, or him, or them a letter.

I'm not talking about sending it to them. You're not going to send this letter anywhere; or e-mail it, text it, message it, nothin'. That is not the point. *They* are not the point here.

You are. You are the point.

Write them a letter. Tell them how you feel about what they did. Write it from the kid that you were then. Or write it from the adult you are now. Even better, it's often very useful to write two letters – one from each of you.

Remember this is for you. No one else will read it unless you want them to. You can say whatever you want. What I hope is that you will say everything you need to say, think everything you need to think, and feel everything you need to feel.

If writing a letter doesn't fit with your experience, and there are lot of stories for which the letter isn't appropriate, here's what I'd like you to do instead.

I'd like you to think about what happened to you. I'd like you to think about a child who you know now and care about, who is the age *you* were when it happened. You might know someone that age who you care about very much. Or you might just have to imagine one. The child/kid/teenager could be your own son or daughter, your niece or nephew, a friend's daughter or son. Imagine that your experience happened to them instead of to you. Exactly the thing that happened to you. Think about how they would feel. What it would be like for that child you care about.

Now I'd like you to think about what you could do to take care of them. Think about ways you could help them. Think about what you as an adult might say to them. Or do with them. Hug them. Hold them. Reassure them. Give them support. Give them permission to cry, to sob, to howl at the heavens, to pound on a pillow until the feathers fly. Imagine the many kinds of loving, caring support you can give that child to deal with the experience.

And write about that. Write about taking care of that child. Write about taking care of that version of you.

You might even try both assignments… See what you discover. Good luck.

Take care, all.

Chapter nine

Ants in the Sand

Hi, again.

How was that? Painful as hell? Gloriously satisfying? Somewhere in between?

Please read the letter or letters out loud. Or read out loud the thoughts you wrote for helping your child. Slowly. Pay attention to what you're reading – to what you've said. Pay attention to how you feel.

*　　*　　*　　*

I hope writing it gave you something. I also hope that reading it out loud gave you something as well. Don't be surprised if your reaction while reading it is different from when you wrote it. Often, when you're hearing your words out loud, you feel things that you don't feel when you're writing them. Perhaps it's more like hearing someone else's story. You're not pouring it out. You're taking it in…

Don't be surprised if you're crying. What happened hurt you. And don't be surprised if you're feeling angry. Again, what happened hurt you. You may be feeling more calm. Getting it out after all this time can quiet things. You might even be feeling gleeful, if you finally talked about something that's been festering for ten or twenty, thirty, fifty years. You could be feeling pretty much anything. Or nothing, of course. Sometimes that happens.

There's no right or wrong answer, here. Remember?

I do hope you got something from this. If it was important enough for you to write about it when I asked the question, then it's important enough to do whatever you can to heal it. Or take a step towards healing it. Or simply remember and acknowledge it. It stuck around. That kid who you were when it happened is still right there inside you, feeling everything that happened. That child needs to be heard by you.

It wasn't okay what happened to you. It's important that you know it. It's important that the adult you looks at the child it happened to and tells that child it wasn't okay. Helps that child. Takes care of that child.

Believe it or not, if you take care of that child, that child can end up taking care of you – by not loading you down with the feelings that come from *then*...

*   *   *   *

The next step. We are now going to take a look at another important –

BUMP:

Art is useless, pointless. I'm wasting my time...

My simple response to this rather profound particular bump is that it's story time. Do you remember the story of the Ant and the Grasshopper? I'm going to tell you two versions of the story; then you get to decide which one you prefer.

The first version is taken from Aesop's fable.[25] Here goes:

It was a beautiful summer day. The sky was blue, the grass was green, and the sun was a warming yellow glow. A large group of ants was busily working. They were building their home and gathering their food, storing it away for winter. Soon they would be well-prepared to face the harsh cold time. Suddenly they heard a lovely sound coming from the meadow nearby. Music was soaring through the air, enticing them. They decided to take a brief time out and go looking for the source.

Off into the meadow they went until they came upon a grasshopper, sitting on a rock, fiddling away on his violin.

"Mr. Grasshopper, Mr. Grasshopper," they all chimed together. "What are you doing? Your music is lovely but winter is coming. You need to stop frittering away your time. You need to get ready. You need food and shelter. Water, too."

"You're right, dear friends. You're absolutely right," the grasshopper responded. "But I love my music so. I need to play."

After pleading with the grasshopper a few more times, the little ants marched away, shaking their heads.

The cold winter came and the ants were snug as bugs in their little home. Well-fed and protected.

Suddenly a knock came on the door. They pushed hard against the door, which was being pummeled by the winter wind and snow, opening it as little as possible to protect themselves. Outside stood the grasshopper, grey-looking, thin, and shivering.

"Hello, dear ants," he said. "As you warned me, winter has come and I have no food or shelter. Can you please help me?"

The ants looked at each other sadly and shook their heads. "We're very sorry, Mr. Grasshopper. But you are much too big to come in to our home, and you would use up all our food in a minute. There's just nothing we can do for you. We wish you the best."

The grasshopper nodded his head and walked away.

When spring came, the ants exited their home, and stumbled across the grasshopper, lying dead on the ground.

The moral of Aesop's story is that it is important to work hard, to plan for tomorrow and not waste time on "frivolous" things.

*   *   *   *

Image by Edward de Deene[26]

And here's a lovely illustration of the story from 1567!

*   *   *   *

But now the second version of the story. Some people believe that this is the true version, one that got changed with the coming of the Industrial Revolution.

The first half of the story is identical to the previous version:

It was a beautiful summer day. The sky was blue, the grass was green, and the sun was a warming yellow glow. A large group of ants was busily working. They were building their home and gathering their food, storing it away for winter. Soon they would be well-prepared to face the harsh cold time. Suddenly they heard a lovely sound coming from the meadow nearby. Music was soaring through the air, enticing them. They decided to take a brief time out and go looking for the source.

Off into the meadow they went until they came upon a grasshopper, sitting on a rock, fiddling away on his violin.

"Mr. Grasshopper, Mr. Grasshopper," they all chimed together. "What are you doing? Your music is lovely but winter is coming. You need to stop frittering away your time. You need to get ready. You need food and shelter. Water, too."

"You're right, dear friends. You're absolutely right," the grasshopper responded. "But I love my music so. I need to play."

After pleading with the grasshopper a few more times, the little ants marched away, shaking their heads.

The cold winter came and the ants were snug as bugs in their little home. Well-fed and protected.

Still, the day finally came when the whole group of ants gathered in the middle of their living room to draw straws. The little ant who drew the shortest straw sighed deeply. The other ants gathered around him, wrapping him in as many layers of warmth as they could, and muttering words of encouragement.

They walked to the front door and pushed it open carefully, just enough to allow the bundled-up ant to push through into the blizzard roaring outside. He walked and he walked and he walked until, finally, he spotted the grasshopper.

"Mr. Grasshopper, Mr. Grasshopper, won't you please come home with me. We're dying of boredom! We desperately need to listen to your lovely music or we'll never make it until spring!"[27]

*   *   *   *

You can define your own moral for this version. It is certainly my answer to the idea of art being either pointless, useless, a waste of time, or frivolous.

*   *   *   *

Now we're going to do another visualization. (Remember an audio file is available for listening or downloading – go to the website http://www.theartofbecominganartist.com/visualizations and enter the word – Beach – where it asks for the code word.)

I'd like you to find a place where you can sit or lie down comfortably and quietly. Then listen to the Beach Journey or read the script on the following page.

*   *   *   *

BEACH JOURNEY

Okay remember how to get comfortable. Turn off the lights. Get as comfortable as you can, sitting or lying down, whatever works best, and breathe. Just like we did last time. Breathing. Relaxing. Breathing. Relaxing. Taking the breath into your body and letting it out again. Breathing. Relaxing. Breathing. Relaxing. Adjust your body so that you are as comfortable as you can be. And breathe.

I'd like you to imagine that you're at the beach on a tropical island. It's very hot, but not too hot, and you're comfortably dressed.

What is the beach like?

Walk around a bit. Feel the sand under your toes.

What color is the sand? What does it feel like? What does it smell like? What does the air taste like? How does it feel on your body? How do you feel being there?

You notice there are some trees at the edge of the sand. Walk towards them and feel the bark. Now feel the leaves. What are the trees like?

Walk through the trees for a moment. You toes feel something on the ground. You bend down and look at it. What is it? Do you want to take it with you?

Okay, walk back out onto the sand down to the water's edge. Feel what the water's like. Feel the water touching your feet. What are the waves like?

Look down at where the water touches the sand and notice what has drifted in on the tide. You can look through what's there and take whatever you like. Explore the shore for a while on your own and see what else you can discover.

Now I want you to look out at the ocean and see something. It's on the horizon, just a bit too far to make out what it is. Closer – it's coming closer. Now you can see it.

What is it?

Finally it comes all the way in and arrives at the shore. Explore it. Think about how it got there, where it came from. Walk around it. Touch it.

Now imagine you *are* it. Be it. Experience it. Now you know how it got there. Now you know what it feels like to be it.

Then return to yourself. Do you feel anything different about it?

Continue walking along the beach 'til you see a spit of rocks leading out to sea. Climb the rocks. They're not very high and they're not slippery. Suddenly you see a hole in the rocks. It's the perfect size and the perfect shape. You can leave something in that hole. Whatever you want to leave there.

Glancing around, you see another rock that will just fit into the top of the hole to protect what's inside it. It will be safe there now, once you put the rock in place. You can leave whatever it is there forever, or come back for it whenever you want.

Keep climbing across the rocks until you discover another beach. A lovely, small cove. A wise being from the sea sits on the sand in the middle of the cove. The being clearly has all of the wisdom of the oceans.

Walk to the being, sit down across from the being, and ask something; anything you want. Listen to the answer.

As you get up to leave, the being reaches behind, pulls out something, and gives it to you.

Now return over the rocks, making sure you are paying attention to the route so you can return here whenever you want. Walk back along the beach to where you started, and pause to look around you. Again, knowing you can come back whenever you want.

Then slowly come back here.

*   *   *   *

Homework Assignment

Draw or paint or write something from the journey you just took. It can be the whole trip, or one piece of it. Or something else entirely that comes, somehow, from the journey.

Please remember to do bumps!

By the way, since this is a Homework Assignment, meaning you will be going away from the book for a bit, please do three things…

Remember the three things that you take from your list and "do" that may help you feel creative??? Do them.

See you later.

*   *   *   *

If you wrote something, please read it out loud. If it's visual, place it somewhere where you can really look at it. A piece of music? Listen to the sounds you created.

Did you enjoy the journey? Did you discover something interesting? Or find something, or receive something valuable?

Maybe you just couldn't get into it at all? This time…

This piece was your imagination at work.

Remember all those students who said they were not creative at all in the very first class. So many of us often, or always, have a fundamental belief that we are not creative and have no imagination whatsoever. We'll continue to talk about this a great deal as we go further along.

This time, however, whatever you saw, or felt, or found, or heard from the wise being, or decided to leave in the hole in the rocks,

WAS ALL STRAIGHT FROM YOUR IMAGINATION!

Pretty amazing, huh?

Take care, all.

Chapter ten
The Moment of Truth

In Class Exercise

Reminder: it's an In Class Exercise, so please do it right now for about twenty minutes.

Please choose a Moment From Your Life...

and write about it.
(or draw it, or paint the scene. Or carve a piece of wood. Whatever you want to do to reproduce this moment.)
Make it as accurate and as real as you possibly can. Everything should be as close to the exact occurrence as you can make it.
For this assignment writing may in fact be the best option, so if you can possibly manage it, I hereby encourage you to create a written piece. Obviously, if that's not okay, please create whatever replication of the moment you prefer.
(NOTE: I'm officially asking for your trust again. You will understand shortly why I am making this request. I would like you to choose a moment, any moment you would like to write about. Except!!!! Please do NOT choose one of the most important, meaningful, significant moments in your life.

It can be a good moment, a meaningful moment, or a bad moment. Just DO NOT let it be one of those extraordinarily powerful, pivotal moments one has in one's lifetime.)

OK, pick a moment. Remember to make it as accurate as you can. And please do bumps!

See you in about twenty minutes.

*   *   *   *

How was that?

Did it bring the moment back for you? Did you notice anything interesting in the bumps?

Please stare into it now, or read it aloud, giving it full feeling as you do.

*   *   *   *

Okay, without another word about this piece, I would like to give you your Homework Assignment.

Homework Assignment

Take the piece you just did about that moment in your life, and change something...
You can change a little bit. Or a lot. However you want.
The key here is to take that accurate and real moment you reproduced and change it in some way so that it is *not* accurate or real.
Please feel free to groan at me...

And *please* do bumps. And do three things.

See you later.

*   *   *   *

How was that?

Are you groaning at me? Did you hate it or love it? Was it fun or hateful?

Please read it aloud. Or gaze into it. With feeling, of course.

*   *   *   *

How was that?

The reasons people hate this assignment are numerous, while the reasons people love this are often singular and very straightforward. We'll talk more about it in a few minutes, but first I have something important to say.

WELCOME TO FICTION!!!!!

Yup. That is what you just did. You just wrote fiction.

Or painted or carved abstract art.

Many of us think of fiction as something we create whole cloth from our imaginations. I think pretty much the exact opposite. I believe that everything we create, or almost everything (I wouldn't want to be too absolutist here), comes from our lives. Transformed, transposed, transported, metamorphosed, altered. That's what art is. A variation on a theme. The theme is "you."

I've surprised myself a thousand times. I write something that is complete, absolute fiction. Completely invented. Created it from nothing and nowhere. It's the essence of my imagination.

But.

Something about it keeps echoing inside me; a word, a phrase, a location. A feeling. I've no idea why. Or what. Where it's coming from. It just keeps echoing. Until sure enough, *almost* completely silently, a little while later, I'll realize what the echo is. What it's about. Where the piece is actually coming from.

For me, the single most bizarre example was a scene I wrote in a science fiction piece. Four or five years after I'd finished writing it, I had the horrifying experience of remembering something awful that had been thoroughly hidden from me for my whole life, from the instant it occurred. Talk about suppressed memories. I had absolutely no hint of it in my memory until I was in my mid-forties. It was a stunning shock. I spent a very long and painful time recovering the memory and researching the event. (I was very mistrustful of memories until I realized that I always ended up coming up with evidence that the events had actually happened.) I worked hard at dealing with it, and recovering from it. Until finally, I came to a sort of quiet (or at least quieter) place inside me around the event.

Then one day, months later, I was once more thinking about the experience when a phrase started going through my head. It was part of the memory itself. It was a phrase that I'd kept repeating to myself when I was in the process of remembering the events. A phrase from the memory.

This time the phrase sounded familiar in a different way. I had no idea what or why. Where it was familiar from. It wasn't the words that were familiar. It was the rhythm of the words. The "chorus" kept singing in my head, over and over and over. For weeks...

Until one day I figured it out. I went digging for the science fiction piece I had written several years before, and turned to the right page. On that page was the line I'd kept hearing in my head. Different words entirely. Still, the rhythm and, as it turned out, the *meaning* of the line, were identical to the profound repressed memory I had finally recovered, several years later.

I had written about the memory in my fiction long before I had any idea what had happened. Without even consciously knowing it had happened.

I was simply writing my life. Six hundred years into the future, in my science fiction.

After that it became almost a game for me to write something entirely fictional, and then, usually after I finished it, to figure out what part of my life I was "rephrasing."

I've spent my entire life thinking about how fascinating human beings are. (Other animals, too, of course, but I can't quite get into their minds the way I can get into ours.) We're amazing. Understanding how we work is one of the passions of my life. And this business of constantly reproducing our lives in our imaginations is a truly magical one.

*   *   *   *

Okay, before we continue this discussion, I'd like you to do an In Class Exercise.

In Class Exercise

"When I create something that isn't the truth, I feel…"

This one is definitely a writing activity.

(See you in twenty minutes.)

*   *   *   *

How was that? Did anything surprise you? Do read it out loud, please.

All right, let's get back to the discussion of writing fiction and telling the truth. Often it's seen as writing fiction VERSUS telling the truth. That turns out to be a problem for many of us.

Please keep in mind that for some of us, transforming the reality of our lives into something different, something imaginative, is just plain fun from the get-go. It makes you laugh. It makes you happy. It gives you the opportunity to rewrite something you *like* the idea of rewriting. Maybe a happy ending instead of a sad one. A success instead of a horrifying failure. You get the girl instead of losing her. You win the lottery.

Yet for many of us, when we first start changing the truth of our lives to something that isn't true, we flinch…

"That's not what happened. I can't say it is."

"I can't draw that because it's not the way it actually looks."

"I'm not supposed to lie."

"And I'm certainly not allowed to MAKE THINGS UP!"

How many times were we accused of "making things up," as kids. Of fibbing. Of lying. Of being overdramatic. Or avoiding telling the truth.

This was somehow, no matter what the context, the worst thing we could do. A lot of us have a whole world inside of us yelling at us about always telling the truth. When we try and create something that isn't the truth, that isn't realistic, all of those memories, and accusations, and all of that training on the evils of lying, come up on us.

That does NOT make for good art.

This problem comes up so often in my courses.

I had one student, in a course that continued on for almost two years, who gave my worst (favorite) example of this topic.

She was a lovely woman in her forties, very bright, a professional who worked in education. And she wrote beautifully. Every sentence she crafted was perfect. Every single one. She wouldn't read her piece in class until and unless every word, phrase, and sentence, was just so.

The desperately sad part of this process was that almost every perfect sentence she wrote and read for the class, related to her complete inability to write. She would always explain, absolutely apologetically, that she simply could not do the homework. In the most perfectly crafted prose. Week after week.

Until one Saturday morning, my student, let's call her Alana (since this is a rather long narrative, and I don't want to just keep calling her "she"), announced that she had started to write the actual homework. She had been very excited about it, and the piece was flowing along happily, but then she had to stop. She couldn't keep writing it. No matter what she tried.

The Homework Assignment was similar to your last In Class Exercise. I'd asked the class to write about a moment in their lives, this time from their childhoods. (This time, however, I did *not* add the request that it be a truly accurate moment.) Alana had started writing about all of these wonderful things she'd done as a child that had taken place in a lush tropical park just a block away from her house. She'd spend her time lying in the grass reading, being frequently distracted by the birds flying overhead. She'd play with her dog in the park, throwing pears for him to run after and fetch, which he'd actually do without eating them, and then he'd bring them back to her. She wrote about sitting there with the sun shining down on her, daydreaming, writing short stories in her head.

She was having a glorious time writing about these wonderful memories from her childhood. Writing and writing and writing. Finally. After almost two years of sitting in my class, week after week, she was pouring words onto the paper.

Continuing the piece, she started writing about the coloring book extravaganzas she'd had with another little girl, her dearest childhood friend, sitting in that tropical, flower-filled environment, the two of them happily coloring away together.

That's what stopped her in her tracks.

We all waited for the explanation. Why did writing about fun coloring book sessions with her best friend stop her from writing? "Why? What happened?" we all asked, mystified and disappointed for her.

"Because we *never* colored outside," she explained. "We always did that in the playroom inside my house, not at the park."

Oh.

"Okay," I responded slowly. "You changed the setting a little bit. Can I ask why that stopped you?"

"Because it wasn't true," she answered.

"Therefore?" Once more I asked her slowly and very very gently.

"What if she read it? She'd be so upset!"

"Because????"

"Because it isn't true!"

"Okay," I responded. "So…"

"You don't lie!" she interrupted, forcefully. "You don't lie!"

"Okay…," I started again with the "okays," (I was truly a bit flummoxed). I took a breath, then continued. "I think something is going on here, Alana. Do you agree?"

My student of two years nodded. This time *she* was a bit slow with her response, as she started to reflect on what she was saying so forcefully.

Alana was not a stupid woman. Nor naïve. She understood perfectly that art is art, and if I'd asked her to define poetic license, she would have had no trouble with either the definition of it, or the practice. Yet here she was, practically crying, because her childhood girlfriend would have been devastated to read that their coloring book "parties" had happened in a slightly altered location.

"How do you feel about exploring this a bit further?" I asked.

Alana nodded.

This class had been together for almost two years and the trust and safety level was very high.

"Good," I responded, moving over to the flip chart and picking up a marker.

"You don't lie," I wrote.

"Okay, you don't lie. What happens if you do?" I asked.

"It grows," she responded quickly. "It gets bigger."

I wrote, and waited.

"You get found out!"

I wrote and waited.

"You get punished."

Again.

"You feel embarrassed and ashamed!"

This time she breathed out deeply, and sat back in her chair.

"All right," I said, giving her a moment. "Can you, in fact, remember something like this happening? Does it feel familiar?" I finally asked.

Alana nodded her head slowly. She looked down.

"You want to tell us about it?"

She nodded one more time.

We waited.

She took a breath and told us the story.

She was in junior high school, the seventh or eighth grade (so she was about thirteen), and she was walking out of school with this same best friend, who was *very* upset. Her friend's math teacher, a man, had been looking down her blouse during class. Then he'd put his hands on her shoulders in a very uncomfortable way. He had done it at other times, with other girls in her class as well. None of them knew what to do about it. But they all hated it.

A key thing to remember here is that this happened during the 1970s, before the concept of sexual harassment had taken hold. I'm not sure the phrase even existed in the popular culture back then. Legal charges were just beginning to take place in the court systems. The term was barely recognized by the rest of us. Keep that in mind.

Back to her story.

Alana was very upset by what had happened to her friend. So upset that, instead of doing her homework that night, she wrote about it. The next day at school, the piece of paper fell, unnoticed, out of her notebook and was found by a teacher who promptly turned it in to the principal. Alana had not put her name on her writing.

(Please note: this is a practice I strongly discourage. I always want everyone to put their name on their art. It's your art! Though this time, I thought, perhaps it was lucky that she hadn't.)

Not so much, it turned out.

That afternoon her best friend was almost as distraught as the previous day. Group after group of girls who were in this particular teacher's class had been pulled into the principal's office for a handwriting test. To see who had written the piece about the teacher!

Of course, they couldn't find the writer. Alana, fortunately, was not in his classes.

Still, she was very upset about the whole thing, and about what was happening to the girls who were in his class, so she went home that night and told her mother what was happening. To this day she can't remember what kind of reaction her mother had. The next day, however, her mother went to see the principal to explain that it had been Alana who had written the piece. That afternoon Alana herself was summoned to the principal's office.

The principal stood in front of her, and told Alana over and over and over, "You don't lie."

That's all Alana said about that moment.

Her next memory took place in the girl's bathroom. She stood in front of the sink, washing the blood off her fingers. Turns out that, while instructing her about lying, the principal had repeatedly hit Alana on her knuckles with a wooden ruler. Hard enough to make them bleed!

Suddenly, Alana added that in addition to the blood, she was washing paint off her fingers, as well. She'd been in her art class when she'd been summoned, it turned out. That fact made the event even more painful for Alana to remember.

The final memory, she burst out with, accompanied by a painful gasp, was that the piece she had written was a *poem*. Apparently, writing the piece in the pure art form of poetry was even more heartbreaking for her.

Given the outcome.

She sat back in her chair, looking overwhelmed and grief-stricken. She also appeared completely flummoxed.

After a few minutes of silence we continued talking.

I repeat, Alana was a bright, conscious woman. She knew it had been a very difficult moment telling her mother about the writing. She knew that it was even more difficult when she got verbally and physically punished for it at school, an experience that had never happened to her before.

Yet, she was shocked when I pointed out to her that the teacher had been sexually harassing his students, an illegal act, and that in this day and age, it would have been the teacher who got in serious trouble, who would have been called on the carpet and probably disciplined, perhaps even fired. Not Alana. That today, she would probably have felt protected by the concept of the whistle blower's safety for revealing an illegal and unethical truth about the teacher... Not punished.

None of that had occurred to her, even while she was telling us this story, all these years later. It never occurred to her that it was the teacher who had done something wrong. That it was the principal who had done something wrong. That Alana was, in fact, practically a hero.

None of that occurred to her. She was still thinking about the incident, reliving her feelings, like the child she had been.

She was, while she was telling us the story, talking about something bad and wrong and terrible that she had done.

She had simply never connected the dots.

All she knew, up to that moment, was that "YOU DON'T LIE!"

The image had been frozen inside her brain and her being, all those years before. And stayed there. Every single time she tried to write fiction.

*   *   *   *

How utterly sad and awful!

What she was left with instead was the ability to write beautifully crafted prose about her inability to write fiction.

These kinds of connections that we have never transported into the future of "now," happen all the time. These events that we have never re-examined as adults, that we've never applied to the world of art, live inside us. I've heard the stories endlessly from students. I've seen it in my own life. It is, of course, an incessant, integral part of the therapy I do as well.

We will continue to explore all sorts of different versions of this in the context of various topics as we go along. It keeps coming up.

Remember the story of my student from Japan who had to write about what a particular fictional character was thinking at a particular moment? There was only one right answer. Only one truth. Even in fiction.

Telling the truth is one of the most fundamental values we are taught as children. By our parents. Our teachers. Everyone.

Still, for many of us it has left a terrible residue that *interferes* with our imagination.

Imagination becomes labeled as a bad thing; a lie, instead of the essence of creativity that it is. Plus it is often the most extraordinarily creative way of getting to the truth.

It's vital to be aware of this when you're trying to create art. In art there are many versions of the truth. Many versions of reality. That's one of the essential things that art is.

One more time:

Welcome to fiction.

*   *   *   *

Now I want to reassure you, beyond your words, or mine, or those of my other students, that telling the truth is a topic for many artists, so here are some lovely quotes from other artists.

> "When I was a little boy, they called me a liar, but now that I am grown up, they call me a writer." Isaac Singer[28]

There you have it, from Isaac Bashevis Singer. What you learn about lying as a child. What you then *have* to learn about it as a writer...

William Faulkner described writers as having an innate incapacity for truth telling... That's why we label it fiction instead!

Mark Twain's take on it:

"…most writers regard truth as their most valuable possession, and therefore are most economical in its use."[29]

A couple of slightly off-center views on where the creativity comes from in the first place:

"The secret to creativity is knowing how to hide your sources."
Albert Einstein?[30]

"I always write about my own experiences, whether I've had them or not." Ron Carlson[31]

Probably the most profound observation of them all:

"Fiction is [a form of writing which] reveals truths that reality obscures." Jessamyn West[32]

Think about that for a minute.

Frequently, what we're trying to do when we create art is to make a point. Create art about something we've learned, something we believe is important. Say something meaningful. Even when we're supposedly "simply" writing fiction or composing a piece of music. Painting. Whatever we're doing, we're trying to communicate something.

But. When the events happen to us in our actual lives, it often takes us forever to understand what they meant. Or what we're taking away from the experience. Days, months, years. We think about it, dream about it, write in our journals, talk to friends, go to therapy. The meaning is so often subtle. Buried in layers of "stuff." What we actually take away from the experience takes work, often years of it, to figure out.

That, however, isn't going to work when we're creating art. One of the points of the art is to communicate that insight. To share it. To express it. Therefore, when we write about it, we labor mightily to make it more available. More accessible. Hopefully not too "in your face," but we are working at making the connection of that art to that point.

Which can't happen when the "stuff" gets in the way, *unacknowledged*.

Ironically, this suggests that we often tell more about the actual truth when we're making it all up...

Take care, all.

Chapter eleven
Let's Go On an Adventure

In Class Exercise

Let's start this chapter with an In Class Exercise. Or, of course, as usual, a drawing or painting exercise. Whatever works. Hell, compose a piece of music for this one. Choreograph a dance. A comedy routine. My guess is that this particular assignment lends itself to almost any art form.

Here's the topic.

"I'm afraid to do my art because..."

*   *   *   *

Then when you're finished, turn the page.

*   *   *   *

Okay, please read out loud, or look at, or perform, or play your homework.

I'm hoping, really hoping, you didn't come up with a complete absence of fear. You could. I've known it to happen. I always try to convince myself that the people who are absolutely positive that they have no fear of their art or their creativity, are right. They simply are not afraid of it. I always try. Here's the best I can come up with for those of you who feel you feel no fear.

Right now, at this moment in time, working on this particular piece, in this particular place, you are not afraid.

But. I think you'll probably realize that what I'm actually saying here is: IT'S THERE SOMEWHERE, SOMEWHEN, SOMEHOW. Some fear exists.

If I'm completely wrong and there simply is no fear whatsoever inside you about your art, at any time, in any setting, with any piece of work, then I apologize. I am sorry for not completely believing you. I need to trust you when you say it.

The second thing I'll do is celebrate the miracle that is your relationship to your art.

Overall, however, I almost *entirely* believe that every artist on this planet and likely, in this entire universe, encounters fear of their art in one way or another or another. OR ANOTHER.

I mean to say, it is ENTIRELY NORMAL!!!! Fear is pretty much intrinsic to the creative process. For almost everyone. Fear of anything. Fear of everything.

In fact, let's do a whiteboard. You've already done your personal and preliminary whiteboard with this assignment. "You're afraid to write because..." Now I'll show you a whiteboard comprised of only SOME of the responses my in-person students (*and I*) have given to the question, or statement, "I'm afraid to do my art because...."

*   *   *   *

Whiteboard
I'm afraid to do my art because…

it's bad   it sucks   I have no talent

i'm scared of what will come up

I'm scared of what I'll discover   I'm scared what people

will say   So and so will be upset   I'll hurt them

I'm terrified of exposing myself   I won't be able to do it

I'm scared of exposing so and so   Scared I'll go crazy

I'm scared of spending so much time alone

of what I'll find out   I'll fail   I have nothing to say

I'll have to do it over and over and over again

It won't make sense   the point will be unclear

the wording will be unclear

the painting will be unclear

it'll be over the top, stupid   it'll be under the top, boring

It won't be new   it will be trite and hackneyed   too long

too short   I WILL BE NAKED AND EXPOSED

It will show ugly realities   I hate being judged

I'll make all sorts of mistakes

Don't want to explore THAT   Don't want to go HERE
I'm a coward   I'll be a failure   I won't live up to
people's expectations   I won't live up to people's beliefs
about me   I have no flare   I have no imagination
What if my work gets dismissed   I don't want to be
disappointed   I don't want to think about that topic
People will think I'm cocky   It will destroy my image
            What will I find underneath –
    it will be all dark and sticky and moldy and gross
            It will be disgusting I'll go blank
I'M NOT REALLY AN ARTIST, I'M A FAKE
            just another whim
I'll start doing it, put in time and effort and commitment
and then I'll quit   I'll throw it away
 I want to mine my art for gold, but what if I find coal
See, I'm crazy,   I'm weird.   I'll be so disappointed
NO ONE WILL BE INTERESTED IN IT
I'm not honest with myself   I'm afraid I'm too lazy
            I don't want to be criticized

I'll lose my privacy   I'll discover all my limitations
I prefer to keep it in my brain memory dish where I can
wander alone   It will stir up memories
          it will bring up all my doubts about myself and
what happened to me
I don't want the witch on my shoulder to show me how evil
I am   *I HAVE NOTHING TO SAY*
It will be silly   *WHAT IF NO ONE LIKES IT*
I won't make any money from it   It will be mediocre
I won't fit in   I'm too different   I will be condemned
for my behavior if I write about it because I will be
                    wasting time
          it will break up my relationship with my mate
it will break up my relationship with my parents, siblings,
family in general, friends.....   It will *KILL* my mother
     I just don't know what I'm getting into!
I don't know what's going to happen. Don't know where
I'll end up.   I don't know what's inside me.
     I don't know what's going to come out of me

And on and on and on and on… Fear of anything. Fear
of everything.

*   *   *   *

Please Note: In this whiteboard I have only gone through my notes on this assignment from FIVE classes! I've done close to one hundred classes. I suspect you get the idea... Bottom line: Art is scary.

Going to the place where you create art is often frightening. Remember what I've said about jumping off a cliff. Well, **_even_** if there is water down below or you're attached to a parachute, jumping off a cliff is scary as hell. That's one of the reasons people do it. It's an adrenalin rush. The good kind of scary

But, way too often, going to our art feels like *just* jumping off a cliff. The really bad kind of terrifying.

*   *   *   *

We'll talk more about fear in a minute. Hell, we'll be talking about fear in one way or another for a huge part of this process. It keeps coming up in fascinating and convoluted ways. First, however, I'd like to share some of my favorite quotes from other artists about fear.

"I am not inclined to apologize for my anxieties, because I have lived with them long enough to respect them ... ", E.B. White said. "A writer's courage can easily fail him," he commented while accepting an award from the National Book Committee. "I feel this daily...I admire anybody who has the guts to write anything at all."[33]

"The solitude of writing is also quite frightening. It's quite close sometimes to madness. One just disappears for a day and loses touch." Nadine Gordimer[34]

Donald Murray in his book *Shoptalk*; "They were silent. Empty. They felt anxiety. Panic. Terror. 'Good,' I'd answer. 'You are a writer. You are at the place from which writing comes.'"[35]

Ernest Hemingway is responsible for one of my all-time favorite quotes on the topic, largely because of who he was. Hemingway is probably equally well-known for being both a writer AND an adventurer. He was in the First and Second World Wars, the Spanish Civil War (in varying capacities), he was a deep-sea sports fisherman, went on African safaris, ran with the bulls in Pamplona (or at least went to see them – the facts are unclear). He did many things that would frighten – even terrify – most of us. An adventurer for sure. Now here is his response in an interview:

Ernest Hemingway, when asked what was the most frightening thing he had ever encountered, answered:

"A blank sheet of paper."[36]

Pretty cool, no?

I do have a response to those of us who are afraid we will discover that we are crazy if we get into our art:

"Insanity – a perfectly rational adjustment to an insane world."
R. D. Laing[37]

So there!

*   *   *   *

The whole idea of fear of the unknown is a big topic for many of us. I also think many of us are taught from early days that it is something to fear.

"You know one thing. You know you will not be the same person when this voyage is over. But you don't know what's going to happen to you between getting on the boat and stepping off."
James Baldwin[38]

To repeat: considerably too often, going to our art feels like just jumping off a cliff.

*   *   *   *

Fear is such a fascinating (and terrifying) topic. Here is my very favorite quotation on the topic, told to me in a university social psychology course by my most beloved professor ever, Dr. Peter Suedfeld (and repeated to me quite recently while we were out having dinner together, at least a hundred years later...☺).

"You know you're having an adventure when you wish that what you were actually doing was sitting at home in your own living room, in front of your own fireplace, reading about someone else doing it!"[39]

Let me elaborate.

An adventure is, essentially, *by definition*, both scary and exciting. If it were only scary, it would just be unpleasant. A frightening event. Whoopee... Who wants to do things that are terrifying, but not fun? You have to, sometimes, but you generally do it because you have to. Not because you want to.

If you were going to do something exciting, that would be fun. It's fun to do things that are exciting. It's fun to do things that are fun. It's obvious, right? However, fun things are not actually adventures. They're just fun.

Ergo, adventures, in order to be actual adventures, are *both* dangerous and exciting.

Here's an interesting piece of research.

In 1962, two rather well-known psychologists of the time, Stanley Schachter and Jerome Singer, ran an experiment[40] in which subjects were given an injection of epinephrine, more commonly known as adrenalin. Only some of the subjects knew what the injection contained. (This study was done in the days prior to the more modern "informed consent" ethical requirements of research studies.) Adrenalin usually results in entering a state of physiological arousal.

Think "fight or flight" or freeze responses. Anger or fear. Now, believe it or not, the other response one can have to a physiological state of arousal is happiness or euphoria or, you guessed it, excitement. They all have very similar physiological responses, including increased heart rate, increased blood pressure, heavy breathing, increased blood flow to muscles, etc.

These subjects were then sent into a room with another person, supposedly another subject, but actually a research assistant acting out an assigned role. A shill. The assistant was told either to act as if he were angry or to act as if he were happy. Upon completion of the experiment, the real subjects were asked to rate their emotional state. The results were quite striking. Those subjects who were in a room in which the "stooge" acted as if he were angry, reported feeling angry. Those who were in a room with a happy stooge, reported feeling happy.

Schachter and Singer interpreted these results essentially in terms of human beings functioning as information-processing mechanisms. We experience an unexpected physiological response and then cognitively search for an explanation for it. In this case, input from the other person in the room was the major explanation the subjects had as to why they were in a physiological state of arousal. Consequently, they mirrored the other person's emotion, without actually having any reason – other than physiological – for feeling it.

Why do we care? All right, let's go back to having an adventure!

Many of us tend to feel more comfortable, or are at least more accustomed to, feeling one particular negative emotion over another. (Or at least, what's considered negative; I might disagree.) As a therapist I see it all the time. For example, some people respond to certain kinds of difficult circumstances with sadness. They won't feel at all angry, even if one might think they should. Others, in the same situation, get angry instead. Really, really angry, without a drop of sadness. Again, their reaction is opposite to what one might think was appropriate. I work very hard to help my clients "give unto Caesar that which is Caesar's." Some sadness, some anger. Both emotions are often present (as well as several other ones), and entirely appropriate, in the exact same situation. Many of us, however, feel more comfortable feeling and expressing only one or the other of those emotions.

I believe the same is true of excitement and fear.

Personal story: For years, I was almost incapable of feeling fear. I'm pretty sure that happened as a result of my crappy childhood, in which fear was unceasing and intense. I didn't like being so afraid all the time, so I responded to the *unpleasantness* by shutting down my ability to feel fear. Not consciously, of course, but very sensible in its own way, I think. Sort of. I was just never afraid of anything. (Except cockroaches…)

In retrospect, it was a bit of a dicey way to live. A bit! Not necessarily survival-oriented. (I do have to add I am very grateful that I did survive it.)

Anyway, one effect of it was that I was a *great* adventurer back then. I could afford to be. I wasn't afraid. Even of things I should have been afraid of…

I only rediscovered my fear when I went to bed because of my back, during those "bad years", and it was often excruciatingly terrifying.

The point is that I had spent all of the years before that, thinking everything I did, all my adventures, were just profoundly exciting. Never scary. As I say, thank goodness I survived that.

What I eventually came to understand was that I was always actually feeling the excitement *and* the fear. Both. Still, I gave all my feelings away to the excitement. I called all of that physiological adrenalin arousal state – excitement.

The same is true for the other side of this particular coin. I have discovered that many people do things in the other direction. If they are about to embark on an adventure, they can only feel the fear! The anxiety! The terror! They shut down on the excitement side. They don't see their adventures as anything but scary.

The truth is, if they dig deeply enough, they will often discover that a lot of their fear is actually happiness, joy, and excitement! Remember Schachter and Singer's study. These arousal emotions – fear, anger, excitement/happiness – physiologically, feel very much the same. Very easy to confuse them.

The point of this all? The name of one of my courses was:

"Writing: the Other Word for Adventure."

*   *   *   *

I think I could keep writing the rest of the book about fear. It's so pervasive for so many of us when we're trying to do our art. (Much less trying to live our lives…) But *for now* just a few more words on the topic.

Believe it or not, fear is often much easier to deal with than we think. Even just naming the fear out loud, or expressing it in writing or painting or movement, can reduce its power.

It's often the stuff that stays inside us; the images inside our heads and the buildup of the feelings inside our bodies because of them, that feel the most powerful. Moving those feelings and images and thoughts and terrible lessons to the outside of ourselves, into the air, can sometimes reduce the power of the fear enormously.

"Many of our fears are tissue-paper-thin, and a single courageous step would carry us clear through them." Brendan Francis[41]

But one of the most important things I have to say about fear pertains to a giant "should" that is so, so, *so* frequently out there in our universe. There are many, many versions of it, from many perspectives, and I have to say that I fundamentally disagree with all of them.

The "should" – the "*shouldn't*," actually… ☺ – is **"YOU SHOULDN'T BE AFRAID!"**

"Don't be afraid." "You don't have to be afraid." "Don't be a wimp, a coward, a scaredy cat, a chicken." "Fear isn't good for you!" "Stop being such a weakling."

I don't think I know anybody who doesn't wince when they admit they're afraid of something. Fear always seems to be thought of as something you should be ashamed of.

But fear is very useful! It's essential to our survival. Hardwired in. One more time, think fight or flight or freeze. It's how we keep ourselves safe. (It's that bungee cord…)

"There are times when fear is good. It must keep its watchful place at the heart's controls." Aeschylus[42]

Most important of all, the bottom line of deciding where we go and what we do with our fear is simply that we need to be able to make our own choice. Choice: one of the most important words I know! In this case, that usually requires looking at our fears, exploring them, and understanding them.

"Who is more foolish, the child afraid of the dark or the man afraid of the light?" Maurice Freehill[43]

Take care, all.

Chapter twelve
A Funny Thing Happened

Do not panic as you read the following Homework Assignment! (Remember we can work with fear...)

Homework Assignment

Write or draw or do something funny.

You've panicked anyway, right? At least a lot of you have. Paralysis. Blank brain. Let me guess at some of the thoughts going through your head, if you have any...

"But I'm not funny."

"I'm not a comedian!"

"I don't know how to do humor!"

"I've *never* been able to tell a joke decently."

"I'm not a funny person."

"Humor is a specialty. Just not *my* specialty."

"No way can I write something funny."

And on, and on, and on...

Okay. Think about this. Has anything that's ever happened to you in your entire life, ever made you laugh? Anything? Anything at all?

Now think about this. Have you ever told anybody *else* about that thing that happened in your life that made you laugh?

And finally: When you told them about that thing that happened in your life that made you laugh, did they crack a smile?

Of course, they did! I guess you must actually be funny…

Did you just smile? Even a little? Well, then, I guess *I'm* funny. EVEN THOUGH I'M **NOT** A COMEDIAN!

Now go write down that thing that happened in your life that made you laugh, that you told someone else about, that then made them crack a smile. Or draw a picture of it. Or perform it.

That's your Homework Assignment … Remember: bumps and three things.

See you later.

*   *   *   *

How did that go?

I have to admit a guilty secret. This is one of the assignments that I most wish I could hear you read out loud. That I wish I could see.

I love it when we do this in my classes. I get to spend the whole class laughing. Almost every time. Because pretty much every single person comes up with *something* funny! Even if they aren't funny, humorous, a comedian, a "specialist…!"

I really do wish I could have the opportunity for you to make me laugh. But I can't.

Although *you* can, so please do proceed to exhibit your humor.

Did you laugh while you were showing it? While you were performing it? While you were reading it? I bet you did. So much for the jumping off a cliff terror!

*   *   *   *

It's so interesting.

We have a whole pile of entirely magical beliefs on the subject of humor. As though it's something mysterious that only a few people are capable of. As if you have to possess some special talent, or ability, some secret into the world of funniness.

Most importantly, so many of us believe that only a very few special people are capable of creating something that makes people laugh. It's why almost every student I've ever had panics when they hear this assignment. "I'm just a regular mortal. I can't do humor."

Think about it. Almost every day, something will make you crack a smile. Or chuckle. Or laugh. Actually laugh out loud. Heck, there's even an acronym for that now…. Of course! (For those of you who are retrogrouches – it's LOL.)

Obviously there are times in our lives when this isn't true. Painful times. Difficult, horrible times.

The fact of the matter is, however, that the research suggests we laugh about fifteen times a day. Fifteen times. Then we tell somebody about it. We make them laugh. Then you can write it down. Or paint a silly picture. Or dance some funny move. Which would make you, officially, a comedian. Creating art that makes people laugh.

If it's part of your life, it can be part of your art:

"Common sense and a sense of humor are the same thing, moving at different speeds. A sense of humor is just common sense, dancing."
William James, 19th century psychologist and philosopher[44]

YOU ARE FUNNY! ARE TOO!!

Take care, all.

Chapter thirteen
Stuff, Stuff, and More Stuff

Hi, again.

Now I want to return to the subject of fear.

Whoopee, no?

Let's talk about a topic that comes up repeatedly in the assignment, "I'm afraid to write because…" It comes up in class discussions, in brainstorming the whiteboards. It actually comes up quite consistently, whether students are talking specifically about fear, or something else entirely.

Let's start with a long list of excerpts from the whiteboard discussion of the assignment "I'm afraid to write because…"

*   *   *   *

I'm scared of what will come up,
I'm scared of what I'll discover,
I'm scared of exposing myself
I'm scared I'll go crazy
I'm scared of spending so much time alone
I'm scared of what I'll find out
I WILL BE NAKED AND EXPOSED
It will show ugly realities and mistakes
I don't want to explore THAT
I don't want to go THERE
I don't want to think about that topic

What will I find underneath - it will be all dark and sticky and moldy and gross It will be disgusting.
See, I'm crazy.
I'm weird.
It will stir up memories.
It will bring up all my doubts about myself and what happened to me.
I don't want the witch on my shoulder to show me how evil I am.
I don't know what's inside me.
I don't know what's going to come out of me.

*   *   *   *

Quite a list, no?
I'm going to call this topic:

"Self-Exposure And/Or Painful Memories"

It's a fear many of us have.
Perhaps, even more frequently, it's a *fact* about doing creative work.
Doing art often brings up events and feelings and memories that we don't want to think about. Or talk about. Or feel. Or even have as part of our lives. It even brings up topics and feelings and memories we don't even know we have inside us.
A lot of these feelings and memories are painful as hell. They're sad and difficult, infuriating, frightening. They make us want to run. As fast and as far away as possible.

> "It's nervous work. The state you need to write in is the state that others are paying large sums to get rid of." Shirley Hazzard[45]

It's so true!
If this weren't already perfectly clear to me from my personal experience of shutting down on writing, then opening up to it again with

everything that erupted out of me, it became abundantly clear after I started teaching.

It was quite fascinating, really. I saw it frequently in my students. I see it frequently with my clients. It simply goes back to what I said in the very beginning of this book. "Stuff" can come up when you're going towards your art!

Here's Anne Truitt's perspective:

"The most demanding part of living a lifetime as an artist is the strict discipline of forcing oneself to work steadfastly along the nerve of one's own most intimate sensitivity."[46]

I love this quote. I can picture that nerve. My own most intimate sensitivity runs along the inside of my arm when my palm is turned upward. It's the physical manifestation of my internal being.

My art is always bringing up the most personal, sensitive, memory-filled part of my being. I have a theory as to why this is true. Of course. (Theories are my tendency, right?) Why art brings up this part of our world. The painful, self-exposed part.

It's simply because the fears that so many of us have about this happening are completely valid and absolutely real. As I've suggested throughout this book:

DOING ART BRINGS UP STUFF!

Here's my theory:

*   *   *   *

Dari's theory

Creativity and emotional work come from the same place.

There you go. That's the theory in the proverbial nutshell. Creativity and emotional work come from the same place… Done.

No? A bit more information, maybe? Awwww. Really? It's just so clear.

I'm kidding. (I'm hoping you've figured that out by now…)

Anyway, here I go.

Proposition #1: Creativity is one of the most personal and powerful things we are capable of. It's creative. Therefore, it's original. Therefore, it's unique. Therefore, it is all about me. Or in your case, you. Absolutely personal.

Obviously, art can be immensely powerful. One of the most precious and powerful parts of you, your personal history, and even our shared human heritage. Masterpieces of paintings and literature, music, architecture. We create the knowledge of our universe. Science. Physics. Medicine. $E=mc^2$. Technology. How much creativity did it take to transmit sound from one distant place to another? To invent the Internet? To remove a heart from one human being and place it into another? To even think of such a thing? To invent a piano and then make transcendent music with it?

I find myself laughing a bit as I try and justify that creativity is one of the most powerful parts of our universe! Therefore, I'm going to stop trying.

I believe it is. You can decide if you agree with me or not.

Since creativity is such an extraordinarily powerful process, that would suggest that it comes from an extraordinarily powerful place inside us.

Proposition #2: In order to deal with life's challenges, one needs to access a very powerful place…

Let me elaborate.

Remember my earlier story about my abysmal childhood. There I was, a small child, suffering enormously and trying to survive in the most effective ways possible. I was a small child. I had no resources to deal with the abuse. No ability to look at it and analyze it and understand it and deal with my reactions to it, or my feelings, even my thoughts. NO WAY at all to do anything that would change things. There was simply nothing I could do about it. Except:

It turns out that, in my case, one of the most effective ways of dealing with it, and thus surviving it, was to shut it down and put it away.

Not deal with it. Not think about it. Not react to it. Just sort of go away from it all. A very effective method, as it turns out. The official jargon calls it avoidance.

At certain points in our lives, this is one of the most useful survival techniques imaginable. Just go away from it. Make it disappear. Get on with what you can get on with, and leave the rest of it alone. Run from the mindless beast.[46] Super effective! An interesting point to keep in mind, however, is that after you've gone through it, whatever it is, as long as you keep staying away from it, by definition that means you're not dealing with it…

Still, if you actually have no way of dealing with the torment at the time as, for example, when you're a child with *no resources*, then shutting it down and putting it away often works brilliantly.

If you stop and think about it, however, if you do have a horrible childhood, or a deeply traumatic event, or even a series of terrible events as an adult (war, famine, prison), and you do have to put it all away somewhere deep and dark and hidden because you do not have the capacity to deal with it at the time, you require a pretty powerful place to store it. That place has to hold extraordinary pain and suffering, sorrow, grief, fear, anger. It has to keep it locked away from you, concealed, hidden, and out of sight. In addition, it has to keep you *safe* while it's holding it all. That's the purpose of secreting it away, remember, shutting it down. To keep yourself safe.

Oh my goodness! That had better be one heck of a sturdy storage container.

Conclusion: I believe that the powerful place in which you store the pain (until you're prepared to deal with it), and the powerful place from which your creative universe arises (when you're prepared to deal with it), is the same powerful place.

When I pictured that place for the first time, it was actually very clear to me where it was. (In my theory, anyway...) Directly above my pubic bone. I knew it instantly. (It took at least a year for me to make the connection that that is where my womb is. The place from which creation actually comes. What can I say...) By the way, guys, when you start out as a fetus, you have a womb as well. Both genders are identical.

Okay, so picture this. You're an artist. You have no idea about this "powerful place." You just want to paint, or write, or compose. You want to do your art. If you're lucky you start doing exactly that. (Although only maybe lucky. In the circumstances that we're talking about there are both advantages and disadvantages to doing your art versus not being able to!)

There you are. You start creating your art! But...Your artistic universe is coming from exactly the same place where you've stored all that other, horrible, stuff.

So, wham, there you are, as well, banging brutally hard against those terrible, secret, horrible things. Since it's all coming from the same place.

You went to that place to do a painting of a soothing mountain lake, and WHOOSH. There's an ocean with twenty-foot waves crashing down on your canvas, crushing you against the rocks. You're writing a poem about walking down the street, and whoa, a Cyclops jumps in front of you, threatening to rip you into shreds. You're composing a lyrical ode to trees, and you have a panic attack. A drawing of a leaf, and the image gets stuck in your throat and chokes you.

You try and do your art, but while you're doing it, the hidden stuff blindsides you, torpedoes you, sinks you into a maelstrom.

STUFF THAT HAS NOTHING WHATSOEVER to do with the art you're trying to create.

Or so it seems...

You have no idea what's happening. Why it's happening. What the hell is going on. Yet you are, in one way or another, completely freaking out. That is so often the beginning of what happens to so many artists. It stops many of them dead in their tracks, perhaps never to recover.

Some of us know enough to be really scared of what's going to come up on us. To expect it. Like Anne Truit; to try to manage and control it.

Let's go back to the list from the whiteboard. One of my favorite, or least favorite comments. Familiar in any event.

"I don't want the witch on my shoulder to show me how evil I am…"

I submit that, contrary to popular belief, the last thing you're going to discover is how evil you are. Still it's often one of our greatest fears when we're encountering all that awfulness.

But my belief won't stop you from being scared of it. There you are, trying to do your art, and all this other stuff is coming up on you. You have no idea what it's about.

Let me go sideways for an instant and tell you how I came up with the theory in the first place. It was sort of in the middle of my bad-back years. I was visiting my father (remember he wasn't the problem…) in Miami Beach, lying on the grass by the water in the warm sub-tropical sun, staring at the puffy white clouds in the sky. I was busily making those pictures in the clouds that I talked about a few chapters ago. Something I used to do when I was a little girl, though I hadn't done it in years! I started to think about that. About why I'd stopped. Because it really was fun! Also wonderfully creative. (To be perfectly fair about this, I had been living in Vancouver for a very long time. Not a lot of white puffy clouds in blue sky. That's just not the way Vancouver skies generally work. Still…)

I also started thinking about what I'd been dealing with during this difficult time. All seriously difficult. Abruptly I thought about my beloved Vincent. Vincent Van Gogh is my muse. Don't ask me why. Though I love his art passionately, there's more to it than that. He just is. My muse.

I imagined him doing his art. Working so hard on his beautiful paintings. And banging against his pain every time he did. The joy of the art. The pain of the rest of it. Express yourself. Suffer. Express yourself some more. Suffer worse.

The theory came to me.

So many artists go crazy. Abuse drugs. Abuse alcohol. Kill themselves. It's true. A horribly painful true.

I think that place I'm talking about in my theory, is part of it. That powerful place that holds the pain.

And holds the creativity.

Shortly after I came up with the theory, I was having lunch with a friend of mine and received a profoundly painful sort of validation. She was a single mom whose only child, a teenager, had died in a car accident the year before. We were talking about art and artists, and I told her about my thoughts on the theory. She instantly agreed, and I can still see the gesture she made with her hands to describe what she was saying.

She told me that after her son died, while she was trying to pretend to deal with it, she felt an enormous pressure inside her, pushing against the pain. Not letting it come. She said it was as if there were simply no room in her being to take in the pain. Her hand described a capped volcano waiting to explode. She was holding down the explosion. Yet she had to let whatever it was come out, in order for her to be able to go inside herself and cope with the unbearable tragedy of losing her son. She knew she had to go to that place, and she described the childhood torment she'd experienced that gushed out of her when she went there. This was what allowed her to cope, however much she could, with losing her own child.

Something inside me had stopped me from writing for all those years. And, sadly, it had been the right thing for me to do. I couldn't afford to go to that place and discover what was in there waiting for me. I wasn't ready. I'm not entirely sure what would have happened if I had gone there, but I'm pretty positive I wouldn't have survived it. Not in any even faintly acceptable way. Plus I would have had NO IDEA what was happening.

It's important to me when I'm talking about this, that you understand two critical aspects of what I'm saying.

One: My childhood was, in too many ways, extraordinarily bad. Sometimes I feel self-conscious saying that because of the unbearable horrors so many people have gone through, but it's true. My childhood was very painful. When I worry about comparing myself to others, I remember one of the most valuable gifts my advisor gave me when I was in my early twenties. The conversation happened when I was telling him how uncomfortable I felt talking to him, a child survivor of the Holocaust, about my own crappy childhood.

His response was simple: "torture is torture..."

Hopefully, most of you reading this don't come from those kinds of circumstances. Going to that place inside you, therefore, will not be quite *so* extremely painful. Or it may be perfectly okay for you go there because you've done so much of the emotional work you have to do. It may be difficult, but not horrific.

Two: The second, and in many ways, even more critical aspect of this theory, is what I said about having NO IDEA what was happening. Vincent likely would have had no idea that that was what he was coming up against. Nor would I have had. It would have come at me out of the blue.

Hopefully that isn't true of you anymore. Not if you're reading this!!!

You'll have an idea what's happening. You can be aware, can delve, can work with it.

Subsequently, if you do your art and difficult things come up for you, there's a really good chance you can deal with them. Get support from wherever you can get support. (Remember I even said this in the very first chapter of this book... GET SUPPORT.)

Family, friends, therapy, organizations. Any of it. All of it!

Stuff comes up! And you can get help! And you can probably start to work it through. You can learn to understand what it's about.

It's your stuff. It can get in the way. Hopefully you can go through it and come out the other end. One of my favorite things in life. Going through it and coming out the other end.

Then the art can flow.

The most crucial thing about all of this for me is that, if it all stays buried, a part of me stays buried. Since it's part of me and part of my life, keeping it shut away is having an impact, often an enormous one.

I think it is painfully hilarious that of all the sentences I have uttered in all of my courses and all of my columns, the single one that has made it onto the Internet in the most locations is the following:

"If you ain't driving it, it's driving you."

So often, once you go there and start working it all out, it finally stops running you.

And not being run by all your history is glorious!

Of course, being able to go there and do your art is the other glorious. Absolutely amazing.

But there's even more good that can come out of it.

Even with the side of this that means difficult things do come up, the other side of it is that, quite frequently, the stuff coming up isn't at all bad. *Good things* come up, too. Joy actually gets buried under the pain. The fun, the happiness, the magic, gets lost. When you go digging out the rubble, it's amazing some of the wonderful things you might remember.

I even remembered that my father had a terrifically sweet pet name for me. Something I hadn't remembered for a minute until I turned thirty-five. The happiest memories are often tucked away in that place, along with the pain.

And that happiness can affect your art as well.

One of my very favorite comments on the wonders of doing this work came from a lovely young woman, twenty-three years old, I think, who stated, "Every single time I 'get there' I feel a place in my mind go *still*."

It's hard to go to the hard place. But it's so often sublime to come out the other end.

"I like to remember that October morning. I like to go back into it from the 'future,' where I now live, and retrospectively paint into it all the prescient signs of my belated emergence. For years of my life I developed my negative propensity for time travel. At a moment's notice I could plunge into some awful moment of the past (or some awful fantasy about the future) and come back with enough material to take a lugubrious bath in. I am now becoming adept in making the positive trip as well. I send my mental spaceship to points past or future and it frequently comes back with old buds of present blossomings (like that October morning): or sometimes a bold design for fruits to come." Gail Godwin[47]

Sometimes, the art can even flow effortlessly.

"That's how art should be. It should go on in the midst of life and not be put on a pedestal. It should be what you do between sips of tea."
Emma Thompson[48]

Take care, all.

Chapter fourteen
So Who Are We?

Good morning. Good afternoon? Evening? Middle of the night! Okay, then. Hi! How are you? Are you ready?

Today we're going to do another whiteboard. Or two...

I'd like you to sit/stand/lean/lie, whichever, and do a whiteboard about:

What is your image of an artist?

Or, to put it another way, what are artists like?

*   *   *   *

Whiteboard
Your Image of an Artist
Write down anything, *anything* that comes to you.

*   *   *   *

How was that? Did you have many images? Many ideas?

Why don't you take a bit more time and imagine everything you've ever thought about artists, or heard, or read, or seen (don't forget movies and TV images), about who artists are, or are supposed to be. What they're like. How they act. How they look. Who are those beings who do all that creative work?

Think about it a bit more and see if you have anything to add to your whiteboard.

*   *   *   *

Did anything surprise you?

Or was it pretty clear from the start what your perceptions are?

Here's a sample of what other students and I have come up with as our stereotypes. Because they *are* stereotypes.

It's natural, I guess, that most of the people who do this particular whiteboard come up with many of the same answers. That's what stereotypes are... I'm still always a bit taken aback by how consistent our perceptions of artists are. How similar everyone's lists tend to be.

*   *   *   *

Whiteboard
Stereotypes/Images of Being an Artist

Artists are loners   Solitary

They're poor

They are avant garde   Free-spirited

CRAZY.   They're always crazy.

They're dirty   and sloppy   Old time hippies

Alcoholics

Drug addicts

Promiscuous   Irresponsible

conceited   egotistical

arrogant

Megalomaniacal

Shabby   Suffering   Unhappy

Self-destructive

Suicidal!

And they always wear black...

Now, first things first. They really *do* wear black!!!

Personal story. I'd been hired to write a screenplay for a film production company. To get into the proper mindset, one of the things I did was to go to a script-reading with my husband. It was my first one. The reading took place in a theater and was attended by two or three hundred people. Every single one of those people, including me – though I hadn't consciously thought about it! – was dressed all in black. (Except for my husband who was in blue jeans...)

It was pretty funny. Dennis' blue jeans were actually quite striking in contrast.

Anyway, back to the *other* stereotypes.

Look at the list. Some of it's good. Mostly, it's very, very bad.

This is what artists are. No. This is what our image of artists is.

Now go look in the mirror. You are involved in this particular book because you want to be an artist. Or because you are an artist…

If you want to be an artist, however, or if you are an artist, according to our whiteboard (and I'm guessing that you had at least *some* of the same stereotypes on your board…), you have to be alone, poor, suffering, addicted, self-absorbed, crazy, and suicidal. Yup. In order to be an artist you have to be fundamentally miserable!

Remember what we were talking about in the last chapter? There are all sorts of reasons for some of these stereotypes. Certainly I believe in "Dari's Theory" on where art comes from, and that some of the suffering is bound to happen. Has to be true for some of us.

However, to think all artists are on the verge of self-destruction is absurd.

Because, on the other side of this particular coin, is the **FACT** there are all sorts of perfectly lovely, happy, even NORMAL people, who are artists! Hell, you may even be one of them.

I know I am, of course… ☺

In addition, while art is often not the highest paying profession (except for the very few rich ones who are the "stars"), especially in the beginning, lots of artists have ordinary jobs they use to support their art; so they just ain't poverty-stricken.

I've actually never noticed a relationship between artists and their resistance to showers. I mean, *really!*

Many, many, *many* artists are incredibly warm and kind, and even helpful and giving to others. Just think of all the artistic donations you've seen at fundraisers, silent auctions, and so on. Artists helping and mentoring and working in groups with other artists is almost a given.

The problem here is that, if one wants to be an artist, and at the same time is carrying around this rather horrific stereotyped perception of what it means to be an artist, IT IS GOING TO INTERFERE with your ability to be one. It will sabotage your motivation (who wants to be miserable all the time?), or your ability to take yourself seriously as an artist if you *aren't* like that… Or at the very least, it will push you in some very weird directions in your attempt to be a *real* artist.

So, here are my thoughts on being an artist:

You can be creative and still love people, a lot!
You can be talented and still be physically self-caring.
You can work for a living at something that actually pays you
a salary.
You don't have to sleep around (more than you want to).
Or be an alcoholic.
Or a drug addict.
You can be kind, and gentle, and sensitive to other
people's feelings.
You can live a long, non-self-destructive life.
And you can be perfectly sane.

*   *   *   *

Those are my thoughts, and I'm sticking to them!

Think about what your thoughts are on who you are… and consider your options.

*   *   *   *

Next topic.
New Whiteboard. Very straightforward.
Name all the arts and the crafts you can think of.

*   *   *   *

Whiteboard
Arts and Crafts

*   *   *   *

Whiteboard
Arts and Crafts

Painting
Sculpture
Weaving
Writing
Pottery
Composing
Cooking
Musician
Gardening/Horticulture
Architecture
Knitting
Embroidery
Jewelry Making

We'll stop with those, though there are obviously many others. These are some of the ones that usually come up first.

Okay, now I want you to separate this list into which of these are the arts and which are the crafts.

I'm now going to make assumptions on which category you placed each item in, based on the numerous classes who've done this.

*   *   *   *

Whiteboard
Arts and Crafts

ART	CRAFTS
Painting	Weaving
Sculpture	Pottery making
Writing	Cooking
Composing	Knitting
Musician	Embroidery
Architecture	Jewelry Making
Photography	Gardening/Horticulture

Let's do something interesting here. I'm going to ask a couple of questions, and, when you're answering the first two questions, I would like you to imagine all of the major museums and art galleries that you've visited or with which you are familiar.

Who does the painting? Men or women?

Who does the sculpture? Men or women?

For the next question, imagine the concerts and the operas, the symphonies you've heard.

Who composes the music? Men or women?

Imagine the buildings you've seen in New York, or Paris, or London.

Who does the architecture? Men or women?

Until *very* recently, the answer is that men do the vast majority of the painting. The sculpting. They are the serious composers. They are the architects.

At least in the public eye!

For many of us, it's still true of the *images* in our heads as well.

Even in writing, believe it or not, there is still a great deal of evidence of gender bias, although the statistics are definitely improving!

Now answer the same question for who is most likely to do the crafts. The quilting and the pottery, the embroidery, and the jewelry making. Women, no?

Cooking is seen as women's work for sure. *Except*, of course, when the cook is a chef! In that case we're far more likely to think the chef is a man. It is then, and only then, when cooking becomes an art form.

Gardening gets done in the afternoon by women. Unless it's horticulture. Or architectural landscaping.

It's the second decade of the twenty-first century. Yet all of this is still mostly true, a lot of the time. There's been progress, of course. Great progress. It's still true, however, to a shocking extent. And still absolutely true of the images we have of it!

My *question* is, if quilting were done primarily by men, would it be considered an art? You can guess my answer. Of course it would.

Men do art. Women do crafts.

That's how we see it. A lot. Still.

The point of this exercise is that these categories are another stereotype we have of artists. An important one. Whether you're a man or a woman.

I always used to think this way myself. Especially about crafts. Crafts were done by women and were profoundly less profound than art. Real art. I was just like everyone else. All those activities listed under crafts were something else. Certainly not real art. Certainly they were *less*.

Until one day...

I had a student who had been quilting for thirty years. She talked about her work with the same love and passion I talk about writing. The reason she had signed up for my class was that about ten years previously, her husband of many years had died. She had not sewn a single stitch since that moment.

She'd been halfway through a quilt when it happened, and it had hung there in her quilting room, all that time. Halfway done. She was determined to get back to it, but she couldn't. No matter what she tried.

Until a glorious moment finally arrived (for both of us...), a few months into our course. She started working on the quilt. She finished it. And she felt joy.

I couldn't have felt more gratified. I asked her if she would bring in the quilt to show us.

Look, I'd seen quilts before. I liked quilts – if I *noticed* them, which mostly I didn't. Until this student walked into the classroom with this large piece of work she had finally finished. She struggled until she found a way to hang it on the wall.

Abruptly, shockingly, I felt like I had entered into a sacred space. (You choose the nature of that sacred space: church, temple, mosque, synagogue, a star-filled vision of the night sky.) Whichever you want. But there, right in front of me, was a mystical universe. A quilt. Exquisite. Art of the highest form.

That was the moment I recognized the stereotypes I had about "art."

That was the moment I recognized the stereotypes I had about "crafts."

In the next moment I realized how common they were. How many of us hold the same MIS-perception?

*   *   *   *

More stereotypes? You bet. There are many of them. I'll just talk about a couple more.

This is another gender tendency – more in the past than the present, but it's still going on. If there is big art – I mean big in a physical sense – to be done, men do it. If small, tiny art, it's most likely done by a woman.

I remember the first time I saw a Louise Nevelson's *Sky Cathedral* piece at the Museum of Modern Art in New York. It was exquisite, sculpted, and carved of wood. And it was huge; about ten feet by ten feet. I remember actually feeling shocked when I found out it was done by a woman artist. In hindsight, that is horrifying. Yet true.

Many of the women artists I know talk about their time in art school and the gender biases they encountered there. Not taken seriously, discouraged, and on and on and on. Still, the oddest one to me was this bias against their ability to do large pieces, large installations, large sculpture, even large paintings. They were supposed to work on small art.

Cameos, embroidery, small portraiture.

For heavens' sake, women should be allowed to do large art, and men should be allowed to do small art without feeling weird…

I think that big art may also be thought of as Big Art – i.e., important, monumental (in all senses), significant. In our world, the sheer size of it may imply, for many people, profundity.

Another gender difference, some of the time, is the male tendency towards planning out their art. It's a bit funny, actually. Many wives and girlfriends will think this particularly humorous because of a relationship-stereotype, which goes something like this.

Wife/Girlfriend: "We need to sit down and talk about what we're doing this week."

Husband/Boyfriend: "Grunt."

Wife/Girlfriend: "Really we do. We need a plan."

Husband/Boyfriend: "It'll be fine. Don't worry about it."

The idea of thinking of planning as a *male* artistic bias is a bit odd.

I first connected with the planning art idea when I was a kid in school. Having since checked it out with many of my students, I've discovered that even now it's a commonplace theme when training writers. It goes something like this:

You're in an English course discussing the art of writing and the teacher (often a male, in this case) informs you that the correct way to write is to plan it out. It doesn't matter if it is an essay or a novel, an article or a screenplay, or even poetry. The first thing you need to do is to write an outline. For scriptwriting, it's called a storyboard. You organize the piece you're planning on writing, and you figure out what's going to happen in the beginning of it, the middle, the end, as well as everything in between. There's even a fundamental saying about it, a commonplace quote: "If you don't know the ending, you can't write the beginning."

Huh?

Wait, it keeps going.

After you have your outline finished, you need to develop a character sketch of all your characters. Their backstory. Who they are, what they're like, what their history is. You need to *know* the people who populate your stories.

You pin this all up on your wall, with maps, architectural depictions, and place images, as well. The whole thing!

We are often taught that this is the only proper way to write something. Anything at all.

Well, whoops.

There I was when I started writing. I sat down, typed a phrase which became the title of the piece, and wrote a sentence. Then I wrote another sentence. I had no idea before I sat down that I was going to write a piece of fiction. NO IDEA. I had no idea what it was, what it was about, where it was going, who was in it, where it took place. Nothing. I just kept writing sentences. Until I got tired. Which is when I went away. A few days later, I came back and wrote another sentence. Then more. I kept doing it. Gradually a science fiction novel unfolded.

Now, the whole time I was engaged in this particular writing process, I heard those voices in my head from all the different English courses and writing courses I'd ever taken, of how I was **supposed** to be doing it.

But I wasn't doing it that way at all.

So?

So, I felt stupid. I felt like I was wasting my time. Like I was a total dilettante. A dabbler. That I wasn't taking my work seriously. That I was just *amusing* myself.

In any event, I kept amusing myself until I finished the novel.

Still, I was definitely NOT a serious writer.

Until one day at The Vancouver Writers' Festival (I'm pretty sure it was in 2001), I attended a panel discussion with Ursula Le Guin. She's one of my favorite science fiction writers and has published numerous novels and non-fiction works on the art of writing, won myriad awards, and been translated into various languages. A rather serious writer...

And SHE announced to the audience that she wrote her many, many novels, ONE SENTENCE AT A TIME!!!

Imagine!

No planning. No outline. Nothing at all. Just one sentence at a time. I was so happy!

I could take myself seriously as a writer. Without planning out the entire thing. It simply doesn't come to me that way.

Here's another quote by Le Guin. When asked in an interview, "Do you map out your writing projects ahead of time?" she replied, "No, I have lots of good intentions, but no control over my writing."[49]

Planning be damned!

Unless, **OF COURSE**, planning is what works for you. It has to be your way. Remember?

The point is, planning doesn't work for all of us. Yet you still get to consider yourself a real artist even if you don't plan.

One caveat on this point. I'm assuming that if you're an architect, say, planning does become critical at a certain stage. This is probably true of many art forms… Allowing your art to flow at certain stages, however, may also be critical, even in architecture.

The gender part of this discussion is that in casual surveying of many of the artists I know, guys seem significantly more likely to plan their work than women do. Even though women seem to be the ones who want to plan out their weekends…

Okay, one last topic on the subject of stereotypes of artists and art, specifically in the visual arts.

If I were to ask any group of adults what single instruction they remember most about how to do visual art "properly," in grade school, or what they did wrong when they were doing their art as a child, I'd bet real money that the most common answer would be:

'You have to color inside the lines!'

Or "I wasn't any good because I couldn't color inside the lines."

It's like a magic phrase.

You *must* color inside the lines…

Uh-huh… It goes on from there. I'm not an artist because:

"I can't draw a straight line."

"I can't do perspective."

"I don't know how to do shading."

"I don't know how to do anatomy."

"I can't make a face look like a face."

"I'll never be an artist because I don't know how to draw."

"Because I've never been to art school."

"I'm never good in art class 'cause I can't do it the way the teacher says."

I'm not an artist.

Visual artists often become convinced that there is only one correct road to take in order to become an artist. You have to learn the correct way to draw. First and foremost. Forever. And only then… ONLY then can you start messing around and becoming more creative. After you have all of the basic skills, first. You have to know how to do it the right way. First.

But, here's my problem.

I know many wonderful artists who suck at drawing a straight line. Who hated art school. Even failed at art school. Couldn't draw an accurate piece of anatomy if their lives depended on it. Who still, to this day, can't, or can't stand, coloring inside the lines…

Yet when I look at their drawings or paintings or etchings, I'm enraptured. Mesmerized. Joyful.

I kept thinking about this idea. It was kind of like the way I used to think about planning a novel. There's a right way and a wrong way. Isn't there? Ya gotta know the ending before you can write the beginning, right?

No. I already put that whole thing to rest, right?

Yes!!!!! RIGHT!!!!

What does that mean, therefore, about learning the proper rules and regulations for drawing and painting? Here's where I went with that.

My husband is weird. He's a nature photographer with one little hitch. You can never figure out (or hardly ever) what the photograph is. And no, it isn't because he has played with it on the computer. He does not alter it digitally.

It's a flower. Oh. Are you sure??? Maybe not, maybe it's a rock…

It's very unusual art. In my own humble opinion, it's very beautiful (and many, many people agree). Still, it's unusual. Why is it unusual?

Because with photography, you can usually tell what the hell you're looking at.

That's kind of the point, I thought to myself, when I was pondering this idea. (I wasn't quite sure where I was going, but I just kept thinking about it.)

You see something and you take a picture of it. And that is the thing that you have a picture of.

Ahhhhh. I suddenly realized where I was going with this. Bear with me.

The first photograph in history was taken in 1826.[50]

Prior to that moment in time, there was no way to reproduce an image other than with some form of visual artistry. If you wanted to preserve a picture of a landscape, it had to be drawn or painted. A building, drawn, painted, or sculpted. A picture of a person? It had to be a portrait, sketched or painted by someone who could draw or paint. Maybe a bust or figurine.

It was the only visual record we could have.

Strange to think about that way, but that's the truth of it.

In order to have a visual record of anything, one was required to find someone who could reproduce the image in some artistic form (not including photography), that actually looked like the "anything."

So if you wanted a record of something, or a picture of a loved one, or an image of a beloved garden, or cat, or building, or mountain, you truly did want it to look like the thing you wanted the picture of.

Ergo.

The ability to reproduce an image on paper, or canvas, or a cave wall that would represent, as closely as possible, the "imagee," required skill. Accuracy. Perspective. Lighting. Shading. The ability to draw something that truly evoked the subject you were drawing, was highly valued and profoundly sought after. Even necessary

Artists studied and learned the skills as effectively as they could. It really, really, really mattered for them to have the ability to draw inside the lines. As perfectly as possible.

Until in 1826, the camera arrived. It developed and became more utilized as the century progressed.

Then what happened? Impressionism hit the art world. Now it could afford to! It wasn't necessary to reproduce reality with a paint-brush anymore. Art could go exploring. Which, of course, it did.

The world of Romanticism, Impressionism, Post-Impressionism, Expressionism… Abstract art became more and more popular. Became more and more varied and unpredictable and strange; eliciting reactions unimaginable earlier.

Interestingly, what did not change was the *expectation* and the demand for artists to have traditional training in accurate reproductions.

Sometimes we're a little slow to catch up with progress…

Think about computers for a second. As digital technologies become ever more powerful, some of the underlying techniques that were once so important have, rather unexpectedly, and perhaps sadly, become redundant. Writing script is no longer taught in many grade schools. Students don't need it, because all they do is type on their laptops or tablets or smartphones. (Very few bother learning to touch type.) Hand-drawing a straight line isn't very important when a CAD/CAM program can do it for you, and better. It colors inside the lines too.

Among other things, this may free us up even more to color outside the lines ourselves.

I suggest that traditional training for artists can be profoundly useful. Can be profoundly helpful. It can lead to creating great pieces of work. Masterpieces.

I also suggest that there are other ways to produce masterpieces.

For some people, it's just not good to learn how to color inside the lines. Or to write an outline for your novel. Or even to write it one sentence at a time.

You may be noticing a trend here. We have all sorts of assumptions about who does art, what art is, and how we're supposed to do art.

What works for you is what matters.

Take care, all.

Chapter fifteen
The Inappropriate I

In Class Exercise

"When I write about myself, take a photo of myself, draw a picture of myself, and so on…"

Then when you're finished, turn the page.

*   *   *   *

Okay, there are definitely two sides to this particular coin. When you flip it, it may land on heads or tails or both. Let's talk.

We'll start with the "glorious" version of what happens when you do your art about yourself.

*　　*　　*　　*

Whiteboard
The Good Parts Version
Write down anything, *anything* that comes to you.

I feel free.

Good.

I'm emptying the mud out.

Comfortable.　　　Excited.

I'm exploring unchartered territories.

It's satisfying.

Commenting on life.　　Celebrating my voice.

I go deep. I want to explore rip off band-aids of time.

I can focus.　I can stop time.

I can discover more about me.

I grow wings to set free in me.

I learn things about myself.

It's like if I empty out all the thoughts I have and the feelings I have and I can then get to the other kind of writing.

I'm like a giant walnut in the sea.

I get to see who I am and I can decipher my emotions.

I can flaunt my peacock feathers.

I'm totally honest.

I learn things.

I give myself love and attention.

Relief.

I get to look at my feeling and opinions.

I can look at my reactions and see if they are logical.

I'm happy, usually.

My most honest,   both critical and positive.

It's my way to help myself and get my deepest understanding.

It's exciting looking back. It all goes way too fast.

Exploration, explanation and discovery.

A relief to get it down.   Let the cat out of the bag.

No more secrets.

Writing about "me," creating a self-portrait, taking a selfie!!!, can be some of life's truly satisfying experiences. It can open you up and be a world of discovery: it can "Set you free."

It's your chance to say or show whatever you want about the experiences you've had, the adventures you've been on, the adventures you want to go on.

In my universe, it's also one of the most *therapeutic* things I can do. It's partly like talking to your best friend. Even better some of the time. You *always* get the response you choose.

I've taught many courses specifically on journal writing, which is one essential version of "writing about myself." ("Writing the Road Inside" is one of my favorite course names.) So many people have always wanted to keep a journal for one of a million or so reasons. Yet they don't – for a million or so reasons. This course is designed to help them do that. Teaching it has been great fun and wonderfully fascinating. (There has to be something fascinating in a million or so reasons!)

One day in class, I abruptly realized how deeply rooted the whole topic of journal writing was for me, even more so than *"simply"* a lifetime of writing in one.

It goes to when I first returned to my writing. I wrote a science fiction novel about the future, set in the year 2613, in which the world had become "Holistech." It had integrated a holistic approach to humanity, *with* technology. No more human vs. techie battles! (I know… shocking!)

A major example of that integration in 2613 was the "Identity Source Computer," an exact imprint replication of our beings, brains, and every other aspect of us, but wayyyyy faster, with more instantaneous access to all parts of our being.

Writing this chapter, I realized that this might actually be the best way I would have answered this assignment myself.

So, herewith, an excerpt from my book, *One Step Into Time.*

"My journal has always been crucial to my well-being… In severe moments I've even held it to my body, taking direct comfort from… the knowledge that my deepest self exists on its pages.

But… one thing I've always wanted from it, whether that want has been fervently strong or just a humorously whispered wish, it has never been able to do.

It has never spoken back to me.

It has never answered my questions, evolved my process or identified my patterns… My journal has almost always been profoundly useful in helping me find my way, since it holds the purest concrete reflection of my spirit that exists... But it has never, by itself, accomplished any of it.

But my Identity Source Computer has. It talks back to me all the time. One day I pour thoughts into it. The next day it's evolved a step further, mirroring back the essence of what I'd said but hadn't seen."

Okay. My fantasy ideal computer doesn't exist yet, even though we're getting closer and closer. The fact of the matter is, however, I'm pretty sure I was completely wrong about one thing. I think the journals we keep, here and now in the twenty-first century, talk back to us all the time. Journals – "writing about myself" – can organize our thoughts, help us grapple with our hopes and problems, and find solutions in unique and very, very powerful ways.

It's a way in. A way out into the world. A way to delve into what you're feeling. A way to understand what you're feeling when it's hidden from you.

Here's one of my very favorite quotes on this topic (one of my favorite quotes period).

"The world is horrid right straight through and so am I ...every bit of me is tired. I'm old and ugly; stupid and ungracious...I want to grouch and sulk and rip and snort. I am a pail of milk that has gone sour. *Now*, perhaps, having written it all down, the hatefulness will melt off to where the mist goes when the sun gets up.... Writing is a splendid sorter of your good and bad feelings, better even than paint."[51]

That quote is by Emily Carr (thus the reference to "better even than paint..."), and perhaps the best statement I've ever read about one of the great reasons for writing in a journal. There are many other reasons, of course, other than sorting your emotions. You can keep a record of your life, your work, your exercise, make observations on the universe, plan your future, and on and on and on.

Still the whole thing comes back to, what are some of the things that happen "When I write about me…"

It's often, as can be seen if you're "*doing*" this book, a direct route into your creative world. "When I write about me…" is often invaluable, precious, and filled with joy.

$$*\qquad*\qquad*\qquad*$$

But now we need to go look at the other side of the responses to this assignment.

A whole other topic, about what happens, "When I write, or do any art about myself…"

$$*\qquad*\qquad*\qquad*$$

Here's a sample of some of the less than ecstatic responses.

$$*\qquad*\qquad*\qquad*$$

Whiteboard
The not so good parts version…
Write down anything, *anything* that comes to you.

I have to stop exploring why.

I just do defense mechanisms.

It's just self-masturbation.

I'm uncomfortable. Self-conscious. A whiny, snively rat.

Danger to go deep.   Sink into pit of doom.

I make a fool of myself. I make a fan of myself. Yuck.

Validating right to victimhood.

What's the point?

I should be positive.

I feel self-conscious.   Selfish.   Self-indulgent.

Incessant commentary about life.

Get a life.

It's freer to write in the 3rd person.

It's all so fundamentally about me!!!

It may not be of interest.

Not fiction.   Fact-based.   Too analytical.

> *I wouldn't.*
>
> *I'll focus on larger stuff.*
>
> *Complaining.*
>
> *Torture chamber or root canal.   Exercise or exorcism?*
>
> *I'm such a Diva.*
>
> *I'm too analytical.   Sob story.   boring*
>
> *It's flowery.   I'm just embellishing.*
>
> *I'm misrepresenting everything.*
>
> *OMG. It's so all about ME!*

Doesn't sound like fun...

Nope.

First of all let me say very clearly, a lot of people HATE, *hate,* **hate,** creating art about themselves. Despise it, dread it, abhor it, turn away from it, flee from it, get nauseous at the thought of it. Or, to put it simply, some people do not like doing art about themselves.

Some people even love it and hate it at the same time. Or at different times.

Guess what? Yup. There's no right answer.

Let us explore.

When I was at university, in my first-year English literature course, I got an assignment to write something meaningful about a book I cared about. I had discovered an author who, at that moment in my life, couldn't have been more important to my emotional well-being. The author was Ayn Rand. The three books that captured me were *Fountainhead, Atlas Shrugged,* and the little-known science fiction novel, *Anthem.* In today's world, Ayn Rand is seen as standing for other topics related to her writing, politically and economically, and you can, of course, think whatever you want to about those aspects of her work and philosophy.

The gift she gave to me, however, after my painful childhood, was permission, for the first time in my life, to think that "*I*" mattered. That it was **okay** for me to matter. It was even important. Profoundly so.

I decided to write that English literature paper on that very subject; Ayn Rand and the subject of "Self."

The first thing I did was look up the word "self" in the dictionary. (It was an actual paper dictionary. This was a little while ago...) What I found there were words like "self-absorbed," "self-centered," "self-important," "self-indulgent," and, of course, the all-important, "selfish."

(Let's keep in mind that there are hundreds of words with "self." I am not referring to all the words that are strictly neutral, factual, or descriptive. I was looking at the words that were evaluative, which contained judgments; either overtly or implied.)

Well, either overtly or implied, I found numerous words that were utterly, utterly negative. Again, starting with the all-important one, "selfish." To continue with the list, there was: self-engrossed, self-involved, self-focused, self-pitying, self-interested, self-righteous, self-satisfied, self-serving, and so on, and so on, and so on.

Focus on self was bad! Caring about yourself, being involved with yourself, being absorbed or interested in yourself, feeling yourself was important – all BAD.

Next there were words like self-conscious, self-abasement, self-defeating, self-effacement. Those were the ones where the self was putting down the self, so to speak.

The truly good, positive words – the words that mean that you are doing something RIGHT; something for the benefit of you and the world in general in pretty much all contexts – were words like "self-less," and the truly wonderful "self-sacrificing." Giving up of self is the ultimate good.

It was pretty astonishing for me to see all that implied judgment in black and white, right there in the dictionary! Not just inside *me*. That's certainly how I perceived it. Anything focused on me – bad. Anything focused on other people – good. No matter what.

I believe this concept is a major part of our culture. Many other cultures, as well. Focusing on other people is a good thing. Focusing on yourself is bad.

I kept thinking about it. Knowing there was something wrong. It felt so good when I thought I mattered. But the world kept telling me it was bad.

Here's what happened next.

A phrase kept running through my mind while I was obsessing about this. The phrase was:

"Thou shalt love thy neighbor."

You've heard the phrase, right? We all get taught it at one point or another. In one way or another. I actually thought it was one of the Ten Commandments. Turned out it isn't, actually. It is simply a quote from the Bible.

"Thou shalt love thy neighbor."

Profoundly important. One of the ultimate good statements in our universe. But, guess what? That's not the whole quote.

You know what the quote actually is? Is a hint of an echo coming back to you when you think about it????

The actual quote:

"Thou shalt love thy neighbor as thyself."

AS THYSELF!

In all the years I've taught, in all my classes, not one single person ever remembered, on their own, that that was the full quote! The official biblical quote. The verse from the bible, The Old Testament. Leviticus 19:18. "Thou shalt love they neighbor, *as thyself.*"

Have I emphasized it enough yet? I figure all those students who were from other cultures, cultures that were not Judeo-Christian, had an excuse. Some excuse. Although most of them were very aware of the "Thou shalt love thy neighbor…" *part* of the quote.

What excuse, however, do those people have who *were* from Judeo-Christian cultures???

What a fascinating omission from so many of our memories. And depressing as hell. In my book, anyway. And, oh, yes – this is my book.

Consequently, the actual meaning of the quote, a true foundation for what we see as one of the most fundamental moral values in our world – loving thy neighbor – is that the benchmark, the guideline, the criterion for how we are supposed to feel about, and care about our neighbors – all the other people in the world – how we are supposed to love *them*, is based on, described, and demonstrated by how much we love *ourselves*.

That is the ultimate moral objective!!!

Yet hardly any of us even remember that loving ourselves is a critical part of the concept. That *this* is what teaches us *how* to love our neighbors.

Okay, here's the point (*if* it isn't clear yet…). I believe that we as a culture, don't think or believe that it is morally important, or even morally correct, to care about or focus on ourselves.

Look at the quotes in this particular whiteboard, entitled, "When I write about myself…"

It's a sob story, it's boring, I'm embellishing, I'm being too analytical, I'm whining, I'm snively, I'm a rat, I'm selfish, self-indulgent, incessant (as in **bad**) commentary about life, get a life, I have to stop exploring why. I'm validating my right to victimhood… It's self-masturbation, for heaven's sake!

The final example, it's so all about ME!

Translation. When we write about ourselves we often judge that as being the worst, most self-absorbed, stupid, indulgent thing we can do!

These feelings are not coming out of nowhere. We're generally judging ourselves as bad for thinking about ourselves, in the first place. Extra bad, if we actually go exploring it.

A lot of us are doing it to each other, as well. And we are often put down, insulted, or laughed at for being too analytical.

Overly analytical!!! Pretty much any level at all of self-analysis can be judged as *overly*. Thinking about yourself, much less feeling anything at all about it, is just silly...

Here are some of the phrases you may have heard:

"Stop being so analytical!"

"You're making it too complicated!"

"Stop thinking about it so much."

"Get on with it!"

"Get over it!"

"You have to let it go!"

Plus my personal favorite...

"Stop navel-gazing!"

*   *   *   *

Okay, so first, you're not supposed to love yourself. Next, you're not supposed to think about yourself. You're not allowed to dwell on yourself. Or explore, feel, analyze yourself, and so on and so on.

For art, this translates into, you are not supposed to write about yourself, or paint things about you, or do music or lyrics that are "all about you!"

So. So?

For starters, if any of your art is coming from anything about you, you're going to feel bad! This set of bad feelings is going to shut down your art. Logical, right?

Also, since I believe that everything we do in art fundamentally comes from inside us – variations on a theme, extrapolations out into the universe – we're in deep doo-doo if we aren't allowed to look at "I."

It's truly fascinating. Our culture, a lot of the world, in fact, values learning and studying and understanding how everything in the universe works. Education is one of the be-alls and end-alls of success in our world. We worship academia. Physicists are among the highest order of intelligence and respectability. Mathematicians, as well. Scientists of every type, in fact.

These people spend their lives studying the most precise, miniscule minutiae that exist in the world. It gets more and more infinitesimal how tiny a thing science can examine, and study, and measure, and experiment with, and strive, and struggle, endlessly, to understand. Hell, the atom was considered tiny, a very long time ago. Now we've gone totally beyond that to the array of subatomic particles. This is considered a great thing; an important, powerful, necessary, and fascinating thing to study. To analyze. Most importantly, to understand!

Of course!

I suggest that living beings are even more complicated, more complex, more mysterious than atoms. Or even subatomic particles. I suggest that we are probably one of the most mysterious and complex things that exist in the universe.

Even so... We are supposed to go through life studying and analyzing, exploring and analyzing everything, *everything*, but us.

Anything but us.

If we do study ourselves, we are **NAVEL GAZING.** Obviously one of the worst, most wasteful, self-indulgent (look at the word I just used!) things we can do!

Think about it. Think about the most significant problems facing you. Think about the most significant problems facing the world.

Many, many, many of them would be dealt with better if we functioned better with ourselves and with each other. If we analyzed. If we understood how we humans really work....

Telling us not to examine or explore ourselves seems ludicrous to me.

*   *   *   *

So here is my image for the day:

I want you to picture telling Albert Einstein to STOP being so analytical.

*   *   *   *

That is my perception of how "bad" it is for me to love and care and think about me.

NOT!

*   *   *   *

Okay, so we've looked at the good parts version, and the bad parts version, of "When I write, or paint, or do my art about me..."

I cannot predict which type of response you will have.

The joy of self-discovery, the expression of self, the bringing your insides joyfully out onto paper, or canvas, the freedom of, *finally,* saying it all out loud (so to speak...),

or......

"Get over it!"

To make things more complicated, you may very well have both sets of reactions.

There's no right answer, of course. They are what they are. Your feelings that is. Your thoughts on the subject.

Still, I do want to suggest something.

If your work reflects all the good aspects of doing art about yourself, which is terrific, why don't you take another five minutes and do some more digging, and see if you come up with any other ideas. See if there are any other feelings or judgments on the topic buried deep inside you. If you don't, that's great. Don't think for a moment that I'm unhappy with you being ecstatically joyful about doing art about yourself!

I'm actually being a bit protective of you, just in case there is a secret, more negative view skittering around inside you. Please check and see if anything else comes up.

If, on the other hand, you are stuck in the mire of how awful and evil and terrible you are when your art is focused on you, take another five minutes and see if there is any happy part hidden deeply away.

In the end, however, if your assignment expresses nothing positive about "When I create art about myself..." I want to assure you, you are not alone. Way too many of us feel that way.

And maybe, the more you think about it – how sad it is that it's not all right for you to think about yourself, the more it may change.

Take care, all.

Chapter sixteen
Let's Talk

In Class Exercise

I want you to write a piece of dialogue.

This is another "Please, don't hate me" one. Just try to trust me for
the next twenty minutes.
Also, this is one of the exercises that is definitely more focused on the
writing type artists who are doing this book.
My husband suggested that the visual artist version of this might be
drawing or painting two people having a conversation. He thinks
most of you will hate me for making you draw faces… Might be
worth a try.

See you soon. Please, especially for this assignment, don't
forget bumps!
Then when you're finished, turn the page.

*   *   *   *

How'd that go?

This time I'm going to show you a whiteboard that consists of some of the *bumps* students have had from this assignment.

Whiteboard
Bumps **from writing dialogue assignment**

This is hard.   I don't know how to do it.

I'm analyzing how to do it.

I'm overthinking this.   I have no idea what to do.

At first I had HUGE resistance.

I realized I was writing a description.

I instantly was afraid.

It's very short.   Very bad.

I compared it to Robert Parker's dialogue His is so light!

Hard. I don't like it.

Hard. It's very internal.

It's hard to have two different characters.

I can't write it complexly...

This is vulgar.

I can't.

Is this a real conversation?

I just don't know how to write dialogue.

Whenever I give this exercise, I always think about the assignment I gave you about being funny. Remember? Pretty much everyone freezes when asked to create something funny. "I'm not funny." "I don't know how to be funny." "I'm not a comedian." "You have to be a comedian to write something funny."

Oddly, or maybe not oddly, the same thing often happens when I ask people to write dialogue: "I don't know how to write dialogue." "I've never been taught how to write dialogue." "I have to learn how to write dialogue."

Far too often, the first reaction everyone has when trying to write dialogue is to freeze.

Blank page. Blank brain.

I don't know if you remember what I said about trying to write something funny, but let me remind you.

I suggested that maybe, perhaps, sort of, sometime, something funny had actually happened to you within the last week. I then suggested that, maybe, for your assignment, you could simply do something with that.

Pretty much the same thing is true this time. About dialogue.

Online, Dictionary.com defines dialogue as: "conversation between two or more persons," or "the conversation between characters in a novel, drama, etc." Thus, my question to you is, have you had a conversation with one or two other people anytime within the last, say, five years? Probably, eh? (The Canadian part of me slips in every now and then…)

How come you didn't just write *that*?

My point? I'm guessing you've probably already gotten my point. Probably...

Dialogue does not have to be some intensely studied, planned, mapped out and regulated writing activity. It can be as simple as what you said on the phone to your friend this morning. Then what they said back to you.

Maybe you could try and hear the two people talking in your mind. Just write down what they say. Or say it out loud if it helps. Does it sound like something you would say? Yes? Voila! It's dialogue…

Congratulations.

Now go do it again. Hopefully without the brain freeze.

*　　　*　　　*　　　*

How did that go? Better? (I'm guessing it was.)

Good!

If it wasn't, you can try it again. Just remember to imagine *any* conversation you've ever had.

Of course you can work on your dialogue in a million ways. Still, just hearing a conversation in your head, and putting it down on paper, is a wonderful way to begin. There is a music, a rhythm to it. Work at listening to the melody of the words.

*   *   *   *

An issue that came up for me around dialogue when I started writing, had to do with what I call "context."

From the beginning, my written dialogue always sounded very natural, real, like two people actually talking to each other. It may be partly because I'm a therapist. Two people talking is something I do a lot. A lot! I can hear it endlessly in my head.

I put it down on paper. It actually sounds like two people talking. BUT!

I had a strong tendency to write just the words of the conversation. Just the words, and *nothing* else. Back and forth. First, the one person's words, and then the other's. Nothing else.

I came to call it Talking Heads. One head talks. The other talks. The other head talks back.

I wonder if you visual artist types have any tendency to do the same thing.

But that is not what is going on during a conversation. It's not just words coming out of people's mouths.

There's a whole world of elements going on as part of that conversation.

Let's try a brief list. We'll start with the setting:

Where are the people?

What are they doing?

What's happening around them?

Think about it.

"I'm tired. I can't believe how tired this makes me feel."

"Me, too. I could just curl up in a ball and go to sleep."

See how different this brief conversation sounds and what it signifies in the two very different settings.

First setting. The two people are lying, stretched out on a sandy beach in bright sunlight.

Second setting. The two people are standing on an assembly line at an automobile manufacturing plant.

Context.

Next context. Who are the people?

Gender?

Age? Children or adults?

Relationship? Strangers. Friends. Lovers. Work colleagues.

"Take me to your leader."

All right. Which is it? Children playing in their back yard? Or aliens arriving on our planet…?

I think you probably get the idea. There's a world of topics to talk about in terms of the context of a piece of dialogue. Think about the emotional tone of the conversation. Who's feeling what? How do they show it?

Think about facial expressions, gestures, body position. Movement.

Pencil tapping gives a lot of information in the right context. Pacing the floor is so different from sitting cuddled up in another person's arms.

Context.

Context, context, context.

How I learned to avoid Talking Heads was by giving my dialogue context.

Who are the people who are talking? What are they doing? What do they look like? Where are they? How are they acting? How are they feeling? What's going on around them? And on, and on, and on.

Think of that conversation you had the other day. When you do, I'm guessing you are imagining the whole thing. The words and the context.

Why don't you try it now.

Darylynn Starr Rank

*　　　*　　　*　　　*

In Class Exercise
Dialogue with context

*　　　*　　　*　　　*

That really was different, wasn't it?

Unless you knew all about this in the first place, and included it in your first piece of dialogue (some people do!), I'm guessing it probably was pretty different.

Keep that in mind when you're working on dialogue. It is not, usually, two heads talking to each other in the immense, colorless, empty reaches of outer space.

Two heads dangling in an otherwise blank painting.

Conversation and context!

One more time, congratulations and welcome to a world where you actually can create dialogue!

*   *   *   *

Now for your homework. A *very* different topic.

Homework Assignment

"The reason I don't paint, or dance, or write (or, or, or) more, or as much as I want to, is because.....”

Take your time with this one. It might be really interesting. Do try and remember bumps.

Take care, all.

Chapter seventeen
The Reason I Don't

The question for the Homework Assignment was, "**The reason I don't paint, or dance, or write (or, or, or) more, or as much as I want to, is because...**"

Before we look at what you wrote and explore it, I want to talk about my motivation here.

First, let me say that some of your explanations may be perfectly accurate. They may reflect the true reality of your life, your circumstances, or your emotional state. This may be a very useful exercise for you strictly in terms of getting a clear, down-on-paper picture of what's going on. Your answers may provide a grounded, pragmatic explanation of the reasons that you do not do your art as much as you want to.

Or they may not.

What I was partly asking for was for you to tell me how you *explain* to yourself the reasons for you not doing your art as much as you want to.

This is often an entirely different matter.

When you give that explanation, one of the things I'm most looking for are what I call the "Pit Words" you use to describe your lack of sufficient artistic endeavor.

I know... What the hell are Pit Words?

Let me explain by backtracking a bit. The most striking thing that has always surprised me the most every time I gave this assignment is that I kept expecting every single person to have a unique response. I expected to hear something like, "I don't write because I have four kids and they keep me very busy. Too busy, actually." Or "I don't play the guitar because I work full time." Or "I want to write in English but I've only been speaking English for three months." Or "I don't sculpt because I broke my wrist two years ago and it hasn't healed properly, so I'm waiting for them to schedule the surgery…"

Or, reasons along the lines of emotional/historical delving: "I don't paint because, when I was eight years old my father came home when I was coloring in my coloring book and he grabbed all my crayons and melted them in the fireplace, ripped up all my coloring books then threw them in the fire, told me that was the worst coloring he had ever seen in his entire life, then told me that if he ever saw me drawing anything ever again he would be very very angry! Now every time I sit down to draw, I get a terrible stomachache and start throwing up in fear."

I expected something, anything, about the particular and specific circumstances of each individual's existence.

You know by now how I feel about every one of us being unique. About how every single one of us has special, personal, historic reasons, causes, roots, etc., etc., etc., for every single aspect of our art.

Thus, with this particular assignment, I always expected, assumed, anticipated, knew, absolutely for sure, that there were going to be a million answers to this particular question.

Obviously. But.

On this particular question, for some very odd reason that I haven't quite figured out yet, I get, so to speak, hoist on my own petard.

There are almost always…

Wait. Yes. I get it. You're going to be *absolutely* the exception here. You're going to have written utterly unique, complex, and personal responses to this question, that are precise and specific to you and your life, which means, consequently, that this section of the book will have absolutely no relationship to you whatsoever. It will be a complete waste of time….

Right? (Okay. I admit it. It's true. I was smiling as I wrote that.)

Even if you are that exception, you might still find this discussion vaguely interesting anyway. It might explain why your best friend doesn't dance as much as she wants to. Now you can be a know-it-all and help her with her art. Or your spouse is suffering because his photography has been put aside. Maybe you can help.

Or you might have written something that doesn't actually explain why you don't do your art as much as you would like to, but that you have thought of once or twice in your artistic life, which might be vaguely related to you and your endeavors. Might…

Maybe you will still want to give this section a read, just in case there is something more.

As I was saying, the oddest thing about this assignment is that there aren't, usually, thousands of different reasons among my students. There are usually only four or five reasons that come up regularly in people's answers. Maybe even only three or four. (We will, of course, explore those stated reasons a little further on.) We all seem to be surprisingly consistent when we struggle to understand or explain, to ourselves and to others, why we don't do our art more than we do. Why we don't do our art as much as we want to. Or as much as we think we should. Or as much as we try to.

Three or four or five answers, *very* consistently. And that doesn't make a lot of sense in my universe.

I'll repeat one last time (in this section anyway…), that we all have utterly unique and personal reasons for who we are, and what and how we do our art. That started me thinking.

Something about the whole process felt familiar. Really familiar. It was something about the *consistency* of the explanations. The consistency of what the problem was in student's worlds, about their ability to do their art. I kept circling the topic, and circling it, but it wouldn't come.

Suddenly I thought about my niece.

I have several nieces, blood and surrogate, so I'm thinking that fact will offer this particular niece some anonymity as I proceed to talk about her personal world in this chapter in my book. I hope so. (Hey, you, niece! No one you don't know will have any idea it's you. Also I hope you will feel okay even if someone does figure out who you are. In any event, I am now going to e-mail you this chapter to get your permission… OK, she responded and granted me permission to write this. Phew!)

Many years ago, this niece was going through some very difficult times, in several different areas of her life. Abuse, drugs, major failures in her education process, relationships, and more. I, of course, committed a great deal of time and energy and effort to helping her. Translation: we talked constantly. In person, on the phone. Endless hours of therapy. She'd talk, she'd cry, she'd get angry, sobbing, panicking – major, heavy, intense conversations, that went on for hours. And hours.

And hours.

Yet almost every single minute of those conversations was about her relationships with guys. The guy she was dating, or living with, or breaking up with, or was interested in, or was rejecting her. Whatever.

Since she's a great deal like her aunt, me, she would analyze it all in intense detail, struggling to understand, explain, work through, and get sane, around each particular relationship problem.

Of course I would work right along with her. Especially because it was all so very real and powerful. She's not a stupid woman. When she had a problem it was tangled and complex, worthy of the struggle. Worthy of the analysis.

Still, the conversations were never quite satisfying. To me, anyway. Like we never quite got where we were trying to get to.

At the end of our conversations, I would always demand one minute to talk about other things. About what was happening at school. Or at work. Or with substances. She'd tell me how things were going with each particular topic, but they generally got pretty short shrift; a brief offhand comment about other events, experiences, and traumas, that were often unbelievably harrowing. Yet her comments were throwaways, really. Please note, the *comment* was the throwaway. Not the topic.

By this point I'd be out of time to talk, or she would. Yet some of the time, a lot of the time, actually, what we were talking about would be momentous. Significant. Serious. We just didn't have any more time. Frustrating and upsetting as it was, we often just had to leave it. And that really was frustrating and upsetting. For me, if not for her!

So every so often, I'd sit back down and continue the conversation anyway. And she would, too. This time she would really lose it. Big crying, or big panic around this new topic. Because it truly was a vital point in her life.

We would struggle. We would grapple. We would talk forever more. And quite frequently, by the end of *that* conversation, we would figure something out. Something important. My niece would feel better. Calmer. Breathing better. Plus I would feel profoundly satisfied. We'd gotten "there!"

It took me a while to figure it all out because she was always absolutely convincing when she was talking about her suffering from her relationships. The problems were real, the analysis complex and intense, reasonable, logical, and smart. As I said, my niece ain't stupid.

That's why it took me a while to understand it. Finally I did. I figured it out. Next, I came up with a name for it. I'm a writer. I like to give things titles…

Boys – later men – were a pit word for my niece.

"Pit Word."

This is how I pictured it.

Imagine a giant hole in the ground. All the dirt dug out of it. The hole is sitting there empty. No soil, no nothing.

Now think about everything in the world that is bothering you. Really think about it. Now put every single thing that you came up with into the hole. Just throw it in. Into the pit. Then think about anything else that's bothering you and throw that all into the hole too, on top of the first batch. Keep throwing. It's a really big hole.

Next step.

Pick a word, an idea, a concept, a topic, an *issue,* that has real meaning for you (though you may not yet, truly, understand what all that meaning is…), a word that has true significance in your universe, and place that word on some kind of sign or placard, which you then put on top of that gigantic pile of wretched things that you've thrown into that hole. That is the official title of the hole.

That word, concept, idea – title – that's the pit word.

My niece, unknowingly, of course, had long ago chosen the word "boy." Thus I labeled it her "Boy Pit." The instant I did that, a great deal of her world became clearer to me.

My niece was a young woman, then in her late teens and later in her twenties, who cared very much about the relationships she had with guys. Nothing very unusual about that. When she started living with her boyfriend, it became one of the most important things in her life. Of course she thought about it a lot. She struggled with their relationship a lot of the time. She worked tremendously hard to understand the relationship, and improve the relationship, and make it work. When they broke up she was devastated. She was sad and upset and panicked and she thought about *that* a lot, as well. It made perfect sense, all along the way, that we discussed boys. Perfect sense.

BUT!

It was not the only thing in her entire life. Boys were not the only thing that mattered. Boys were not the only thing that she cared about, worried about, got hurt by, or panicked about. There were other parts of her life that were profoundly important to her as well. Many other parts.

It's just that, for whatever reason, and I do think safety in some weird way is a big part of that reason, boys were the topic that was acceptable for her to deal with. Boys were okay for her to talk about, think about, struggle with, cry about, and panic about. In some way, her problems with boys were either less traumatic – or more interesting – easier – *something* – for her to grapple with than all the other stuff.

That was why, pretty much no matter what else was happening in her life, we talked about boys. Only. It was her Boy Pit. The man in her life was the obvious, concrete, "go-to" reason, for what she felt were the problems in her life.

To hell with school, or drugs, or family, or work, even her health. Boys were the bottom line. The *official* problem.

That is how the concept of the pit word developed.

That is also how, after a lot of circling around with the responses people in the courses *kept* giving to this particular homework, I finally arrived at the concept for this assignment. Because I realized we artists have pit words, too. (By the way, my niece is a wonderful artist as well...)

I have now come to think of this particular assignment,

"The reason I don't paint, or dance, or write or, or, or, more, or as much as I want to, is because...."

as the **"Pit Word"** assignment.

It's how it's labeled in my course outline, and how it's labeled in my head.

When I give you the homework, part of what I am actually asking is for you to dig around in your psyche for your pit word (or words) about why you don't do your art nearly as much as you want to.

Because I think we all have pit words. They become the more **obvious**, more **concrete**, **"go-to"** explanation, for what is happening to us. We use that word to explain ourselves.

Please listen carefully to the following statement. It's important.

There is always something absolutely true about the pit word. It truly does matter and it truly does mean *something!*

I don't question that for a minute. I don't think you should question it either. My niece really did have boy issues. Relationships mattered to her enormously, and she had a great deal of difficult history to deal with around them. It was not, however, "the whole truth and nothing but the truth." It was only part of the truth.

For this homework, what I'm actually saying here is that I hereby officially, question your answers.

For some of you anyway. For some of your answers.

I am, indeed, a bit skeptical about what you give as your reason or reasons for not doing your art as much as you want to. Tricky this, obviously, as I've never met you, and I haven't seen your answers, so I have to ask for some good faith belief on your side! Also, as you know, this is very unusual for me. My whole point is that you are the official authority on you, and the single entity who most knows what's going on inside yourself. On this one assignment, however, I am going to just plain suspect your answer. At least a little bit.

*   *   *   *

Now on to the actual responses. Finally, eh?

The following are the most common answers people give for the assignment:

"I don't do my art as much as I want to…"

"Because I'm lazy."

"Because I procrastinate."

Plus, most frequently of all: "Because I have no discipline." Or "I'm not disciplined enough."

Sometimes people will also say, "Because I don't have enough time."

This last one is the one answer that I'm most likely to believe is more of a true reason, and less of a pit word. We're all way too busy these days. Going to school, taking care of kids, working, taking care of aging parents. Managing way too much, too much of the time.

Still. There may be an element of "not enough time" that is still a pit word.

There you have it. I believe that most of the time, those answers listed above are actually the word, the label, that you have placed on top of all the other things that you have shoveled into your pit, about all the actual reasons you don't, in fact, get to your art as much as you would like to.

I believe that the pit words – lazy, or undisciplined, or procrastination – whichever (and of course there are many other pit words), are what you have chosen (for any number of reasons), in your head, as your *explanation* of why you don't get to your art. That you repeat it over and over and over to yourself, as to why you are such a bad person, as in, why you are such an insufficient producer of your art.

That pit word is your official explanation.

The one you don't have to question, or think about, or explore. A catch-all phrase that, like all catch-all phrases, has one truth, yet hides a wealth of complexities, subtleties, round-abouts, non-linearities, histories, misdirections, and (probably) "stuff." All of which you then don't have to think about. Or feel about. Or fix.

So, to be extremely blunt about it, I don't buy it. I simply do not buy it. Hardly ever!

Let's take a look at some of those words.

*   *   *   *

Let's start with the word "lazy."

It's a funny word. You'd think it was bad enough to simply call yourself lazy. Yet we often have such heavy-duty add-ons with it. Lazy slob. Lazy-good-for-nothing. Lazy bum. It's really quite a powerful put-down.

Though surprisingly common. Especially given how hard we all seem to work these days.

One night in class, I was especially surprised by a particular student who used the word to describe her inability to do her art. She wasn't the sort who you would guess could even *be* lazy. She seemed like a very active, very focused, high-functioning, type of woman. Almost too high-functioning. A very intense person in both the good ways and the bad. Not, in any way, someone you would think of as lazy.

I decided to investigate.

I asked her to describe the last time she had felt too lazy to do her painting.

She described an evening that she had set aside as her time for "getting to" – her expression, not mine – the abstract landscape that she had been working on, "a little…" (again, her word, not mine). There she was, sitting in her living room with nothing else to do, trying to convince herself to stand up, walk to her easel, pick up her brush, and begin. And she tried. She imagined herself standing up and going there, but she didn't move. She started talking to herself, urging herself to get up and get to it. She was eager to do it. Looking forward to how much fun it would be. Excited that she was actually getting close to finishing it.

Yet she didn't move. No matter how much she encouraged herself.

She insisted in class that she was just being a "lazy bum." Too lazy to get to her art. A "good-for-nothing, really," she said.

I asked her how she felt about not doing it.

"Relieved," she said, "but really, really, really disappointed."

Hmph, I thought. *What's going on here?*

Slowly the late-summer evening, Vancouver sun glowed in through the window of the classroom and I had a thought. (Sun has a tendency to make my brain work.)

I asked, "Can you describe what you were doing before you were sitting in the living room wanting to paint?"

"Uh, putting the kids to bed."

"Two, right? A girl and a boy?"

"Uh-huh."

"And before that?"

"Cleaning up after dinner, I guess."

"Okay," I said, deciding how not to prolong what I was pretty sure was going to be the outcome of this conversation. "Let's go back to the beginning of your day."

"Okay," she said. "What do you want to know?"

"Can you describe your day for us? What did you do that day, before that moment on the couch?"

I'm guessing, you, the reader, are starting to figure this out, just like I did.

This woman, in her early thirties, a single mom, proceeded to describe a day that started with waking up at six a.m., feeding her two kids, getting dressed, getting the kids dressed, making lunch for them, getting everybody out of the house on time, driving them to school, going off to her job as an elementary school teacher, teaching all day, picking up the kids, taking her daughter to her gymnastics class and her son to his hockey game, and on and on and on. The day culminated with dinner, clean up, helping the kids with homework, getting them set up to go to bed, and finally, sitting down on the couch at 9:30 that night.

"Oh," I said.

She looked at me suspiciously.

"All right," I said, trying not to sound tooooo sarcastic. "Do you think you could find another word beside lazy to describe how you were feeling when you were sitting on the couch?"

She grimaced. The rest of the class was trying not to laugh. (Hey, listen. We were a very close group. The teasing was always VERY gentle.)

"Uhhh???"

"Come on," I urged. "You can do it."

"Tired?" she suggested timidly.

"Maybe," I responded. "Just a little bit."

She nodded.

"Exhausted?" I suggested.

She nodded.

"Completely and totally wiped, perhaps?"

My lovely student sat up straighter in her chair, looking way less timid, AND WAY LESS defeated about her artistic endeavors.

"*Completely!*" she blurted. "Why do I have to put myself down like that?"

"It's a question," I answered. "One we need to explore a bit, probably."

"Yes," she agreed.

"At least now you get that it has **ABSOLUTELY NOTHING** to do with you being lazy. While it does have absolutely everything to do with you being exhausted because you are doing a great deal in your life and it's a bloody miracle that you manage to get to your painting at all, ever. I think the last thing you need to do to yourself is put yourself down for that fact. What do *you* think?"

The deep, relieved breath she took was lovely to hear and feel.

So, please, dear person reading these words, pay attention to all of the various reasons you might be accusing yourself of being "lazy." AND get off your own back!!!!

This whole process is hard enough without you putting yourself down for it.

Thanks for listening. We'll talk about more pit words in the next chapter.

IT'S NOT LAZINESS IF YOU'RE COMPLETELY EXHAUSTED!

Take care, all.

Chapter eighteen
Maybe Later

More Pit Words

Procrastination.

"I procrastinate too much."

"I always procrastinate."

"I'm such a procrastinator."

Like "being lazy," procrastination is one of the more common explanations people give as to why they don't do their art. A perfect pit word.

It's much like being lazy, especially emotionally. You don't get to it because you put it off because you're bad. A bad person. A bad artist.

This perception is quite prevalent in our culture as well. Procrastination is bad. Very, very, very bad.

The absolute worst quote I've ever seen on this topic was:

(Though, yes, I agree. It's sort of funny…) Sort of.

"Procrastination is suicide on the installment plan."

Ah, but now, an interesting aspect of this quote is where I saw it…

I was teaching a "mini" creativity course in a Small Business Development Program. I say mini because it was just a few classes in the middle of a full program. The program coordinator was being quite open-minded, suggesting to his students that it was important to access their creativity in this process. Business may be business, but he thought adding creativity into the model would be surprisingly beneficial in the process of creating a start-up firm.

(An interesting note is that I have never received such extraordinarily polarized responses in a course evaluation, as I did on that program. Participants either adored what I was talking about, calling it a "wonderful gust of fresh air," or "the most inspiring part of our program," or they despised it. "Utter waste of time." "Irrelevant." "Pointless.")

Anyway, I'm sitting in the front of the class while the students are writing an assignment, my eyes wandering around the room looking at the posters and signs up on the walls, and there it is. "Procrastination is suicide on the installment plan."

One *has* to get down to *business*, I presume.

Procrastination is bad. Or so the world declares.

If you go online and look for other quotes on procrastination, you will be flooded by the variations on this negative theme. I won't include any more of them here because I don't want to reinforce the perception. We already all believe that procrastination is wrong. Wrong, wrong, wrong.

Just bad.

Well, not so much, maybe.

Go back to the early stages of this book, and of this process of getting in touch with your creativity. Remember the work we did on ways to enhance your creativity. How to stimulate your art. Think about some of them. I asked you to come up with ideas, activities, actions, that would help you get to your art. There were scads of them.

Taking a walk.

Doing a meditation.

Looking at other art.

Playing a computer game.

Staring at the ocean.

Staring at a sand picture as the grains of sand float down the framed glass, for heaven's sake.

What could look more like procrastination than that???

Okay. Maybe sharpening your pencils. (Very funny note to me. Just before starting this writing today, I realized that I had not one single pencil either in my studio or my whole house, and so I just – honestly,

I did – I just sat down at my writing table and sharpened seven pencils to scatter around.)

I did not, really I didn't, realize I had just done that, while I was writing the previous sentence... Ah, the unconscious machine.

The point is that an enormous amount of what we call procrastination is, in reality, our way of preparing ourselves to get into that place where we create our art. Becoming still. Moving away from the noise and busyness of the world. Focusing in. Trying to be receptive so that we can hear our internal voices.

But we have been taught, *so* well, that procrastination is such a bad thing, that when we observe ourselves doing these activities we instantly assume that we are just wasting time. Just putting off what we are supposed to do because... Because we're bad, I guess. Remember what I always have to tell the class about the homework they didn't do? "Observations On Your Fallow Time."

So what really happens?

There we are, sharpening pencils, or reading, or playing computer games, staring out the window, or listening to music. Maybe we're tidying up because we can't stand the idea of working in a mess. We get on the computer and do a defrag. We stare at the canvas and decide our brushes are a hard, sticky mess, so we start doing a proper clean on them. Or we start organizing our sheets of music into some kind of system, instead of actually picking up the guitar.

Hell, maybe a short workout would help. Or going into the kitchen and grabbing a mug of... something. Tea, coffee, beer.

Whatever!

The important thing is, do we actually say, oh, I'm preparing myself to paint? Or, I'm getting myself in the mood to write? Or, heaven forbid, I'm working on enhancing my creative environment so I can do my art?

Of course not! Hardly ever!

What we actually say is, "OMG, I am such a procrastinator." Read "loser," at least when it comes to doing our art... The world has taught us well. If you want to do a task, hop to it. Just do it. If you don't, you're faking it. You're putting it off, so you don't have to do it at all.

But hey!

What if, just maybe, you are actually doing something vital, something you need to do, to leave the regular world, the working world, the taking-care-of-your-house-and-your-family world? What if, what you are really, really doing is getting yourself into the mood to do your art?

Here is one of my favorite quotes on procrastination. One that fits in perfectly with my perception of how we get to our art.

"As a writer, I need an enormous amount of time alone. Writing is ninety percent procrastination: reading magazines, eating cereal out of the box, watching infomercials. It's a matter of doing everything you can to avoid writing, until it is about four in the morning and you reach the point where you have to write." Paul Rudnick[52]

What if that really is what you're doing????

Take care, all.

Chapter nineteen
I Don't Have Any

Okay, the last pit word we're going to talk about is discipline.

As in, "I don't do my art as much as I want to, or as much as I think I should, because I have absolutely no discipline."

None.

Zero.

I am an undisciplined human being. I only know how to waste time. I do everything and anything I am not supposed to do.

An undisciplined loser!

"Discipline" is a funny word. I have a bit of a complicated relationship to it.

The Merriam-Webster dictionary has six definitions. I'm going to list all of them.[53]

*   *   *   *

dis·ci·pline - *noun* \'di-sə-plən\
Definition of *DISCIPLINE*
1. punishment
2. *obsolete*: instruction
3. a field of study
4. training that corrects, molds, or perfects the mental faculties or moral character
5:*a*: control gained by enforcing obedience or order
b: orderly or prescribed conduct or pattern of behavior

c: self-control
6. a rule or system of rules governing conduct or activity

*   *   *   *

Doesn't that just all sound soooooo creative????

Here are some of the synonyms: control, inculcation, indoctrination, limitation, restraint, self-control, subordination, chastisement, and of course, comeuppance…

Even more creative, right????

The first three *antonyms* the dictionary lists for discipline are disinhibition, incontinence, and unconstraint…

Yikes!

When I started writing full time I would spend most of every weekday (I worked hard to maintain weekends as weekends) in my studio, writing. Five days a week, six or seven hours a day.

And pretty much every single person who discovered that was how I was spending my time, would ask me one of two questions. Sometimes both.

One of the questions was, "Don't you get lonely?" or "Don't you get crazy from being alone?" or "How can you stand being alone all the time?"

My answer to this question will come in a different chapter.

The other question, however, is the point of this chapter. "How do you find the discipline?" "How can you be so disciplined?" "Where did you learn to be so disciplined?" "OMG. That must take so much discipline."

All right. The truth of the matter is that for a very long time I hardly registered the question. It just didn't compute. I get that that sounds a bit odd, but it didn't.

So I sort of shrugged it off.

I actually felt a bit dumb, because I simply didn't know how to respond. I couldn't really figure out what they were talking about. It was the oddest thing. I just didn't have any idea how the hell to answer the question.

Until one day, probably the twentieth time I got asked the question, I blurted out, "What are you talking about? What does getting to write all day have to do with discipline?"

In turn, the dear friend who was asking the question this time looked at me like I was nuts, and responded, "You go out there to your studio and sit there for hour after hour, day after day, working on your stories. That has to take so much discipline. I'd run out of there screaming."

"Okay," I said, "This is ridiculous. Let me think for a minute."

This time I spent some energy thinking about the word discipline for the first time ever in relationship to my writing.

I almost immediately realized what the problem was.

"It's got absolutely **NOTHING** to do with *discipline*!!!!" I exclaimed. "**NOTHING!!!** I get to go out to my studio every single day, hour after hour, and **PLAY**. I get to invent worlds, create people, immerse myself in adventures and excitement and fascinating universes. (Or at least they're fascinating to me.) I get to live in my very own fantasy land. Go where I want. Do what I want. Make up stories all day long. How fun is that?

"Hey, wait a minute." I paused and then continued. "I know what *you* did when you were younger, so here's my question for you. How did you find the discipline to go tripping on acid?"

In unison we burst out laughing.

"Seriously," she asked. "That's what it feels like to you?"

"Seriously, " I answered. "That's what it feels like to me.

"It has absolutely never occurred to me that what I'm doing requires discipline. I'm always just so happy I get to go out there and do it.

"I mean, sometimes I'm miserable, like when it doesn't come, or when I hate how it sounds, or when it feels like the stupidest idea in the whole world. At least I get to keep doing it – and making it better. It sure as hell doesn't feel like discipline!"

We both thought that was fabulously interesting.

Now let me ask you. I mean really.

Think of something you love to do when you have the time, the money, or the opportunity. Something you really have fun doing.

You grab the time whenever you can to do it. Or you go on some huge vacation to do it as much as possible: scuba diving, hiking, cycling, wandering around Europe or New York, visiting every museum and art gallery you can, or shopping non-stop at every cool boutique or gear store. Maybe your passion is skiing or kayaking. Whatever.

Now ask yourself. How much discipline does it take to do it?

Huh? Once more.

Huh?

If it's something you love or feel passionate about, doing it is simply not about discipline.

That's my point.

*   *   *   *

However it's not the only point.

I have, over time, come to consider the true depth of the concept of discipline. Okay, yes. It's a bit more complicated than what I've presented here. I even ended up writing a column about it during the years I was a newspaper columnist. I'm including it here.

Take a look at the part that does validate the useful aspect of the concept of discipline, and then we'll continue exploring the use of the word in the context of using discipline as a pit word.

*   *   *   *

Life and Stuff – By Darylynn Starr Rank

Art. Creativity. We have the urge to write, or paint, or weave, or dance, or make something beautiful. Something! Beautiful! And we feel like we can't. Or we don't know how. We're probably afraid of it. And we can't seem to make ourselves get down to it anyway.

And we certainly don't know why that is.

Sometimes I think I'll never really "get it' – art and creativity. I write columns about it. Teach courses. I see clients. I talk about it endlessly with my husband, who's a photographer. I think about it *every* time I sit down to write a piece of fiction.

But still I keep searching to understand. To figure it out. To explain how it works.

You see, I was trained as a social scientist. The scientific method was all-important. Research, research, research. Isolate the variables. Manipulate them. Analyze the evidence. And (or so the idea goes) you come up with an answer. Maybe only a partial one, but an answer that is empirically supported with the appropriate data.

Hmmm.

In creativity… Maybe not.

The fact is, the *one* thing I've figured out for sure, is that creativity is magic…

It happens when I'm sitting in my little rowing boat in the middle of the ocean – a thought, a hint, a breath of an idea. Or when I'm playing with a dog or a cat. Or a piece of string. Maybe I'm talking to my niece on the telephone. Sometimes it even happens when I've been sitting at my computer for five hours working hard at it, waiting for the inspiration to arrive. *Five* hours of nothing. Then "bang!" it comes.

Would it not have arrived if I hadn't been out in the middle of the ocean? Or if I'd shunned my little niece? What if I'd stayed completely away from my computer?

I don't know the answer. But I keep wondering.

One of the ongoing debates in my own world and in my classes revolves around this concept of magic vs. discipline. Free floating inspiration vs. structure and planning. Bolt out of the blue vs. plodding pedestrianism.

One of the most *frequent* comments I hear from students is, "I'm just not disciplined enough." Or (from those making New Year's resolutions) "I need to be more disciplined."

I always react badly. "It's not discipline," I yearn to whisper. "It's got nothing to do with discipline!" I want to yell. And it's true. It's the magic, remember? But deep inside me I know it's not the *whole* truth. Thus I'm always struggling with my conflicting views of how we do our art.

So the other day I was swimming the backstroke in an indoor pool, staring at the sky through the skylight. Thinking about discipline. And planning. The structured part of doing art.

And suddenly – magic! My mind filled with the image of a rocket ship at Cape Canaveral, sitting securely on its gantry (that huge and intricate platform structure designed and built with extraordinary care, planning, and discipline). Suddenly, the rocket takes off, roaring into the heavens with an enormous explosion, riding a brilliant tail of fire and smoke, soaring out into the universe. While down below the poor gantry, the foundation from which this extraordinary flight takes wing, burns to smithereens and disintegrates into smoldering embers.

Ah, the magic of creativity; the struggle, the work, the studying, the grappling, the planning, the learning to create – now invisible. All eyes are on the rocket ship.

Take care, all.

*   *   *   *

There you go. I am conflicted about the concept of discipline. Though not very.

Doing art is not primarily about discipline. I just don't buy it. Or perhaps a better way to say it is: not doing your art probably isn't really about not having discipline.

I'm guessing discipline, the way most people use it in their home-work, is a pit word. I'm also guessing that the pit is filled with all the varied and sundry *real reasons* you don't do your art as much as you want to, or think you should, or wish you could. This may include some actual activities that do require discipline, but not all.

Here's my question. Or maybe simply another one of my "theories."

How much discipline has it been taking you to "DO" this book? As you know, from the very start I have been pleading with you to *do* the book. Not simply read it.

Now, I deeply hope that you are enjoying the process!!! I deeply hope that it is providing you with a wonderful, glorious, fun!!! journey of discovery!

I'm also pretty sure, however, that it has been *somewhat* difficult to do it.

Well, I believe that this is a place where you *are* demonstrating discipline. I believe you are working very hard to explore the things that get in your way. The multitude and myriad of "stuff" that has to be understood and overcome and fought with, and delved through, so frequently when we sit down to our art.

Doing this, I obviously believe, is what is needed in order to give yourself the space and the time and the freedom that allow you to free up your mind, your emotions, and your soul, in order to get to your art.

Still, it's not the discipline to actually *do* your art.

It's the discipline that it takes to finally arrive in that still, magical, receptive, glorious place, where you finally get to play!

*   *   *   *

Official summary of the three pit words we've discussed:

I do believe that sometimes you don't do your art as much as you want to because you're tired, not because you're lazy.

I do believe that sometimes you don't do your art as much as you want to because you mistake putting yourself into a receptive, creative state for procrastination; then you proceed to give up.

Finally, I do believe, that you have a whole/hole lot of real, genuine, important, reasons that interfere with you getting to your art, but that you *interpret* as lack of discipline. (Obviously we've already discussed many of those reasons throughout this book. But I'm sure there are more...)

It's an endless spiraling process. Figuring out how to get to your art. Figuring out what's getting in your way.

NOTE: BTW. I just spent two hours making airplane reservations for my niece (actually the reservations are for the niece who made me invent the concept of the boy pit... Hmmm. How interesting.), playing solitaire, hearts, spades, and Freecell on my laptop, doing some admin work, and cuddling my cat, instead of doing the writing I had set as this morning's activity. I officially got annoyed at myself for procrastinating, being incredibly lazy, and seriously lacking discipline.

In retrospect, I'm pretty sure I didn't want to get to my writing because I don't know what I'm going to write about for the next chapter, and I knew I was almost at the end of this one...

Did I mention "endless spiral???"

*   *   *   *

Homework Assignment

Read through your last assignment one more time: "The reason I don't paint, or dance, or write (or, or, or) more, or as much as I want to, is because..."

Okay, choose one of the reasons you gave as your answer. I'd like you to make a guess as to which one of the reasons looks most like a pit word to you.

(Please note: if one of your words is "lazy," or "procrastination," or "undisciplined," I hope you will choose that word for this assignment. If you want, you can choose another reason as well, and do the assignment twice, or three times. Whatever you want. But do write about one of those three words if you used it.)

The actual assignment is (and I do really hate the word I'm about to use, but for this assignment it does actually work): Deconstruct that word or that reason. Dig into it. Delve inside it. What's going on in your head when you're feeling undisciplined? What are you thinking about when you call yourself lazy? What are you feeling? If you're procrastinating, what kind of dialogue are you having with yourself about it? Then dig deeper. Even deeper.

Dig. And dig. And dig some more.

BUT: Make the assumption that you are absolutely not a lazy person! So why are you accusing yourself of being lazy?
Declare to yourself that you do have discipline in all sorts of areas of your life. School, or work, or exercise, staying in contact with the people who matter to you, cleaning your house. Find an area where you do feel disciplined (there's probably *something*), and figure out what's different about doing your art.

Think about how often you don't procrastinate at all.

Then explore what's happening when you do.

That's your Homework Assignment.

Good luck.

Take care, all.

*   *   *   *

How did it go?

Bottom line. Look, observe, pay attention to the infinite ways you trash yourself around not doing your art. I believe the more you understand what is really happening with it, the more you'll do your art.

Pretty simple, eh?

Not so much. No. Not even a little bit.

But it really may help!

Take care, all.

Chapter twenty
Shhhhhhhhhh

What we are going to do in this chapter is talk about the things we are not supposed to talk about...

No, I don't mean sex, religion, and politics. That's the classic version, right?

It is possible that what you are not supposed to talk about does include sex, religion or politics, but that's not where I'm heading.

Instead, we are going to explore the inside of your being and find out what lives there concerning the topic of what you are not supposed to talk about.

But first things first. Let us proceed with an In Class Exercise.

*　　*　　*　　*

Darylynn Starr Rank

In Class Exercise

This one is a brainstorming session. Please use a whiteboard, use the whiteboard in this book, or imagine your notebook is a whiteboard. I want you to write down **whatever** comes to you.

The topic is:

What are the words, phrases, thoughts, images, or memories that come to you when I ask you to think about the things that stay in your head that keep you quiet?

I am not asking you about the topics you're not supposed to talk about. Or the secrets you're supposed to keep. Or anything at all about the *content* of what you are not supposed to talk about.

I am asking you to think about how you were told, or instructed, or urged, or trained, or encouraged, or chastised, or taught, or punished, to keep your mouth shut.

Words, phrases, gestures, expressions, behaviors, whatever. The things that made you understand that you were supposed to keep quiet!

Take really good care on this one.

If nothing comes, give it a minute.

If something comes, write it down, but then still take a few more minutes. See what else comes.

This one can take time to do the delving.

The information may come to you slowly, and in jerks and spurts.

Then when you're finished, turn the page.

*   *   *   *

Whiteboard
How you were taught to NOT talk about something.
Write down anything, *anything* that comes to you.

*   *   *   *

Did you remember?

Could you hear the words?

See the facial expressions?

It's astonishing what comes up in these brainstorming sessions. For me, as well as for my students. Things I haven't thought about in… forever. Things I had no idea were there. That I hadn't thought about since I was a little girl. Or a teenager. Or even during university.

How I was taught to shut up.

An interesting aspect of this particular assignment is that it is one of the more "action/reaction" topics. By that I mean that students do their own assignments, then we put the answers on the blackboard in class, and then as we do that, almost everyone gets reminded of something else from their *own* childhoods.

"Oh, yeah," they'll say when someone gives an item for the board. "That's what my mother would say, too. I forgot." Or "Right. My father's version of that one was…" "*My* teacher would tell us to…"

This brainstorming session probably takes longer than any other brainstorming we do. It's such an intrinsic, embedded, even un-thought about, topic.

The reason I wished you extra care with this one is that the range of instructions and the range of silences is, to put it simply, extreme. In some families, in some childhoods, it's there in some relatively normal context. It's still there, though. In other childhoods, it's out-right frightening.

We'll talk more about this. Significantly more. I just wanted to mention it now for those of you are having a heavy reaction to this assignment. Of course you are!

Even for those of you who come from the more *normal* version, this may be a bit disturbing to think about.

So, everyone, please keep taking care the best way you can.

*　　　*　　　*　　　*

Here are some of the answers my students and I have come up with over the years. I'm grouping the responses a bit, by type of comment, or some kind of similarity, so I can talk about them more easily afterwards.

*   *   *   *

Whiteboard
What keeps you quiet

Shhhhh.

Be quiet.   Hush up.   Shush.   Stifle it!   Silence!
Stop chattering .
Hold your tongue.   Keep your trap shut.   Stop talking.
Shut up!
Don't wash your dirty laundry in public!
This is family business.   You don't talk about that
outside the family.
If you don't have something nice to say, don't say
anything at all.
Nice girls don't talk about that kind of thing.
Mind your own business
No comments from the peanut gallery.
Keep your opinions to yourself.
You don't know what you're talking about.
You're wet behind the ears.
Father knows best...
You need to learn to suffer in silence.

Remember who you are, darling!   Don't be indiscreet.

Raised voice.   Yelling.   Screaming.

Stop being so emotional.   Boo-hoo.

Stop being so melodramatic.   Stop crying.

Stop crying or I'll give you something to cry about.

Don't say that. Don't even think that!

Stop making things up.

Stop lying.

Stop complaining.

Too much sharing. Way too much.

And now NON-VERBAL

The look!

Index finger to lips.

Grimace.

Head shaking.

Thumb pointing down.

Hands over ears.

The glare.

Tightened lips.

The gasp.
The held breath.
The mouthed "NO."
The sneer.
Closed eyes.
Violins playing.
Fingers to cheek mocking tears.
The fist.
Turning their back.
Walking out of the room.
The raised hand.
The pinch.
The arm grab.
The slap.
The punch.
Ultimately, the beating.

*   *   *   *

Phew…

Hey, that's just a sample. There are way more possibilities. Did you come up with others?

Okay, let's take a look.

The first general topic:

Obviously, most of us have been told to keep quiet at some point or another. At home, at school. Somewhere. Somehow. Probably way more than once or twice. Probably, some of the time with really good reason. For example, you're a kid and you're being too noisy.

But that's not what we're talking about.

Shutting kids up is all too frequent. For all sorts of "not okay" reasons. Even if we don't remember the words, we remember the feelings. And we learn. We learn to shut up.

So: let's look at topics.

There is the whole concept of *"family business."* Not talking about family things outside the family. This usually means the bad things. Very few of us were told not to say, "Hey, my mom won an award for selling the most properties." Or, "My father just ran a marathon." The point is, you're told to keep your mouth shut about anything that's gone wrong. Anything that's upsetting, or bad, or shameful, or wrong that's happened at home. This is for small things, and big things. From silly to serious. It could be anything. You're just not supposed to talk about it outside the house.

I was married for about ten years before I realized something I'd been taught since I was little. I was not supposed to talk about my husband. To anybody. About anything bad. It was supposed to stay strictly between him and me. Husband and wife. There's even legal privilege involved. I can't be compelled to testify about anything he ever told me.

I personally think it's a bloody miracle our marriage survived. How can you live with someone for ten years and never complain about them to anybody else? Crazy... It was, however, the rule. It would have been completely disloyal of me to talk about him.

Another topic. In general, if you're a girl, you have to be nice. Only say nice things. Not be nasty, or mean, or aggressive. Hell, one of the great images of being a good female is to "suffer in silence!"

If you're a boy you'd better not ever be caught crying. Don't cry!!!! Don't be emotional. Don't be a baby.

"Minding your own business" is another great one. Of course figuring out where the line is, is usually pretty tricky. It's your home, your family, it's probably being talked about in front of you, but you'd better not give your opinion. How can you have an opinion, anyway? You're just a kid. Who knows nothing...

"*Don't complain*" is also a big one in all sorts of ways. Heaven forbid you're unhappy about something, or worse; emotional. That continues throughout your life. You're simply supposed to be positive. Happy. A good sport. And on and on and on.

Of course, there's the "*lying*" accusation. We know you're never supposed to lie. Even if you are not lying, the accusation is a quick and effective way to shut you up.

The yelling and screaming gets particularly memorable. Getting yelled at and getting in serious trouble for talking when you're not supposed to.

Obviously, there's a myriad of ways you are verbally told to be silent. About a myriad of subjects.

There are all the non-verbal cues as well.

Sooooo many students used the phrase, "the look." Usually with an exclamation point, or a shudder. A wince, or gritted teeth. Apparently it's a very effective way of shutting up kids, and even adults. Or shutting them down… The power of "the look" seems to stay with us forever.

A variety of gestures teaches us to be very vigilant. Watch for the cues. Figure out when you're speaking out of turn.

Mockery seems to work especially well non-verbally, which I'd never considered before doing this exercise. The violins, the finger drawing the tears, rocking the pathetic baby – you, of course.

Sadly, it can be worse than that, depending on the family you're coming from. It becomes physical abuse. Or what some people call "discipline."

All right. There you go. A quick review of all the various ways you were told as a child to shut up.

Especially at home.

There are also numerous lovely memories students have of school silencing. A lot of the work we did around school experiences related in some way or another to keeping quiet. Being yelled at, of course, in front of the whole class is very effective. *Very* memorable. Being told to stay after class for "talking too much" or saying the wrong thing. Stand in the corner. Rulers on knuckles were much too common. Detention. Being sent to the principal's office.

All in the service of making you be silent.

Please tell me I don't have to repeat the thought that sometimes people need to be quiet. For all sorts of excellent reasons. But it's just not the point here.

The point here, in the context of this book, in the context of this process you are grappling with, is that you are an artist! Art is *about* expression. Expressing yourself in whatever medium you want to express yourself. Pouring yourself into the written word, or the painted canvas. The carved wood, the sculpted clay, the lyrics, the musical chords, the physical movement of your body in dance. The joking of the comedian.

Expressing yourself. Revealing yourself. Fully, freely, flowingly.

Yet the highest likelihood is that you were told, in numerous ways, in multiple settings, and in endless contexts, to stay silent. To NOT express yourself.

Well, to put it as simply as possible, for an artist (for anyone actually, but we are focusing here) having a vibrant set of voices and images in your head telling you to be quiet is profoundly not helpful. To repeat:

HAVING A VIBRANT SET OF VOICES AND IMAGES IN YOUR HEAD TELLING YOU TO BE QUIET IS PROFOUNDLY NOT HELPFUL FOR AN ARTIST!!!

Take care, all.

(Don't worry. We're not finished with this topic.)

Chapter twenty-one

No!

In Class Exercise

This one is another brainstorming session. Please use a whiteboard, use the whiteboard in this book, or imagine your notebook is a whiteboard. I want you to write down ***whatever*** comes to you.

I want you to imagine the following:

What happens when I _do_ break the silence?

To answer this, I'd like you to think about how you feel when you talk about something you're not supposed to talk about. What you think about. What you say to yourself. What happens or what do you think is going to happen, when you break a silence and express something you're not supposed to express?

*   *   *   *

Remember to keep going even after you think you're finished. A lot of the time in brainstorming, the silence of having nothing else to say, is just a pause...

*   *   *   *

Whiteboard
What happens when I do break the silence?
Write down anything, *anything* that comes to you.

Then when you're finished, turn the page.

*   *   *   *

How'd that go? Were you surprised? I was when I did it.

I kept delving and delving and delving and I couldn't quite believe all the different things I felt and thought and experienced when I "spoke out." As well as all of the things I was afraid would happen.

When I started using this process in my courses, again I couldn't quite believe all the different things that everyone else came out with.

Here's a sample of the responses.

*   *   *   *

Whiteboard
What happens when you do break the silence?
Write down anything, *anything* that comes to you.

I feel guilty.

Apologetic. Immature.

I feel like I'm betraying people.

I feel mean. Nasty. Cruel. Insensitive. Not nice.

Like I'm being a shit disturber.

I feel like I'm being too sensitive. Too emotional.

Making things too complicated.

I feel like I'm being irrational.

I feel self-doubt about what I'm saying.

I feel like I'm making it up.   I feel like I'm wrong.

Like I'm lying.

Like I'm being irrational.

I feel like I've got a big mouth.   That I can't keep
my mouth shut.

I feel like I'm always complaining.   Or whining.

I should be nicer.

I need to back off.
I need to soften what I just said.
Or
I need to toughen up!
I feel out of control.
"What the hell did I just do?
I've crossed a line.
I feel tremendous regret.
Embarrassed.
Ashamed!
I feel nervous.   Anxious.   Afraid.
I'm terrified.
I'm having a panic attack.
I'm sick to my stomach, can't catch my breath, my hands are shaking.
And again, what the hell did I just do???
They're not going to like me anymore.
They're going to disapprove of me.

> *They're going to hate me.*
>
> *What's going to happen now?*
>
> *I'm going to pay for this.   How am I going to end up paying for this?*
>
> *What's going to happen to...?*
>
> *How am I going to get punished?*
>
> *(finally, and perhaps most terrifyingly)*
>
> *What are they going to do to me?*

*   *   *   *

Wow! A lot of the time, breaking the silence is a really big deal – a huge deal – a lot of the time.

And when you do break the silence, you pay. Most of us do, anyway. In one way or another. Though not necessarily from the outside world at all! It's what happens inside us that's often the big problem. It's how we feel about doing it that's often the hardest part.

Or, on the other hand, knowing you're going to have to pay keeps us from breaking the silence in the first place. Shuts us up very effectively.

Remember the whole thing about art and expression. Not so good to have to keep quiet!

Let's start at the top of the list.

Guilt is probably the single most common reaction we have when we talk about the things we are not supposed to talk about. In whatever medium you choose to talk about it... The guilts themselves are myriad.

Guilt that you're doing something you're not supposed to do, that you are not a nice person. That you're being a bad person, being mean, that you are just stirring up trouble. Guilt that you're hurting someone. (Especially someone you care about.) Guilt that you're betraying people, exposing them, alienating them. Often, someone in your family. This last one can be a pretty horrible feeling. The one where you're betraying people you love. This one can keep you silent forever.

Questioning ourselves about what we are "really" saying is often another significant reaction when talking about something that is *supposed* to be a secret.

We can do the milder version of self-questioning. Accusing ourselves of being too sensitive, too emotional, making things too complicated. You begin to think that what you're talking about is not really what you know, or what actually happened. The truth must be much lower key. You must be exaggerating, you're just making a mountain out of a molehill.

The more severe version of this self-questioning is when you think you're plain and simple *lying*. Making it up, pretending, remembering incorrectly. Inventing it. This one goes all the way up to feeling that what you're actually doing is what they now call… "False Memory Syndrome."

These kinds of self-doubts are all common reactions to talking about the things you're supposed to keep quiet about.

Accusing oneself of talking too much is another real favorite. Big mouth. Loud mouth. Can't keep my mouth shut. "I'm completely out of control!!!"

The bottom line for me, however, and what I believe is the worst of all of these reactions, is the emotional impact; the nervousness, the anxiety, the fear. Even panic attacks. Pure terror in many cases. And the terror goes along with the potential "punishment." **What's going to happen to me if I tell?** If it's something so important, or so terrible, or so punishing that you've kept quiet about it your whole life, chances are your internal answer to that question will be devastating.

*   *   *   *

A personal struggle of mine with the topic of silencing is that I was taught from when I was very little *never* to write anything bad down on paper. The warning was pervasive. The horror I was warned about was that, once it was down on paper, you could never make it go away. You could never take it back.

Not so good for a writer...........

This particular warning has stuck with me for years and even now affects me when I try to write anything at all. My diary when I was little. My journal as I grew up. Letters were always start-and-stop affairs. Should I say that, or that? Papers in school. Oh, maybe I shouldn't discuss that. It might be revealing too much about who I am. It was certainly a major part of my seventeen years of writing silence. I still struggle with it today. I often check and recheck e-mails I'm about to send, then go back and recheck them, even *after* I've sent them. "OMG. Did I say it okay???"

You should (No, you shouldn't!!!) spend five minutes inside my head as I write this book, wondering every step of the way what to reveal and what to keep my fingers off the keyboard about...

Breaking the silence is obviously a major issue in my work as a therapist. Virtually every client I've ever worked with struggles with silences.

It is also a major issue for all of us artists.

It gets in the way. It interferes with our art. It shuts us down. It makes us tentative and careful. Instead of pouring our internal being into our art, we stumble. Start and stop. Move sideways.

I am not suggesting, not even for an instant, that the proper way to be an artist is to tell all there is to tell. I'm not even faintly suggesting that there is something wrong with your art if you don't express yourself on any and every particular topic. Or that it is bad to keep some things – many things – private!

The essential point is that you need to be able to keep silent about the things you **want** to keep silent about. As long as you are making a choice about that silence. That all-important word. Choice.

Private is precious. Private is your right. Your responsibility to yourself. Hell, freedom of speech means exactly that. Freedom...

To pick and choose what you want to express is critical. To pick and choose what you don't want to express is critical. But you do need to be able to pick and choose.

In order to choose, you need to know what is going on in the back of your being. You need to be able to hear the voices that are trying to tell you what to choose, and especially what not to choose. That are not allowing you any actual choice at all.

Last part of the discussion.

Silencing can happen at any stage in your process.

It can stop you from even thinking about doing your art. It might have made it more difficult for you to pull this book off the shelves in the bookstore, or hit the keys to order it online.

An important point about this: you are not a stupid person.

Somewhere inside you, you understand that doing art means expressing yourself. Therefore, you could easily sabotage that expression, at any step along the way, if you have a giant "shhhhhh" running around inside you. If there's a terrible punishment awaiting you. It's basic self-protection, self-preservation. You're trying, quite consciously or unconsciously, to keep yourself safe.

When you're doing your art, those silencing mechanisms can shut you up entirely. Or shut you down even more.

Often if you try and paint an uncomplimentary image from your childhood that is supposed to be kept a secret. Or if you try and write a story about something bad about a member of your family.

You'll find yourself getting lazy, I bet. Or procrastinating… Certainly you will lack any and all discipline.

If you do manage to allow yourself to express something difficult with your art, you might hit the wall when it comes to allowing someone else to see it.

I was completely flabbergasted to discover where a piece of my own silencing was taking place.

I'd finished writing a novel that was essentially about someone who had spent their childhood being abused. It was a novel. Did I mention that? It was fiction. It looked *nothing* like my own childhood, *nothing*. Hell, it wasn't even mostly about a child. Or a female! It was about a grown-up bad guy. It was a thriller.

But of course it was about my own childhood…

Still, I wrote the whole thing without hesitation. It was one of the fastest pieces of writing I'd ever done. I edited it. Had my husband edit it. Took some of his suggestions, rejected others. I packed it up, addressed it to my agent in New York, called the courier, answered the door when he arrived, and handed him the manuscript. Smiled, thanked him, and closed the door.

Then I stood in the entryway of my house and I started trembling. I started sweating and gasping for air. My heart was racing. I proceeded to do the only thing that seemed available for me to do. I sat down on the floor, paralyzed.

Until I finally I burst out crying. Sobbing, in fact. I was completely panic-stricken.

It actually took me several days to figure out that the book about *my childhood* was heading to my agent in Manhattan. My mother was in Manhattan. My mother who I hadn't seen in fifteen years. Was in Manhattan.

And in that novel, I had broken the silence…

$*$ $*$ $*$ $*$

The voices are there. The training is powerful. I'm hoping you will work at becoming aware of them.

Maybe work at taking back your voice.

$*$ $*$ $*$ $*$

Homework Assignment

I'd like you to do one of two things. Your *choice*, of course.

1. Explore the reasons for talking about the topics, subjects, people, or moments that you are not supposed to talk about.

Or

2. Explore the reasons that it is right and proper for you not to talk about them.

Most importantly, be kind and gentle and caring with yourself.

*   *   *   *

Take care, all.

*   *   *   *

How was that?

What I want to say about the previous Homework Assignment is to be aware. Again, you're not a child any more. I have absolutely no way of knowing whether it is good for you to keep the silence, or if a terrible thing was done to you to shut you up about something that has absolutely no business being silenced.

There may come a time when you are ready to actually break a silence that you have kept for a very long time. To write, or talk, or paint, or sing about one of those areas, topics, subjects…

When you're ready to do that make sure you get the support you need. Get some help. Talk to someone. Partners, friends, therapists. Spend some time with your journal. Go outside and wander around somewhere beautiful.

Sometimes, most importantly for me, I utter the magic words:

"This is not then.

"I am not a helpless child. Or teenager. Or adult in danger. Those particular people, whoever they are, probably cannot hurt me very much anymore. I am a grownup with resources. I really truly probably can take care of myself a lot. This is not then."

Or it may be important for it to be your turn to *decide* to continue to keep the silence. Knowingly. There are all sorts of perfectly sensible reasons for not talking about something.

As long as you're keeping the silence knowingly and through choice, the chances are your art won't be shut down. As long as you're breaking the silence knowingly and through choice, the chances are your art won't be shut down. The key is, do it knowingly.

If you ain't driving it, it's driving you.

When it is driving you, there is absolutely no choice in that scenario…

One more time, be kind and gentle and caring to yourself. That is the best thing you can do for your art.

IF YOU AIN'T DRIVING IT, IT'S DRIVING YOU.

Take care, all.

Chapter twenty-two
Hey! It Really is!

Today's topic is simple:

Art is hard.

It's really, really hard. Or it can be...

Personal story.

When I first, after all those years of silence, started writing fiction again, I went home to Miami Beach for a visit. During the visit I went out for lunch with my closest friend from junior high school. As teenagers we had both been writers. We were in a special creative writing course. We talked about it all the time. She's the one I'd made up stories with in the summertime, lying on the beach, staring at the Caribbean-colored water. Imagining what was in that water.

As adults both of us had stopped writing. At least we had both stopped writing fiction. (She was a public relations writer for a major company.)

The point is my friend was fascinated that, after all those years, I had gone back to it. I, of course, was pretty fascinated by it, too. It was really exciting to talk to her about it. To examine virtually our entire teenagehood as blossoming novelists, and to explore what had happened. We'd started talking about writing at thirteen years old.

Then she asked me a really intriguing question.

"What is it like? What does it feel like, doing it all the time?"

Now, that was a question. The most interesting. The most startling. Yet I had no idea how to answer her.

Everything sounded stupid. Wrong. Inaccurate. Even simplistic.

I kept thinking about it.

Please note, very importantly, here I am not discussing the agony of starting to write in my journal after seventeen years of silence. I am not talking about anything and everything that came up for me when I started putting words down on paper after all that time. I am NOT talking about all the myriad topics that we have been working on throughout this book.

In this case, I am talking about what I experienced when I *finally, finally,* FINALLY arrived at the point where I was actually and actively writing fiction again from my profoundly, though relatively speaking (it's never linear or binary…), "cleared out" inner universe…

I simply kept thinking about the word difficult. Or hard. But I couldn't answer it that way. And I couldn't understand why.

Finally I realized that the major problem I was having in answering her question was the following: Until the moment I'd returned to writing fiction, what the word and idea of "difficult" meant to *me,* was traumatic. It was disturbing and upsetting, sad, terrifying, and miserable. It was my childhood at the time. Or my childhood, as I struggled to deal with it as an adult. This was what constituted the word, the concept, and the nature of "difficult" in my life. Of the word "hard."

Almost always.

Yet that traumatic, upsetting, terrifying, miserable word, "difficult," didn't describe any of the feelings I now had around writing. At all. Writing wasn't traumatic, wasn't hard. It wasn't brutal or ugly, difficult. It wasn't terrifying, hard.

It was just *hard* hard. Simply hard. And for the longest time I couldn't figure out what the hell I meant by that. (Please note: the very straightforward question got stupider and stupider in my mind the longer I struggled to come up with an answer. And once more, please note: "I'm sorry, dear friend. It wasn't your fault I started hating you for asking me the question!")

I struggled for quite a long time with the difference between traumatic and hard. Until finally I figured it out.

Hard, in the context of writing, just meant "toil." It might be very difficult "toil." But not emotionally destructive. Not spiritually devastating.

It was hard work. Difficult work. It was difficult, and exhausting, and hard to get to. It was a struggle. A real struggle. One of the hardest and most straightforward struggles I'd ever engaged in.

After that realization, the fascinating realization of the difference between *traumatic* hard and *difficult* hard, I finally came up with a description of what writing was like for me. Here's the description I came up with.

Imagine you're standing in your kitchen, at your dishwasher – if you have one – which isn't working. There's an enormous pile of dinner plates standing on the floor and reaching all the way up to the ceiling. You have to take care of it.

You reach up to the very top of the pile and you pull down a plate. You turn on the faucet, pick up a sponge, spritz a drop of liquid soap on to the sponge, wet the top of the plate, sponge off the dirt on the top of the plate, rinse the top of the plate. Then you turn the plate over, wet the bottom of the plate, sponge off the dirt on the bottom of the plate, then rinse the bottom of the plate. You turn off the water, put down the sponge, pick up the dishtowel from the towel rack, dry the top of the plate, then turn it over and dry the bottom of the plate, put the dishtowel back on its rack, reach up to the cupboard and open the door, put the plate in the cupboard, and close the cupboard door. Phew.

Then you reach up to the top of the enormous pile of plates and pull down the next one...

And the next one.

And the next one.

And the next one.

That's how I described how hard it was to write a novel. One word at a time, remember?

I've got wonderful quotes on the topic. I think some of the quotes on how hard it is to do art are some of the best comments artists have made.

It's been reassuring to me for me see how many of us are the same. I hope it's reassuring for you.

Take a look.

*   *   *   *

"You don't know what it is to stay a whole day with your head in your hands trying to squeeze your unfortunate brain so as to find a word." Gustave Flaubert, in a letter to George Sand[54]

"Writing is easy: All you do is sit staring at a blank sheet of paper until the drops of blood form on your forehead." Gene Fowler[55]

"When I face the desolate impossibility of writing 500 pages, a sick sense of failure falls on me, and I know I can never do it. Then gradually, I write one page and then another. One day's works is all I can permit myself to contemplate... " John Steinbeck[56]

"Writing is the hardest way of earning a living with the possible exception of wrestling alligators." Olin Miller[57]

"The best part about writing is stopping." Colin Walters[58]

"The writer's way is rough and lonely and who would choose it while there are vacancies in more gracious professions, such as, say, cleaning ferryboats?" Dorothy Parker[59]

"Writing is so difficult that I often feel that writers, having had their hell on earth, will escape all punishment thereafter." Jessamyn West[60]

Now my personal favorite:
"A blank page is God's way of showing you how hard it is to be God."
G.K. Chesterton[61]

*   *   *   *

I honestly believe that during the process of writing this chapter, I have been feeling – or sponging up, maybe – exactly how hard writing is. Seriously, silly as it sounds, I have fought coming into my studio, sitting down, and writing this section.

It's pretty funny, really. It's as if I have to remind myself just how hard writing can be, so I'm not just lecturing you... It feels very difficult to write this particular chapter.

So what else do I have to say about how hard it is to do art?

What else can I say after Steinbeck, Flaubert, and Jessamyn West? Especially after Chesterton's lovely framing?

First of all I can say that, if Steinbeck and Flaubert, West, and Chesterton, as well as pretty much every other artist on the planet, think it's really hard at least some of the time, that probably means it is a perfectly normal thing to feel. Which means there is absolutely nothing wrong with you or your art for feeling that way!

It is often hard. It's sometimes very difficult. Or it can be.

So what else are you going to get out of hearing me, and hearing those great artists tell you how difficult it is to do your art? How inevitably it is going to be difficult? What? You get to be discouraged? Even more afraid than you have been? Exhausted before you even begin? Exhausted after you've finally managed to begin and were hoping things would get easier?

Ah, okay. That's the next most critical point worth mentioning about how hard it can be to do art.

My pile of dishes did, indeed, get smaller.

It didn't stay *that* hard *all* the time. The pile of dishes shrank, and the process of cleaning each plate got easier. A lot of the time.

No, it wasn't linear. Of course it wasn't linear. Nothing seems to be linear in art.

Writing would get easier and easier, and then whoosh, it would take thirty minutes to wash one stubborn plate. A lot of the time I'd walk into the kitchen and the bloody pile would be touching the ceiling, all over again. And every so often I'd struggle like a crazy person to force myself into my studio, onto my chair, fingers to the keyboard. (Like when I'm writing a chapter about how hard it is to do art…), ALL OVER AGAIN!!!

Still, some of the time, a lot of the time, it *would* be easier.

Some of the time the words will flow. Some of the time, the words simply float onto the paper, pour forth, swim, gush, glide on the breath I'm breathing out.

Breathing out. My favorite kind of writing. The words come on a breath, and I write and write and write as long as the breath is suspended in the air. Seconds, minutes, hours, the words flow out on that breath, until the breath is done.

Then I'm finished. Done. For the moment. The day. The week.

Now one more comment on art being hard (or not…).

Back to a thought I mentioned earlier.

Remember when I was joking with my friend about discipline, and I asked her how much discipline it had taken when she was a kid (think nineteen or twenty-ish) to take LSD? To go tripping on acid?

The acid analogy didn't occur to me by chance. It happened one day a year or two after I got back to my writing.

First a bit of background.

When I was younger, pretty much everyone I knew was into drugs of some kind. It was the Age of Drugs. Full out. Almost everyone experimented with weed or hallucinogens as well as all sorts of other drugs. Something. Please know, I was not in any way as pure as the driven snow, but for some reason (a really good one, as it turned out, that I discovered later…), I would not do hallucinogens. No way. Never. Not ever. I just felt like I couldn't afford to mess with it.

During my bad years, when everything from my childhood was coming up on me in a spectacularly out-of-control, overwhelming, and quite terrifying manner, I thought about how smart it was that I'd stayed the hell away from acid. I'm pretty sure I would have been in deep trouble opening the doors to that part of me so early on, way before I was ready.

Consequently, I went through my bad years, did all the endless emotional work I had to do, and then started writing again. As I've told you.

So there I am, writing that day, a year or two after I'm back to writing. And I'm gone. Off in another world.

The words are flooding down the Nile, rushing rapids on the Amazon (yes, there are rapids on the Amazon; I looked it up), geysers on the moon. I'm in another universe, hundreds of years in the future, merging with whales, racing up hills on horses' hooves, smiling, laughing, stars and planets exploding out of my fingers, joy expanding into the universe. Abruptly the thought comes:

This is what tripping must be like!

That is the other side of the discussion about how hard doing your art can be.

Because the difficulty, the toil part, is absolutely not the whole story.

Doing art does feel hard. Almost always, at first, for many of us. A lot of the time, at second. Often the whole way along you feel it sometimes. It comes back and grabs you, even when you're positive you're done with it being so difficult.

That's normal. It's common. Almost all of us feel it, some of the time, a lot of the time! Almost all of us!!!!

But it's the other side that matters here.

It's the joy. And the passion. And the deep contentment.

It's the breathing out.

Take care, all.

Chapter twenty-three
Your Place

One more visualization

(Remember you can download the audio file of this from my website. Go to http://www.theartofbecominganartist.com/visualizations and enter the word – Place – where it asks for the code word.)

We're going to do another visualization. I'd like you to find a comfortable location to sit or lie down quietly. Then play the file, "Your Place" or if you prefer read the script on the following page.

*   *   *   *

Your Place

Okay, turn off the light or leave it on, whichever is most comfortable. Get as comfortable as you can, and breathe.

Breathing. Relaxing. Breathing. Relaxing. Letting the air in through your body, and out again.

Breathing. Relaxing. Breathing. Relaxing. Air moving in and moving out again. In and out, again.

Remember to get as comfortable as you can, adjusting your body however you need, comfortable, relaxed, breathing.

Now I would like you to imagine a truly wonderful place. It can be somewhere real that you've been to, or it can be something from your imagination.

It's a wonderful place. Almost a perfect place. Where you feel good and safe and happy. This perfect place.

Your place.

Breathing, relaxing. Breathing. Relaxing.

What does this place look like?

Look around you and notice what's there. What colors do you see? What shapes do you see? What's in this place? What does it look like?

What can you hear in this place? What sounds are there? Or what sounds aren't there? Listen to this place.

Breathing. Relaxing. Breathing. Relaxing.

Listening.

Looking.

What does this place feel like on your skin? What are you feeling? How does it feel on your body?

What can you smell? Can you smell anything? What scents are there? What odors? What do they make you think of, these smells?

Now stick out your tongue. Can you taste anything in this place?

Breathing. Relaxing. Breathing. Relaxing.

Now reach out with your hand and touch this place. Touch whatever's there. What does it feel like on your fingers? What are the textures?

What are you thinking about in this place? What thoughts are going through your mind? Does it bring up memories? This wonderful place. This safe, beautiful place.

What do you feel? How do you feel here? What emotions are moving through you?

This is your place.

You can come here whenever you want. You can come here for a minute, for a glimpse. Or for a few minutes, anytime you want.

You can come and stay here for an hour.

This is your place.

I want you to remember all of the feelings and the thoughts and the images you have in this place so that you can remember them whenever you come here. You can recreate them in your perfect place.

Your wonderful, safe place.

Now I'd like you to stay here for a couple of minutes, feeling what it feels like, enjoying this place. And when you're ready, come back here.

$$* \qquad * \qquad * \qquad *$$

How was that?

A therapist suggested this technique to me years ago. I was trying to work on something that terrified me. Yet every time I went near it, I'd freak and run away. Sometimes almost literally, though certainly figuratively.

So I'd stop trying to think or feel or remember whatever it was I was struggling with. I would just give up.

Until I created "My Place." Whenever I got scared, I would go there. Sure enough, I would calm down enough and feel safe enough, to continue doing the work I wanted to do.

When I started writing again, I would go there whenever I couldn't get to where I wanted with my writing. When I was nervous. Or shut down. When it wouldn't come. When it simply felt wayyyyy too hard!

Very often, when I came back from "my place," the writing came.

I'm hoping it will do the same for you.

Take care, all.

Chapter twenty-four
So Here's My Other Problem

So here's my problem.

My other problem.

I have to figure out how to end this book.

It's just so arbitrary.

My courses, in the many and varied venues I've run them, have been scheduled in several ways: for a single morning, a three hour session, for a one-day workshop, for an intensive weekend workshop, or for three-hour weekly classes over three weeks, four weeks, six weeks, eight weeks... The scheduled time frames have been highly variable.

The fact of the matter, however, has been that the actual time frames have often been entirely different. More often than not the participants would request that the course continue for a longer period of time. This request is, of course, profoundly gratifying, signifying that the lovely students are enjoying the program, getting benefits from the course, and engaging more and more in their artistic process. (My point, obviously...)

Many of the organizations and institutions where I've taught/facilitated/guided these programs – whatever you choose to call it – have happily extended the courses for another three weeks or six weeks or eight weeks. Then they've done it a second time. Then a third. I believe the longest course sponsored by an organization lasted for about two years.

The rest of the time, if the organizations were unable to continue programming the course, participants were happy to have me present the course privately. We'd do it squeezed into my living room, in what my husband and I always referred to as our lovely, little house (accent both on lovely and *little!*) or, throughout the summer evenings, in my enchanted garden.

These courses often went on for months, many even for several years. It was a glorious experience for me as we delved further and further into participants' creative process. Hopefully just as glorious for the participants.

Please note, the point here is that the courses frequently went on and on and on.

Which brings me back to my problem.

In order for the course to continue on and on and on, I was required to continue on and on and on with my responsibilities as a teacher, or guide, group leader, facilitator – once more, however you prefer to define it. That means I kept continually coming up with more and more and more material, thoughts, exercises, assignments, ideas, constructs, topics, and activities for the group, with which to go on and on and on. More and more individual Homework Assignments, too, tailored to each individual. The students themselves kept coming up with more and more material as well.

Here's the funny part. It was easy! Stuff kept coming up. For me. For everyone. For all of us. There was never a *hint* of a dearth of process work to do, in order for students to get to their art. Never the *hint* of a dearth of material. Never that perfect moment of, "We're done now."

Now you have to think back to the early part of this book where I began talking about "Process, process, process." Do you remember what I said about it? Corollary #1. In terms of getting there?

You don't remember? Let me remind you.

I quote:

"Corollary 1: Finding the things that help you do your art, and finding the things that interfere, are both everlasting processes.

Let me repeat. Everlasting Processes.
You don't "get there." You don't arrive. The process doesn't go away. You don't solve the puzzles, conquer the issues, figure it out, and you're done. I don't think it's ever done. Any more than figuring out your life gets done. You don't solve your life. You live it. And you work on it. It changes as you go along. With each new stage or phase or moment. Each step of your life brings new (you can insert any word you want here: challenges is the current buzzword) issues and worries, joys, topics, people, learning, experiences, desires, adventures, fears, excitements, concerns, ambitions, and so on and so on and so on.
Well, each step of your creativity does the same. Ongoing and everlasting.
Process, Process, Process."

The process just goes on and on.

Of course, as a class continued, it was quite complicated a lot of the time. One student might have something they deeply wanted to work on. A topic about their art that they needed to explore. We'd start exploring it.

Then it would bring up a different issue, and a different problem, for someone else. Something critical to their art. We'd get "sidetracked" exploring that issue.

Then we'd come back to the first one, and grapple with that for a while. We'd want to make sure each person got what they needed. Next, something related – or perhaps completely different – would come up for a third person. We'd have to explore that, too! Because each person was different, and different things came up for them.

Once again, you have to think back to the early part of this book, where I began talking about "Process, process, process." Do you remember what I said about it? In Corollary 2? In terms of the individuality of the creative process. You don't remember? Let me remind you.

"Corollary 2: There is NO correct answer. There can be nothing prescriptive about the RIGHT way to do your art. By its very nature, creativity is about originality. Originality is an individual thing. It's about your thing. YOUR WAY. It has to be.

There are no "shoulds," no rules, no regulations. No laws, or statutes, or edicts, or proclamations.

It's art. It's your art.

And you're the only one in this whole universe who can figure out how you need to create it. How you need to get to it. What you need to do to be able to do it.

There is no RIGHT way. There is only YOUR way.

It's about you.

Period."

The courses rolled on.

*   *   *   *

So back to my problem. Where to end this book…?

How do I decide that you've gotten everything you can from it? How do I decide that you've explored everything you need to explore? Traveled into every corner you needed to travel to? Delved everywhere you needed to delve?

There's so much more to talk about. To examine. To grapple with. So many more topics. More problems. More joys. Exercises and assignments. Questions. Ideas, thoughts, experiences.

There are notes from all of those classes, over all of those days, weeks, months, years, filled with wonderful stories and experiences; discoveries that might give you something. Might help you do your art.

Then there are the bumps. Infinite bumps. Creative lives filled with bumps. Then moving forward. Then more bumps.

Plus, you're not here, and I'm not there. So how do I know?

How do I end? Where do I leave you? What do I leave you with?

*   *   *   *

But this book has to end before we cover all of those topics, and it has to leave you with a message and a process, to continue on your journey.

It has to end before we cover it all, because there is no way to cover it all. Literally. It's simple physics. The universe keeps flowing. So does life.

And so does art.

*   *   *   *

Most importantly of all, so does *your* art.

You're not there yet. Right?

You're thinking as you read this about what to do next, where to go next. How can you actually get to your art? How can you really keep flowing with your art if you've managed to get started?

That's the key. You need to keep flowing. And exploring. And grappling. Getting support when you need to. It's infinite – remember?

You've started. And you'll almost definitely stop, again. And again. And again.

But then you'll start again. Then again. And again.

And that's life.

And that's art.

So the book will end, but your art will not.

*   *   *   *

One more time, because you are not sitting in my classroom, or my little living room, or my enchanted garden, I can't see what you've accomplished since you started this "class." I can't know what you've learned, or explored, or struggled with. I can't know how much you've done your art.

But if you have worked your way through to the end of this book, I'm hoping you've accomplished a lot.

I'm so happy you've stayed with it.

Art isn't easy. Getting to your art is often even harder.

So, congratulations! I hope you are proud of yourself.
Be proud of yourself.

*   *   *   *

Okay, I think I have abruptly decided how to end this book. Quite simple, really. I should have guessed. I'm going to end this book the way I end my classes.

Whenever I end the first scheduled segment of the class, whether it is ending for good or continuing on, I hand out four items.

One is the assignment I gave you right back at the beginning of this book:

"I want to do my art because…"

I don't know if you remember, but I told you that although normally I collect that particular assignment at the beginning, I never read that assignment at the time; instead I put them in a sealed envelope and hand them back on the last day of class. I asked you to do essentially the same thing:

"I would like you to put the piece away somewhere safe. Seal it up in an envelope. Don't look at it again until you've finished doing this book."

All right, you've just about finished doing the book. I would, therefore, like you to find that sealed envelope and take a look at what you wrote in the beginning. You might find it interesting to see what you said at the beginning of this particular journey.

The second thing I hand out is a written copy of all of the quotes I've read in class. Students always want the quotes. An advantage of the book is that you've already gotten a written copy of all of the quotes! That part's easy…. They're in the book…

The third thing I hand out is a brief bibliography of some of the books on creativity (and other things…) that I've found interesting over the years. I say brief because there are so many useful books and I've just chosen a few that were special to me in some way or another. There are many, many other books on the topic that are profoundly worth reading. And I also want to say that I do not feel that everything in every book in my personal bibliography is profoundly worth reading. Nor do I necessarily agree with everything in every book. But there was *something* in every book that spoke to me.

I have included that bibliography towards the end of this book.

The last thing I hand out, quite ritualistically, is a card. In the final moments of the last class, I walk around the room and place the card in front of each student.

I hand out the card and say goodbye to the class.

Then we all say our goodbyes.

The front of the card is a picture that I love. A lot.

Inside the card is a quote that I saw pinned to a tree at an artist's festival in the woods on Pender Island, one of the Gulf Islands in the Strait of Georgia off Vancouver Island.

The quote has never left me. It speaks to my life, to the painful years of losing my writing, and to the joy of finding my writing again.

That quote is what is inside the card.

Then I sign my name.

I can't hand you the card. Or place it beside you.

(And I've also made the difficult decision to not show you the picture on the front of the card in its true glorious color. Including that one color picture would have upped the price of this book by a third. A third! I didn't want to do that to you. So what I will ask you to do instead is to go to my website, one more time, and look at the full color image of the card on-site: http://www.theartofbecominganartist. com/card and enter the word – Flower – where it asks for the code.)

Once again, I can't hand you the card. Or place it beside you.

But I can *almost* reproduce it here.

*   *   *   *

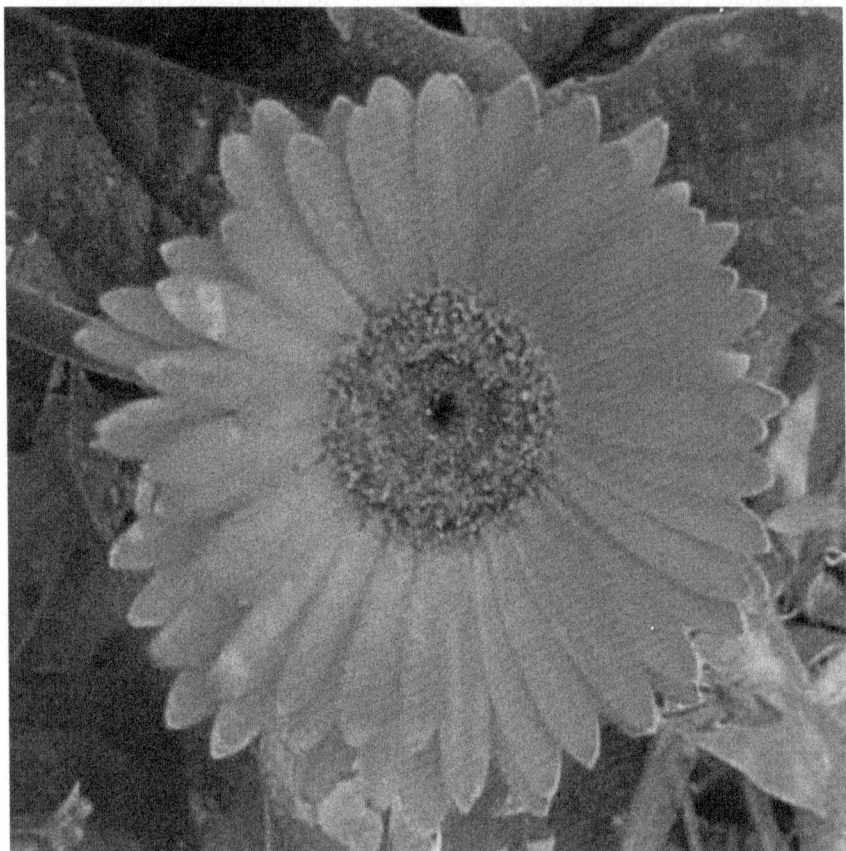

**And the
day came
when the
risk to
remain
tight in a
bud
was more
painful
than the
risk it took
to blossom.**

Unknown[62]

Take care,

Dari

* * * *

Goodbye.

And I wish you the very best.

And I wish you your art.

Take care, all.

My Personal Bibliography

Aron, Elaine N. *The Highly Sensitive Person: How to Thrive When the World Overwhelms You.* First Broadway Books. 1998. Print.

Ascher, Carol, Lousie deSalvo and Sara Ruddick, eds. *Between Women: Biographers, Novelists, Critics, Teachers and Artists Write about Their Work on Women.* Beacon Press, Boston. 1984. Print.

Audette, Anna Held. *The Blank Canvas: Inviting the Muse.* Shambhala Publications, Inc. 1993. Print.

Behn, R. and Chase Twichell, eds. *The Practice of Poetry: Writing Exercises from Poets Who Teach.* Harper Perennial. 1992. Print.

Bradbury, Ray. *Zen in the Art of Writing: Essays on Creativity.* Capra. 1989. Print.

Brande, Dorothea. *Becoming a Writer*, Harcourt, Brace & Company. 1934. Print.

Brossard, Nicole. *The Aerial Letter.* Women's Press. 1988. Print.

Chicago, Judy. *The Dinner Party.* Anchor Books/Doubleday. New York. 1979. Print.

Faly, C. Diane. *The Woman's Book of Creativity.* CelestialArts. California.1999. Print.

Gilbert, Sandra M. and Susan Gubar. *The Madwoman in the Attic.* Yale University Press. 1984. Print.

Goldberg, Natalie. *Writing Down the Bones: Freeing the Writer Within.* Shambhala Publications. Inc.. 1986. Print.

Greer, Germaine. *The Obstacle Race.* Picador. 1979. Print.

Griffin, Susan. *Women And Nature.* Harper and Row. Publishers. New York. 1978. Print.

Keyes, Ralph. *The Courage to Write: How Writers Transcend Fear.* Henry Holt and Company. New York. 1995. Print.

Lamott, Anne. *Bird by Bird: Some instructions on Writing and Life.* Pantheon Books. New York. 1994. Print.

Le Guin, Ursula K. *Ursula Le Guin* interview [sound recording]. 1993.

Le Guin, Ursula. *Dancing at the Edge of the World.* Grove Press. New York. 1989. Print.

Le Guin, Ursula. *Steering the Craft: Exercises and Discussions on Story Writing for the Lone Navigator Or the Mutinous Crew.* The Eighth Mountain Press. 1998. Print.

Neuls-Bates, Carol, ed. *Women in Music: An Anthology of Source Readings from the Middle Ages to the Present.* Harper & Row. New York. 1982. Print.

Olsen, Tillie. *Silences.* A Delta/Seymour Lawrence Edition. Dell Publishing Co. Inc., 1978 Print.

Rich, Adrienne. *A Wild Patience Has Taken Me This Far.* W. W. Norton & Company. 1981. Print.

Rico, Gabriele L. *Writing the Natural Way.* J. P. Tarcher. 1983. Print.

Russ, Joanna. *How to Suppress Women's Writing.* Women's Press. London. 1984. Print.

Schiwy, Marlene A. *A Voice of Her Own: Women and the Journal Writing Journey.* New York. Simon & Schuster. 1996. Print.

Stafford, William. *Writing the Australian Crawl: Views on the Writer's Vocation.* University of Michigan Press. Ann Arbor. 1999. Print.

Sternburg, Janet, ed. *The Writer on Her Work.* Norton and Company. New York. 1981. Print.

Suedfeld, Peter, ed. *Light From the Ashes.* University of Michigan Press. 2001. Print.

Ueland, Brenda. *If You Want to Write.* Grey Wolf Press. St. Paul. 1987. Print.

Walker, Alice, Isabel Allende, Jean Shinoda Bolen. *Giving Birth, Finding Form.* [sound recording] Sounds True Recordings. CO. 1993.

Walker, Alice. *In Search of Our Mothers' Gardens, Womanist Prose.* A Harvest/HBJ Book. 1983. Print.

Acknowledgement for Citations

I would like to thank the authors of these quotations for their brilliance, their insight, their humor, and their validation of what so many of us feel when doing, or trying to do, our art.

I would like to thank the authors, their associates, their publishers, their estate holders, and everyone else who provided me with guidance and help, and who gave me permissions to use the quotations, as well as fair use permissions. Their help was essential and almost endlessly needed.

I would like to thank my husband, Dennis Rank, my niece, Rebecca Handford, and my nephew, Ezra Fieser, for their help with the incredible search to find the sources and contact information for these quotations. I started using them for my courses twenty years ago, and because it was all for educational purposes I did not keep careful track of where I heard or found the quotes... That made getting permissions a wee bit difficult.

And I would like to thank all of the lovely, amazing, creative, incredibly smart, and unbelievably helpful librarians and library support staff all over North America and Europe who helped me find the quotations, helped me find the books, newspapers, magazines, essays, etc., where these quotations originated, and helped me acquire many of them from many, many libraries. I will be forever grateful to ILL... (Interlibrary Loans for those of you, like me, who might have had no idea what that stands for!)

The journey to provide the following endnotes was to my surprise, utterly amazing. An adventure all on its own.

Endnotes

1 Polgar, Alfred. Taken from: Alfred Polgar, KLEINE SCHRIFTEN, vol.4. Copyright © 1984 by Rowohlt Verlag GmbH, Reinbek bei Hamburg, Germany. Originally published in: AN DEN RAND GESCHRIEBEN by Ernst Rowohlt Verlag 1926, p.85-91. Used by the kind permission of Rowohlt Publishing. Translation found at http://depts.washington.edu/vienna/literature/polgar/Polgar_Cafe.htm.

2 Bacon, Francis. From: The Brutality of Fact: Interview with Francis Bacon by David Sylvester © 1987 David Sylvester. Reprinted by kind permission of Thames & Hudson Ltd, London.

3 Poincaré, Henri. THE MONIST, Mathematical Creation, Vol XX. July 1, 1910, No.3, p.10. Found at: https://archive.org/details/jstor-27900262.

4 Walker (Brothers), Alice. Found at: http://www.stcharleslibrary.org/node/1131 through the kind assistance of the library staff at St. Charles Public Library, who provided fair use permission.

5 Sand Toy description from www.jmcutlery.com. Found at: http://www.jmcutlery.com/moving_sand_pictures.htm. Used with the kind permission of J. Mark Cutlery.

6 Referring to Susann, Jacqueline. Cited in: https://en.wikipedia.org/wiki/Valley_of_the_Dolls; and http://www.vanityfair.com/culture/2000/01/jacqueline-susann-valley-of-the-dolls-books.

7 Preston, Don, cited in Seaman, Barbara. Lovely Me: The Life of Jacqueline Susann. P. 286. Orig. pub. 1987 by William Morrow and Company, Inc. Used by kind permission of Seven Stories Press, New York.

8 Saroyan, William. Quoted in Strickland, Bill. On Being a Writer. Sept, 1992. Used with the kind permission of Saroyan estate (University of Stanford).

9 Attributed to Valery, Paul. French critic & poet (1871 - 1945). Condensed from his essay Au Sujet du Cimetiere Marin. (Many versions exist.)

10 Chicago, Judy. The Dinner Party, A Symbol of Our Heritage, P. 24, Anchor Books, Anchor Press/Doubleday, Garden City, New York, 1979. Used with the kind permission of Judy Chicago.

11 Schumann, Clara. (Clara Schumann letter to Robert Schumann, April 23, 1840.) Cited in Litzmann, Berthold and Schumann, Clara. An Artist's Life, Based on Material Found in Diaries and Letters. Trans. Hadow, Grace E. (London: Macmillan, 1913), I:242.

12 Goldman, William. Adventures in the Screen Trade: A Personal View of Hollywood and Screenwriting. Warner Books, 1984. Fair use by the kind permission of the Hatchette Book Group USA, Inc.

13 Attributed to Welliver, Neil. Original source uncertain, but widely believed to have been said by Welliver to his students.

14 Vonnegut Jr., Kurt. Article: Despite Tough Guys, Life Is Not the Only School for Real Novelists. Books Section of The New York Times on the Web. May 24, 1999. Available at: https://partners.nytimes.com/library/books/052499vonnegut-writing.html. Fair use kindly offered by the New York Times.

15 Nesbit, E. A. A Story of the 'Wouldbegoods,' The Saturday Evening Post, Volume 176, Issue 1. Ed G. Graham. P. 22. 1903. Available at: https://google.ca/?gfe_rd=cr&ei=1hquV6WALOvs8wew847AAQ

&gws_rd=ssl#q=%22If+you+can%E2%80%99t+write+a+good+poe
m%2C+for+goodness+sakes+write+a+bad+one.++There%E2%80%9
9s+something+important+there.%22.

16 Eisner, Elliot W. Why the Arts are Marginalized in Our Schools:
One More Time. On Common Ground: Partnerships and the Arts,
No. 5, Fall 1995. © 1997 by the Yale-New Haven Teachers Institute.
Available at: http://www.yale.edu/ynhti/pubs/A18/eisner.html. Used
by the kind permission of the Yale-New Haven Teachers Institute.

17 By permission. From Merriam-Webster's Collegiate® Dictionary,
11th Edition. ©2016 by Merriam-Webster, Inc. (www.Merriam-
Webster.com) Available at: http://www.merriam-webster.com/diction-
ary/synesthesia. Used with the kind permission of Merriam-Webster.

18 Fredriksson, Marianne. Original title Simon Och Ekarna. Trans.
Tate, Joan. Simon & the Oaks. Chapter one0, pp 58 – 61. Orig. ©
1985, Trans. 1997. Trans. first published in Great Britain in 1999 by
Phoenix (an Imprint of The Orion Publishing Group Ltd).

19 Richa A.N, Bradshaw J.L., and Mattingleya J.B. A systematic,
large-scale study of synaesthesia: implications for the role of early
experience in lexical-colour associations. Cognition, Volume 98, Issue
1, November 2005. Pages 53-84 . Used with the kind permission
of Rightslink.com.

20 Aron, Elaine N. The Highly Sensitive Person: How To Thrive
When The World Overwhelms You. Broadway Books, New York,
1997. Reissued with a new preface by the author, 1998. (Multiple
publishers and editions available.) Used with the kind permission of
Dr. Elaine Aron.

21 Buck, Pearl S., quoted by Harris, Theodore F, in consultation with
Buck. Pearl S. Buck, A Biography. Volume 2. Her Philosophy As
Expressed in Her Letters. P. 217. © 1971 by Creativity, Inc. The John
Day Company, New York. Pub. same day in Canada by Longman
Canada Limited. The quote is from The Creative Mind at Work, a
speech delivered at the William Vaughn Moody Foundation Lecture

at the University of Chicago on January 17, 1935. Used by the kind permission of Pearl S. Buck International, University of Pennsylvania.

22 In: Canadian Foundation for Children, Youth and the Law v. Canada (2004) the Supreme Court outlawed school corporal punishment.

23 Descartes, René. The Discourse on the Method of Rightly Conducting One's Reason and of Seeking Truth in the Sciences. French orig : Discours de la méthode pour bien conduire sa raison, et chercher la vérité dans les sciences. (1637). Fair use.

24 Story based on the poem by Buckley, Helen E. The Little Boy. pp 24-25. School Arts Magazine. Oct. 1961. Poem cited by kind permission of School Arts Magazine.

25 From: Aesop's Fables or the Aesopica. Credited to Aesop, a slave and storyteller believed to have lived in ancient Greece between 620 and 564 BCE.

26 Illus. of Aesop's fable of the grasshopper and the ant. 1567. Illus. in: Edward de Deene, De warachtighe fabvlen der dieren, Brugghe, 1567, plate 26. Believed to have been created / published in 1567.Retrieved from the Library of Congress, https://www.loc.gov/item/2005692089/.

27 Source unknown.

28 Singer, Isaac Bashevis. Accessed at Time Magazine online: http://content.time.com/time/subscriber/article/0,33009,950984-2,00.html. Used by kind permission of TCM: syndication@timeinc.com

29 Twain, Mark. Said to Samuel Johnson Woolf when painting Twain's portrait, according to Woolf's book, Here Am I. Random House, New York, 1941. Fair use.

30 Einstein, Albert is a common attribution. Actual source unknown. Variously attributed to several different individuals. Fair use.

31 Carlson, Ron. From a 2006 interview with Carlson appearing in Sun Valley Magazine. Used by the kind permission of Mandala Media doing business as Sun Valley Magazine.

32 West, Jessamyn. To see the Dream, Part 1, Harcourt, Brace & Company, New York, 1956, p. 39. Fair use by the kind permission of Lippincott Massie McQuilkin.

33 White, E.B. Acceptance remarks by E.B. White upon receiving the 1971 National Medal for Literature. Quoted in Keyes, Ralph. Courage to Write. Henry Holt and Company, NY. 1995. Fair use. Based on three sources: (1) "I am not inclined. . ." from Guth, Letters, p. 485. (2) "A writer's courage. . ." from The National Book Award: Writers on Their Craft and Their World. New York: Book-of-the-Month, 1990, p. 52. (3) "I admire anybody. . ." from Plimpton, Writers at Work, 8th ser. 11. Cheever, John, The Journals of John Cheever. New York: Knopf 1991, x.

34 Gordimer, Nadine. Interviewed by Hurwitt, Jannika, in The Art of Fiction, No. 77. The Paris Review, Summer 1983, No. 88. Available at: http://www.theparisreview.org/interviews/3060/the-art-of-fiction-no-77-nadine-gordimer. Used by the kind permission of The Paris Review Foundation.

35 Murray, Donald Morison . Shoptalk: Learning to Write with Writers. Boynton/Cook Publishers, A Division of Heinemann Educational Books, Inc. 1990. Used by kind permission of Heinemann.

36 Widely attributed to Hemingway, Ernest, but exact source unknown.

37 Laing, R.D. Widely attributed to Laing but exact source unknown. Found in many sources and versions, of which the earliest may be in: The Faculty of Philology-History at Universitatea din Timișoara. Studii de literatură română și comparată (1984). Used by the kind permission of Adrian Laing.

38 Baldwin, James. Cooper, Charles R. and Odell, Lee (Eds.) Research on Composing: Points of Departure. Urbana, IL: National Council of

Teachers of English. 1978, pages 101-103. Fair use given by the kind permission of the NCTE.

39 Suedfeld, Peter. Pers comm. In social psychology course, University of British Columbia, 1974. Spontaneously repeated at dinner in favorite Chinese restaurant, November, 2016.

40 Schachter, Stanley and Singer, Jerome. Cognitive, social, and physiological determinants of emotional state. Psychological Review, Vol **69**(5), Sept 1962, 379-399. Public domain.

41 Behan, Brendan Francis Aidan (aka Francis, Brendan). Multiple citations. Fair use.

42 Aeschylus, ancient Greek playwright (525 BC – 456 BC), considered the father of tragedy. Exact source unknown.

43 Freehill, Maurice F. Widely attributed to Dr. Freehill but exact source unknown. May be a variant of a quote attributed to Plato. Fair use by the kind permission of University of Washington College of Education.

44 James, William, 19th century psychologist and philosopher (1842-1910). Quote from roughly 1890, widely cited.

45 Hazzard, Shirley. Quoted in article by Richard Eder: For Writers, Separate Silences by Richard Eder. New York Times. March 26, 1980, page C1. Fair use by kind permission of the New York Times.

46 Inspired by Heinlein, Robert. Podkayne of Mars, Chapter thirteen, G. P. Putnam's Sons, 1963.

47 Godwin, Gail. Violet Clay. Random House; 1st edition, May, 1978. Fair use granted by kind permission of Penguin Random House.

48 Thompson, Emma, speaking to Lindsay Dohan, producer of the Jane Austen film Sense and Sensibility. Used by kind permission of Hamilton Hodell Talent Management, UK.

49 Le Guin, Ursula. Interview with Le Guin cited in Justice, Faith, Steering Her Craft: An Interview with Ursula Le Guin, 2000. Fair use granted by kind permission of http://www.writing-World.com.

50 https://en.wikipedia.org/wiki/History_of_photography.

51 Carr, Emily. Hundreds and Thousands: The Journals of Emily Carr. John Inglis and the Estate of Emily Carr, in the book published by Douglas & MacIntyre, 2006 p. 427. Public domain cited by kind permission of Douglas & MacIntyre (2013) Ltd.

52 Rudnick, Paul. Exact source unknown. Used by kind permission of Paul Rudnick.

53 By permission. From Merriam-Webster's Collegiate® Dictionary, 11th Edition. ©2016 by Merriam-Webster, Inc. (www.Merriam-Webster.com) Available at: http://www.merriam-webster.com/dictionary/discipline. Used by the kind permission of Merriam-Webster.

54 Flaubert, Gustave, in a letter to George Sand. The George Sand-Gustave Flaubert Letters. (1866). Trans. MacKenzie, Aimee. Boni and Liveright Inc., (1921, section XXXII, letter headed "Croisset – Tuesday").

55 Fowler, Gene. Charlton, James (Ed.) Writer's Quotation Book: A Literary Companion. Pushcart Press, 1980. Public domain by kind permission from Pushcart Press.

56 Steinbeck, John. Travels With Charley - In Search of America, page 23. The Curtis Publishing Company, Inc. and Viking Press, Inc., 1962. New York. Fair use by kind permission of the Penguin Group.

57 Probably Miller, Olin. Believed to have been written by Miller (1894-1981) for a syndicated feature, "Dixie Dewdrops", in a newspaper in Thomaston, Georgia. His lines were frequently quoted by others. Fair use, public domain.

58 Walters, Colin, writing for the Washington Times Book Reviews. Fair use by kind permission of the Washington Times Book Reviews.

59 Parker, Dorothy. First used in: Humor Takes In Many Things; In Praising S. J. Perelman's Brand, Mrs. Parker Prescribes for the Trade. New York Times Book Review, January 20, 1957.

The author wishes to thank the National Association for the Advancement of Colored People for authorizing the use of Dorothy Parker's work. Ms. Parker left her estate to the NAACP to benefit its work.

60 West, Jessamyn, To See the Dream. Harcourt, Brace & Company, New York, 1957, p. 3. Fair use by the kind permission of Lippincott Massie McQuilkin.

61 Generally believed to be an adaptation from one or more stories in: Chesterton, G.K. (Gilbert Keith), The Poet and The Lunatics: Episodes in the Life of Gabriel Gale (1929). Fair use, with thanks to the American Chesterton Organization for doing research on the exact source (which could not be found).

62 Widely attributed to Anaïs Nin, e.g., at: http://anaisninblog.sky-bluepress.com/2013/03/who-wrote-risk-is-the-mystery-solved/Source unknown. Fair use. But may actually be from Appell, Elizabeth, from the spring course schedule header at John F. Kennedy University, 1979.

About the Author

Darylynn Starr Rank (most people call her Dari) is a writer, a therapist, and a creativity consultant. In addition to *The Art of Becoming an Artist*, she has written newspaper columns, short stories, novels, screenplays, poetry, and articles, both published and unpublished, and journals, journals, journals. In her clinical practice she works with a wonderful array of creative clients: artistic beings of many sorts. Artists are her specialty.

As a creativity consultant, she gives a massive number of talks, lectures, seminars, workshops, courses, professional development training, private classes, weekend intensives, and online tutorials, all dedicated to the pursuit of our creative process. She presents her programs in universities, colleges, non-profit organizations, businesses, (including one of the largest computer game designers in the world), hospitals, social service associations, community centers, her living room, on the shore of one of the loveliest lakes in British Columbia, at a tropical retreat in the Florida Keys – any kind of venue you can imagine.

The combination of being a writer and a therapist, and of having once been seriously screwed up, is what led to the unique vision she has developed for her workshops and courses…this vision has now been happily distilled into *The Art of Becoming An Artist*.

CPSIA information can be obtained
at www.ICGtesting.com
Printed in the USA
LVOW13s2320070717

540622LV00012B/73/P